AN OVERVIEW OF FEDERAL HOUSING ASSISTANCE PROGRAMS

HOUSING ISSUES, LAWS AND PROGRAMS

Additional books in this series can be found on Nova's website
under the Series tab.

Additional E-books in this series can be found on Nova's website
under the E-books tab.

HOUSING ISSUES, LAWS AND PROGRAMS

AN OVERVIEW OF FEDERAL HOUSING ASSISTANCE PROGRAMS

BRANDON C. SHERMAN
EDITOR

Nova Science Publishers, Inc.
New York

NOTICE TO THE READER

The Publisher has taken reasonable care in the preparation of this book, but makes no expressed or implied warranty of any kind and assumes no responsibility for any errors or omissions. No liability is assumed for incidental or consequential damages in connection with or arising out of information contained in this book. The Publisher shall not be liable for any special, consequential, or exemplary damages resulting, in whole or in part, from the readers' use of, or reliance upon, this material. Any parts of this book based on government reports are so indicated and copyright is claimed for those parts to the extent applicable to compilations of such works.

Independent verification should be sought for any data, advice or recommendations contained in this book. In addition, no responsibility is assumed by the publisher for any injury and/or damage to persons or property arising from any methods, products, instructions, ideas or otherwise contained in this publication.

This publication is designed to provide accurate and authoritative information with regard to the subject matter covered herein. It is sold with the clear understanding that the Publisher is not engaged in rendering legal or any other professional services. If legal or any other expert assistance is required, the services of a competent person should be sought. FROM A DECLARATION OF PARTICIPANTS JOINTLY ADOPTED BY A COMMITTEE OF THE AMERICAN BAR ASSOCIATION AND A COMMITTEE OF PUBLISHERS.

Additional color graphics may be available in the e-book version of this book.

LIBRARY OF CONGRESS CATALOGING-IN-PUBLICATION DATA
An overview of federal housing assistance programs / editor, Brandon C. Sherman.
      p. cm.
  Includes index.
  ISBN 978-1-61122-419-1 (hbk.)
  1. Public housing--United States. 2. Low-income housing--United States.
  3. Housing policy--United States. I. Sherman, Brandon C.
  HD7288.78.U5O94 2010
  363.50973--dc22
                                2010038630

Published by Nova Science Publishers, Inc. † New York

CONTENTS

PREFACE

The federal government has been involved in providing housing assistance to lower-income households since the 1930s. In the beginning, the federal government was involved in supporting the mortgage market (through establishment of the Federal Housing Administration (FHA) and the government-sponsored enterprises) and in promoting construction of low-rent public housing for lower-income families through local public housing authorities. Over time, the role of the federal government has shifted away from providing construction-based subsidies to providing rental subsidies; private developers and property owners now play a larger role; and more federal funding has been provided to states and localities. This book provides an overview of the history and evolution of federal housing assistance programs and policy, information about the main programs, and a discussion of recent issues and trends

Chapter 1- The federal government has been involved in providing housing assistance to lower-income households since the 1930s. In the beginning, the federal government was involved in supporting the mortgage market (through establishment of the Federal Housing Administration (FHA) and the government-sponsored enterprises) and in promoting construction of low-rent public housing for lower-income families through local public housing authorities (PHAs). Over time, the role of the federal government has shifted away from providing construction-based subsidies to providing rental subsidies; private developers and property owners now play a larger role; and more federal funding has been provided to states and localities.

Chapter 2- The population of persons age 65 and older in the United States is expected to grow both in numbers and as a percentage of the total population over the next 25 years, through 2030. In 2002, a bipartisan commission created by Congress issued a report, *A Quiet Crisis in America*, that detailed the need for affordable assisted housing and supportive services for elderly persons and the shortage the country will likely face as the population ages. The Department of Housing and Urban Development (HUD) operates a number of programs that provide assisted housing and supportive services for low-income elderly persons (defined by HUD as households where one or more persons are age 62 or older) to ensure that elderly residents in HUD-assisted housing can remain in their apartments as they age. This report describes those programs, along with current developments in the area of housing for elderly households.

Chapter 3- The HOME Investment Partnerships Program was authorized by the Cranston-Gonzalez National Affordable Housing Act of 1990 (P.L. 101-625). HOME is a federal block grant program that provides funding to states and localities to be used exclusively for affordable housing activities to benefit low-income households.

Chapter 4- Currently, the U.S. Department of Housing and Urban Development (HUD) distributes four Homeless Assistance Grants, each of which provides funds to local communities to finance a range of housing and supportive services options for homeless persons. These four grants—the Emergency Shelter Grants (ESG) program, the Supportive Housing Program (SHP), the Shelter Plus Care (S+C) program, and the Section 8 Moderate Rehabilitation for Single Room Occupancy Dwellings (SRO) program—were enacted as part of the McKinney-Vento Homeless Assistance Act (P.L. 100-77, as amended). Congress appropriates one lump sum for all four grants, and HUD then determines how the funds are allocated among the four programs.

Chapter 5- The Section 8 low-income housing program is really two programs: the voucher program and the project-based Section 8 program. Vouchers are portable subsidies that low-income families can use to lower their rents in the private market. Vouchers are administered at the local level by quasi-governmental public housing authorities (PHAs). Project-based Section 8 is a form of rental subsidy that is attached to a unit of privately owned housing. Low-income families who move into the housing pay a reduced rent, on the basis of their incomes.

Chapter 6- Changes enacted by Congress during the appropriations process in each of the past several years have significantly altered the way that public housing authorities (PHAs) receive funding to administer the Section 8 Housing Choice Voucher program. Prior to FY2003, PHAs received funding for each voucher they were authorized to administer, based on their average costs from the previous year, plus inflation, referred to as "unit-based" funding. Most PHAs were not using all of their vouchers, due in part to rental market conditions, and each year the Department of Housing and Urban Development (HUD) was able to recapture unspent funds. In FY2001 and FY2002, some Members of Congress began expressing concern about the underutilization of vouchers and the amount of recaptures.

Chapter 7- Title V of the Housing Act of 1949 authorized the Department of Agriculture (USDA) to make loans to farmers to enable them to construct, improve, repair, or replace dwellings and other farm buildings to provide decent, safe, and sanitary living conditions for themselves or their tenants, lessees, sharecroppers, and laborers. USDA was also authorized to make grants or combinations of loans and grants to those farmers who could not qualify to repay the full amount of a loan, but who needed the funds to make the dwellings sanitary or to remove health hazards to the occupants or the community.

In: An Overview of Federal Housing Assistance Programs   ISBN: 978-1-61122-419-1
Editor: Brandon C. Sherman   © 2011 Nova Science Publishers, Inc.

Chapter 1

OVERVIEW OF FEDERAL HOUSING ASSISTANCE PROGRAMS AND POLICY

Maggie McCarty, Libby Perl, Bruce E. Foote, Katie Jones and Meredith Peterson

SUMMARY

The federal government has been involved in providing housing assistance to lower-income households since the 1930s. In the beginning, the federal government was involved in supporting the mortgage market (through establishment of the Federal Housing Administration (FHA) and the government-sponsored enterprises) and in promoting construction of low-rent public housing for lower-income families through local public housing authorities (PHAs). Over time, the role of the federal government has shifted away from providing construction-based subsidies to providing rental subsidies; private developers and property owners now play a larger role; and more federal funding has been provided to states and localities.

Today's federal housing assistance programs fall into three main categories: rental housing assistance, assistance to state and local governments, and assistance for homeowners. Most of these programs are administered by the Department of Housing and Urban Development (HUD). Current housing assistance programs include: Section 8 vouchers and project-based rental assistance, public housing, housing for the elderly (Section 202), housing for the disabled (Section 811), rural rental assistance (Section 515 and 521), Community Development Block Grants (CDBG), HOME Investment Partnerships Block Grants, Low-Income Housing Tax Credits (LIHTC), homeless assistance programs, FHA and Veterans' Administration mortgage insurance, and the mortgage interest deduction in the tax code.

Most of the federal housing assistance programs are aimed at making housing affordable for low- income families. Housing affordability—housing that costs no more than 30% of family income—is considered the largest housing problem today. Rental assistance programs, which are the largest source of direct housing assistance for low-income families, all allow families to pay affordable, income-based rents; however, different forms of assistance target different types of households, including the elderly, persons with disabilities, and families with children. Several trends in federal housing policy have emerged in recent decades. As the focus of federal housing assistance has shifted away from construction-based subsidies to rental assistance, block grants, and LIHTC, state and local governments have had greater access to federal resources to fund local housing and community development priorities. This shift in federal funding has also led affordable housing developers to pursue mixed financing: the use of multiple streams of federal funding, state, and local funding, or private financing. Lagging homeownership rates among low- income and minority households have prompted the past several Presidents to promote homeownership-based housing policies.

This report provides an overview of the history and evolution of federal housing assistance programs and policy, information about the main programs, and a discussion of recent issues and trends. It is an expanded version of the Federal Housing Assistance section originally prepared for the 2008 edition of the Committee on Ways and Means publication, "Background Material and Data on the Programs within the Jurisdiction of the Committee on Ways and Means" (informally known as the Green Book). This report will be updated periodically.

INTRODUCTION

The federal government has played a role in subsidizing housing construction and providing homeownership and rental assistance for lower-income households since the 1930s. Today, Congress funds a number of programs to help meet the housing needs of poor and vulnerable populations. The programs are primarily administered by the Department of Housing and Urban Development (HUD), with some assistance provided to rural communities through the Department of Agriculture. The modern housing assistance programs include both relatively flexible grants to state and local governments to serve homeless people, build affordable housing, provide assistance to first-time homebuyers, and promote community development and more structured, direct assistance programs that provide low-cost apartments and rental vouchers to poor families, administered through local public, quasi-public, and private intermediaries. The federal government also makes tax credits available to states to distribute to developers of low- cost housing and provides insurance to lenders that make mortgages to eligible homebuyers. The federal government's largest housing program, however, is arguably the mortgage interest deduction, which is not targeted to lower-income households, but is available to all homeowners who pay mortgage interest and itemize their deductions.

This report begins with an overview of the history and evolution of federal housing assistance policy, followed by a description of today's major federal housing assistance programs, and concludes with a discussion of issues and trends in federal housing assistance policy. This report, which will be updated periodically, does not track current legislation.

HISTORY AND EVOLUTION OF FEDERAL HOUSING ASSISTANCE POLICY

The Beginning of Federal Housing Assistance: FHA and Public Housing

The federal government's first major housing policy was formulated in response to trouble in the mortgage market resulting from the Great Depression. Until the early 1930s, most mortgages were written for terms of three to five years and required borrowers to make payments only on an annual basis. At the end of the three- or five-year terms, the remaining loan balance had to be repaid or the mortgage had to be renegotiated. Another feature of the mortgage market was that lenders would only lend 40% to 50% of the value of the property, so borrowers had to have the cash to complete the transaction or find someone willing to finance the balance (or part of the balance) in a second mortgage. During the Great Depression, however, lenders were unable or unwilling to refinance many of the loans that became due. When borrowers could not pay the loan balances, lenders foreclosed on the loans and took possession of the properties.

It was against this background that the Housing Act of 1934 (P.L. 73-479) was enacted. The broad objectives of the act were to (1) encourage lenders to invest in housing construction, and (2) to stimulate employment in the building industry. The act created the Federal Housing Administration (FHA). FHA insured lenders against losses on home modernization and home improvement loans, created the Mutual Mortgage Insurance Fund to fund the operation of the newly-created mortgage insurance programs, and established national mortgage associations to buy and sell mortgages.

The creation of FHA also institutionalized a revolutionary idea: 20-year mortgages on which a loan would be completely repaid at the end of its term. If borrowers defaulted, FHA insured that the lender would be fully repaid. Eventually, lenders began to make long-term mortgages without FHA insurance as long as borrowers made significant downpayments. Over time, 25- and 30-year mortgages have become standard mortgage products.

As in the case of the mortgage finance market, the federal government initially became involved in the provision of rental housing assistance in response to the Great Depression. In the early 1930s, a housing division was added to President Franklin D. Roosevelt's Works Progress Administration (WPA) as a part of the effort to create jobs and spur economic growth.[1] The Housing Division acquired land and built multifamily housing projects for occupancy by lower- income families across the country. However, the Housing Division's activities proved controversial with local government officials who thought that they were not consulted in the process.

Against this backdrop, the U.S. Housing Act of 1937 (P.L. 75-412) was enacted. It replaced the WPA's Housing Division and its projects by establishing a new, federal United States Housing Agency (a precursor agency to today's Department of Housing and Urban Development) and a new Low-Rent Public Housing program. The new program required partnerships between the federal government, states, and localities. States that wished to receive assistance in building low- rent public housing were required to pass enabling legislation creating new, quasi-governmental, local public housing authorities (PHAs). These PHAs could then apply to the federal government for funding to aid in the construction and maintenance of low-rent housing developments targeted to low-income families. The act declared that it was the policy of the United States:

> ...to promote the general welfare of the nation by employing its funds and credit, as provided in this Act, to assist the several states and their political subdivisions to alleviate present and recurring unemployment and to remedy the unsafe and unsanitary housing conditions and the acute shortage of decent, safe, and sanitary dwellings for families of low-income, in rural or urban communities, that are injurious to the health, safety, and morals of the citizens of the nation.

Housing was a major issue in the presidential and congressional races during 1948. President Harry S. Truman's pledge to address the postwar housing shortage and the problem of urban slums played a key role in his margin of victory.[2] In his State of the Union Address in 1949 unveiling the "Fair Deal," President Truman observed that "Five million families are still living in slums and firetraps. Three million families share their homes with others."[3]

He further stated

> The housing shortage continues to be acute. As an immediate step, the Congress should enact the provisions for low-rent public housing, slum clearance, farm housing, and housing research which I have repeatedly recommended. The number of low-rent public housing units provided for in the legislation should be increased to 1 million units in the next 7 years. Even this number of units will not begin to meet our need for new housing.

The Housing Act of 1949 (P.L. 81-171) declared the goal of "a decent home and a suitable living environment for every American family." The act: (1) established a federal urban redevelopment and slum clearance program, authorizing federal loans of $1 billion over a five-year period to help local redevelopment agencies acquire slum properties and assemble sites for redevelopment; (2) reactivated the public housing program for low-income families (which had been on hold during World War II), authorizing subsidies to local housing authorities sufficient to build 810,000 units over six years; (3) expanded the FHA's mortgage insurance program to promote home building and homeownership; (4) created within the U.S. Department of Agriculture a program of financial assistance and subsidies to improve housing conditions on farms and in rural areas; and (5) authorized federal grants for research, primarily to improve the productivity of the housing industry.

Government Subsidization of Private Development

Through the 1950s, the federal government's role in housing assistance focused largely on public housing, which served a mostly poor population. Congress recognized that a gap existed in the market—few options existed for moderate income families whose incomes were too high to qualify for public housing, but too low to afford adequate market rate housing.[4] Proposals in Congress had been made to address the shortage of housing for moderate income households during the 1950s; however, no legislation had been enacted, in part due to the cost to the government of creating and funding a new program.[5] In order to avoid creating another large housing program with high expenditures, while at the same time finding a way to serve this segment of the population, Congress approved legislation at the end of the 1950s and throughout the 1960s that engaged the private sector in the development of affordable housing.

The Housing Act of 1959 (P.L. 86-372) was the first significant instance where government incentives were used to persuade private developers to build housing that would be affordable to low- and moderate-income households. As part of P.L. 86-372, Congress created the Section 202 Housing for the Elderly program. Through the Section 202 program, the federal government extended low-interest loans to private non-profit organizations for the development of affordable housing for moderate-income residents age 62 and older. The low interest rates were meant to ensure that units would be affordable, with non-profit developers able to charge lower rents and still have adequate revenue to pay back the government loans.

The Housing Act of 1961 (P.L. 87-70) further expanded the role of the private sector in providing housing to low- and moderate-income households. The act created the Section 221(d)(3) Below Market Interest Rate (BMIR) housing program, which both insured mortgages to private developers of multifamily housing and provided loans at low interest rates. The BMIR program expanded the pool of eligible borrowers to private for-profit developers and government entities, as well as non-profit developers. Eligible developers included cooperatives, limited dividend corporations, and state or local government agencies. Like the Section 202 program, the low interest rates in the BMIR program were meant to ensure that building owners could offer affordable rents to tenants.

In 1965, the Housing and Urban Development Act (P.L. 89-117) added rental assistance to the list of incentives for private multifamily housing developers that participated in the Section 221 (d)(3) BMIR program. P.L. 89-117 created the Rent Supplement program, which capped the rents charged to tenants at 20% of their incomes and paid building owners the difference between 20% of a tenant's income and fair market rent.

The Housing and Urban Development Act of 1965 also created the Section 23 leased housing program, the first program to provide rent subsidies for use in existing private rental market units. The same PHAs that administered the public housing program were authorized to enter into contracts with landlords in the private market. These contracts authorized payments to landlords who rented units to low-income tenants. Tenants paid one quarter of their income toward rent in these private units, and the federal subsidies made up the difference between the tenant payments and rent for the units.

In 1968, the Housing and Urban Development Act (P.L. 90-448) created the Section 236 and Section 235 programs. In the Section 236 program, the government subsidized private developers' mortgage interest payments so that they would not pay more than 1% toward interest. Like the low interest rate loans provided through the Section 221 (d)(3) BMIR program, the Section 236 interest subsidies were meant to ensure that units would be affordable to low- and moderate-income tenants, although some units also received rent subsidies (referred to as Rental Assistance Payments (RAP)) to make them affordable to the lowest-income tenants. The Section 235 program instituted similar mortgage interest reduction payments for individual homeowners rather than multifamily housing developers.

Under the public housing program, tenants generally paid rent in an amount equal to the costs of operating the assisted housing in which they lived. Over time, as operating costs rose, there was a concern that the below-market rents being charged to families were too high to be affordable to the poorest families. The Brooke Amendment, which was included as part of the Housing and Urban Development Act of 1969 (P.L. 91-152), limited tenant contributions toward rent in all rent assisted units (including public housing and all project-based rental assistance units) to an amount equal to 25% of tenant income (this was later raised to 30%). The Brooke Amendment is considered responsible for codifying an income-based rent structure in federal housing programs.

By the end of the 1960s, subsidies to private developers had resulted in the creation of hundreds of thousands of housing units. Approximately 700,000 units of housing had been built through the Section 236 and Section 221(d)(3) programs alone.[6] The Section 202 program had created more than 45,000 units for elderly households.[7] The Section 235 and Section 23 leased-housing programs provided ownership and rental subsidies for thousands more. Through 1972, the Section 235 program subsidized nearly 400,000 homeowners,[8] while the Section 23 leased-housing program provided rent subsidies for more than 38,000 private market rental units.[9] Despite the growth in the role of private developers, public housing was still the largest housing subsidy program, with roughly a million units built and subsidized by the early 1970s.[10]

Rethinking the Strategy: From Construction Subsidies to Rent Subsidies

By the early 1970s, concern was growing about the cost, efficacy, and equity of the construction- based housing subsidy programs, such as the Section 236 and public housing programs. Then- President Richard M. Nixon criticized the existing programs as not equitably serving families in the same circumstances, providing poor quality housing, being too costly, and placing some families in homes they could not afford.[11] Out of these concerns, President Nixon declared a moratorium on all new activity under the major housing subsidy programs—except for the Section 23 leased-housing program—beginning in January 1973. Assisted housing activity slowly restarted in response to lawsuits and new legislation.

The Housing Act of 1974 (P.L. 93-383) was the first omnibus housing legislation since 1968 and the first such legislation following the Nixon moratorium. The act created a new low-income rental assistance program, referred to as Section 8. Although the 1960s had seen rental assistance programs like Rent Supplement and Section 23, the scale of the Section 8 program made it the first comprehensive rental assistance program. The Section 8 program combined features of the Section 236 program, which was popular with advocates of construction-based subsidies, and the Section 23 leased housing program, which used the existing housing stock and was popular with the Nixon Administration. Through Section 8, the federal government provided private property owners monthly assistance payments for new or substantially rehabilitated rental units. In exchange for monthly rental payments, property owners would agree to rent to eligible low- income families (defined as families with incomes at or below 80% of local area median income) who would pay an income-based rent. It also provided PHAs with the authority to enter into rental assistance contracts for existing, private market units.

Over time, the use of Section 8 in new construction and substantial rehabilitation projects was found to be more expensive than its use in existing housing. The Housing and Urban-Rural Recovery Act of 1983 (P.L. 98-181) repealed HUD's authority to enter into new Section 8 contracts tied to new construction and substantial rehabilitation, but retained HUD's authority to issue new contracts for existing properties. The act also created a new demonstration program to test a modified use of Section 8, referred to as vouchers. Vouchers were similar to the use of Section 8 rent subsidies in existing housing, but provided more flexibility to PHAs, particularly by permitting families to pay more than 30% of their incomes in rent. The demonstration was made permanent in 1985.

Increasing Role of State and Local Governments

By the mid-1980s, federal housing programs had gone through a number of iterations. Some programs had been scrapped as inefficient, subject to fraud and abuse, or too expensive. Shifting federal priorities—toward reducing taxes and increasing military spending in response to the Cold War—reduced funding available for social programs, including housing assistance. Creation of assisted housing with federal funds was on the decline, with production between 1982 and 1988 slowing significantly.[12] In addition, existing affordable rental units were being lost as use restrictions between private owners and HUD expired or owners chose to prepay their low- interest mortgages and begin charging market-rate rent.[13]

As a result of reduced federal support for housing, state and local governments and private for- or non-profit organizations began to take the initiative in developing innovative ways of providing housing in their communities.[14] Policymakers acknowledged that, in some cases, local communities had better knowledge about how to provide housing than the federal government, and might be able to provide housing more efficiently than HUD.[15] From the late 1980s through the 1990s, Congress acknowledged the value of local control and gave more decision-making authority over housing policy to state and local governments through the creation of block grants and tax credits.

In 1986, the Low Income Housing Tax Credit (LIHTC) program was created as part of the Tax Reform Act of 1986 (P.L. 99-514). The LIHTC was not initially part of the bill that became the Tax Reform Act (H.R. 3838). However, because portions of H.R. 3838 eliminated the favorable treatment of real estate investment income, Members added the LIHTC program to the bill in order to ensure that developers would have an incentive to continue to construct low- and moderate-income housing.[16]

The LIHTC program, intentionally or not, was one of the first major programs to give a good deal of control over housing policy to states and localities. Tax credits are allocated to states based on population. States then have discretion in setting priorities as to how the credits will be used. While states must prioritize projects that serve the lowest income tenants for the longest period of time, they may choose to allocate credits based on criteria such as the tenant populations served— those with special needs, families with children, or those on public housing waiting lists.

In 1990, Congress created another large, flexible block grant to states and localities. The National Affordable Housing Act of 1990 (NAHA, P.L. 101-625) authorized the HOME Investment Partnerships program. HOME was modeled after an earlier block grant, the Community Development Block Grant (CDBG), which was created as part of the Housing Act of 1974 to consolidate several special purpose grants funding many activities other than housing, such as neighborhood revitalization, open space, and water and sewer grants. NAHA directed that HOME funds be allocated to states and localities based on a formula and that funds be targeted to assist families with incomes at or below 60% of area median income. Recipient jurisdictions were permitted to use funds to assist homeowners, construct rental housing, or provide rental assistance, and they were required to establish plans for spending their funds, meet match requirements, and partner with local non-profits.

The Native American Housing Assistance and Self-Determination Act of 1996 (NAHASDA, P.L. 104-330), reorganized the system of federal housing assistance to Native Americans by eliminating several separate programs of assistance and replacing them with a single block grant program. In addition to simplifying the process of providing housing assistance, the purpose of NAHASDA was to provide federal assistance for Indian tribes in a manner that recognizes the right of Indian self-determination and tribal self-governance.

Reforming Rental Assistance

Throughout the 1990s, concern about the state of public housing grew. The public perceived public housing as mismanaged, of poor quality, and dangerous. [17] At the same time, interest was growing in reforming social programs by devolving control to the states and increasing their focus on promoting work and self sufficiency. Concern over the state of public housing—and the influence of the 1996 welfare reform debate and legislation—led to proposals for major public and assisted housing reforms. Several years of debate in Congress culminated with the enactment of the Quality Housing and Work Opportunity Reconciliation Act of 1998 (P.L. 105-276).

The purposes of QHWRA, as defined in the act, were to deregulate PHAs; provide more flexible use of federal assistance to PHAs; facilitate mixed income communities; decrease concentrations of poverty in public housing; increase accountability and reward effective management of PHAs; create incentives and economic opportunities for residents assisted by PHAs to work and become self-sufficient; consolidate the Section 8 voucher and certificate programs into a single market-driven program; remedy the problems of troubled PHAs; and replace or revitalize severely distressed public housing projects.

Specific reforms in QHWRA included increased income targeting in the voucher program, removal of federal preference categories for housing assistance, enactment of a limited community service requirement in public housing, creation of the Section 8 Housing Choice Voucher program (a hybrid of the Section 8 vouchers and certificate programs), authorization of the HOPE VI program (which had been in place, but unauthorized since the early 1990s), consolidation and reform of funding for public housing, and modifications to the assessment systems for PHAs.

TODAY'S HOUSING ASSISTANCE PROGRAMS

Today's system for providing housing assistance to low-income families is comprised of programs that fall into three main categories: rental housing assistance, federal assistance to state and local governments, and homeownership assistance. Rental assistance is provided primarily through rent vouchers that families can use in the private market, below-market rental units owned by PHAs or private landlords under contract with the federal government, and, to a limited extent, construction of new below-market rental units. Assistance to state and local governments comes in a number of forms, including broad flexible block grants that can be used for rental, homeownership, or community development purposes, special purpose block grants, and programs based in the tax system. Homeownership assistance includes direct assistance to defray homebuying costs, as well as mortgage insurance programs to help provide incentives for the private market to meet the needs of underserved segments of the population.

The following section provides a description of the major housing assistance programs that fall into these three categories.

Rental Housing Assistance

Section 8 Vouchers

Section 8 vouchers are a form of tenant-based rental assistance funded by the federal government, administered locally by quasi-governmental public housing authorities (PHAs) and provided to private landlords on behalf of low-income families. (The program is codified at 42 USC § 1437f(o)). Generally, eligible families with vouchers live in the housing of their choice in the private market and the voucher pays the difference between the family's contribution toward rent and the actual rent for the unit. Specifically, a family pays 30% of its adjusted income toward rent (although they can choose to pay more) and the PHA, which receives funding from HUD, makes payments to the landlord based on a maximum subsidy set by the PHA (based on the local fair market rent established by HUD), less the tenant's contribution. Families are eligible to receive a voucher if they are very low-income (earning 50% or less of the local area median income) or low-income (earning 80% or less of the local area median income) but meet other special criteria (for example, are elderly or have disabilities). However, PHAs must provide 75% of all vouchers available in a year to extremely low-income families (earning 30% or less of the area median income). Vouchers are nationally portable; once a family receives a voucher, it can take that voucher and move to any part of the country where a voucher program is being administered.

There are several special forms of Section 8 vouchers. Tenant protection vouchers are provided to families who would otherwise be displaced from other HUD programs. Some tenant protection vouchers, called enhanced vouchers, can have higher values than regular vouchers. PHAs also have the discretion to "project-base" some of their vouchers. Project-based vouchers are attached to specific housing units rather than given to families to use in the homes of their choosing. Another special form of voucher is the homeownership voucher; PHAs have the discretion to allow eligible first-time homebuyers to use their vouchers to make monthly mortgage payments. (For more information, see CRS Report RL32284, *An Overview of the Section 8 Housing Programs*, by Maggie McCarty.)

The voucher program is not an entitlement program. Families that wish to receive a voucher must generally apply to their local PHA and are placed on a waiting list, the length of which varies by community and can range from several months to many years. Congress has authorized and funded roughly two million vouchers. The funding for those vouchers is provided annually by Congress in the appropriations for HUD. The Section 8 voucher program is the largest of HUD's rental assistance programs, serving the largest number of households and accounting, in recent years, for over one-third of the Department's budget. Congress has generally renewed all existing vouchers each year; in some years, Congress also creates new vouchers to serve additional families, referred to as incremental vouchers. The current distribution of vouchers across PHAs results from a variety of allocation methods used in the past: formula-based, competitive, and other. While the distribution of funding to PHAs is generally based on the number of vouchers that they have and the cost of those vouchers, the exact distribution formula has often been modified by Congress in the appropriations process. (For more information, see CRS Report RL33929, *Recent Changes to the Section 8 Voucher Renewal Funding Formula*, by Maggie McCarty.)

Other Tenant-Based Rental Assistance

While Section 8 vouchers are the main form of tenant-based rental assistance, HUD also funds several other types of tenant-based rental assistance. HUD funds special vouchers for persons with disabilities (through the Section 811 program, discussed later) and for homeless persons (through the Shelter Plus Care program, discussed later), and states and localities can use their HOME Investment Partnerships Block Grant (discussed later) funds to provide vouchers.

Public Housing

Low-rent public housing developments are owned and operated by local public housing authorities (PHAs) and subsidized and regulated by the federal government. (The program is codified at 42 USC § 1437.) Generally, families are eligible to live in public housing if they are low-income (those with income at or below 80% of area median income), but 40% of public housing units that become available in a year must be given to extremely low-income families (those with income at or below 30% of area median income). As in the Section 8 voucher program, families living in public housing pay 30% of their adjusted income toward rent.

PHAs receive several streams of funding from HUD to help make up the difference between what tenants pay in rent and what it costs to maintain public housing. PHAs receive operating funds and capital funds through a formula allocation process; operating funds are used for management, administration, and the day-to-day costs of running a housing development and capital funds are used for modernization needs (such as replacing a roof or heating and cooling system, or reconfiguring units). PHAs can also apply for competitive HOPE VI revitalization grants, which are used to demolish and rebuild, or substantially rehabilitate, severely distressed public housing, replacing it with mixed-income housing. (For more information, see CRS Report RL32236, *HOPE VI Public Housing Revitalization Program: Background, Funding, and Issues,* by Maggie McCarty.)

There are roughly 1.2 million public housing units under contract with the federal government, making public housing the second largest direct housing assistance program. The 1998 Public Housing Reform Act (P.L. 105-276) prohibited public housing authorities from increasing the total number of public housing units in their inventory; however, the number of public housing units had begun to steadily decline before then for a number of reasons. PHAs are authorized to demolish or sell their public housing developments with HUD's permission, and since the mid- 1990s, they have not been required to replace those units with new units (although they must provide displaced families with Section 8 vouchers). The 1998 Act also provided authority to allow, and in some cases require, PHAs to convert their public housing units to vouchers. Also, the HOPE VI program has contributed to the demolition of more units than it has replaced.

Table 1. Appropriations for Section 8, FY1999-FY2008 ($ in millions).

FY	Tenant-Based Section 8 Vouchers	Project-Based Section 8 Rental Assistance	Total Section 8
1999	-	-	10,327
2000	-	-	11,377
2001	-	-	13,941
2002	-	-	15,640
2003	-	-	17,116
2004	-	-	19,257
2005	14,766	5,298	20,064
2006	15,418	5,037	20,455
2007	15,920	5,976	21,896
2008	15,703	6,382	22,085

Source: Figures based on congressional appropriations documents and HUD Congressional Budget Justifications.

Note: Figures are not adjusted for rescissions of unobligated budget authority. Prior to FY2005, Congress funded the Section 8 voucher and project-based rental assistance programs jointly. FY2006 figures for tenant- based rental assistance do not include $390 million in emergency appropriations for hurricane relief. Figure for FY2008 tenant-based rental assistance is adjusted for $723 million rescission of current year budget authority enacted in FY2008. Figures shown represent budget authority available in the FY, not budget authority provided (which accounts for differences in advance appropriations from year to year).

Table 2. Appropriations for Public Housing, FY1999-FY2008 ($ in millions).

FY	Operating Fund	Capital Fund	Drug Elimination Grants[a]	HOPE VI	Total Public Housing
1999	2,818	3,000	310	625	6,753
2000	3,138	2,900	310	575	6,923
2001	3,242	3,000	310	575	7,127
2002	3,495	2,843	0	574	6,912
2003	3,577	2,712	0	570	6,859
2004	3,579	2,696	0	149	6,424
2005	2,438	2,579	0	143	5,160
2006	3,564	2,439	0	99	6,102
2007	3,864	2,439	0	99	6,402
2008	4,200	2,439	0	100	6,739

Source: HUD Congressional Budget Justifications, FY2001-FY2009. Enacted funding figures taken from subsequent years' justifications.

Note: An accounting change enacted by Congress led to a one-time savings in the public housing operating fund in FY2005. For more information, see discussion on page 13 of CRS Report RL32443, *The Department of Housing and Urban Development (HUD): FY2005 Budget*.

a. Drug elimination grants were available to PHAs, initially competitively, then later via formula allocation, to pay for safety and security activities in public housing. They were funded from FY1991-FY2001.

Project-Based Section 8 Rental Assistance

Under the Section 8 project-based rental assistance program, HUD entered into contracts with private property owners under which owners agreed to rent their housing units to eligible low- income tenants for an income-based rent, and HUD agreed to pay the difference between tenants' contributions and a rent set by HUD. Families are eligible to live in project-based Section 8 units if they are low-income (having income at or below 80% of the area median income), but 40% of units made available each year must be reserved for extremely low-income families (those with income at or below 30% of the area median income).

No new project-based Section 8 contracts have been awarded since the mid-1980s, although existing contracts can be renewed upon their expiration. Roughly one million project-based units are still under contract and receive assistance. The original contracts were for 10-40 year periods and were provided with multi-year funding from Congress for the length of their contract. Therefore, each year, Congress only has to provide new funding for those contracts that have expired and require annual renewal (although, eventually, all of those long-term contracts will expire so all contracts will require annual funding). (See **Table 1** for appropriations information.) Not all contracts are renewed, so there has been a loss of project-based Section 8 units over time. When owners do not renew, tenants are provided with Section 8 tenant protection vouchers. (For more information, see CRS Report RL32284, *An Overview of the Section 8 Housing Programs,* by Maggie McCarty.)

Section 202 Supportive Housing for the Elderly Program and the Section 811 Housing for Persons with Disabilities Program

Through the Section 202 Supportive Housing for the Elderly program, HUD provides funds to nonprofit organizations which in turn build rental properties for low-income elderly households (those with a head of household or spouse age 62 or older). The program was created as part of the Housing Act of 1959 (P.L. 86-372). (The program is codified at 12 U.S.C. § 1701q.) Section 202 is the only federal housing program that funds housing exclusively for elderly persons, although from approximately 1964 to 1990, non-elderly disabled households were eligible for residency in Section 202 properties.[18] Although the Section 202 program initially provided low-interest loans to nonprofit developers, since the early 1990s, the program has provided nonprofit developers with capital grants, together with project rental assistance contracts (rental assistance that is similar to project-based Section 8). The capital grants are awarded through a competitive process. The current version of the Section 202 program serves very low-income elderly households (those with incomes at or below 50% of poverty). (For more information about the Section 202 program, see CRS Report RL33508, *Section 202 and Other HUD Rental Housing Programs for Low-Income Elderly Residents*, by Libby Perl.)

The Section 811 Supportive Housing for Persons with Disabilities Program was created in 1990 as part of the Cranston-Gonzalez Affordable Housing Act (P.L. 101-625). (The program is codified at 42 U.S.C. §8013.) Until the enactment of Section 811, the Section 202 program provided housing for persons with disabilities. Through Section 811, HUD provides capital grants to non-profit organizations to create rental housing that is affordable to very low-income households with an adult who has a disability.[19] The program also funds project rental assistance contracts to subsidize the rent paid by tenants. In addition, Section 811 makes available "mainstream vouchers" which are similar to Section 8 vouchers and allow eligible recipients to find housing in the private market. Housing built with capital grants may include group homes, independent living facilities, multifamily rental units, condominium units, and cooperative housing. Section 811 developers must provide supportive services to those residing in the units. (For more information about the Section 811 program, see CRS Report RL34728, *Section 811 and Other HUD Housing Programs for Persons with Disabilities,* by Libby Perl.)

Other Rent-Restricted Units

The Section 236 program was a HUD initiative to encourage private developers to create housing affordable to low- and moderate-income households. The program, created as part of the Housing and Urban Development Act of 1968 (P.L. 90-448) was active in promoting new development from approximately 1969 to 1973. (The program is codified at 12 U.S.C. §1715z-1.) The Section 236 program provided mortgage insurance to housing developers for the construction and rehabilitation of rental housing and continues to provide mortgage subsidies to building owners through a mechanism called Interest Reduction Payments (IRPs). IRPs are subsidies to owners that ensure that the owners will only pay 1% interest on their mortgages. Approximately 240,000 developments continue to receive IRPs today.[20] Given the reduced financing costs, owners can charge below-market rents for Section 236 units. Many units also receive rental assistance payments through the Section 8 project-based voucher program, Rent Supplement program, or the Rental Assistance Payments (RAP) program, making the units affordable to very low-income and extremely low-income families.

The Section 221(d)(3) Below Market Interest Rate (BMIR) program was another HUD program that encouraged private developers to create affordable housing by offering FHA-insured loans with interest rates of 3%. The program was enacted as part of the Housing Act of 1961 (P.L. 87-70) and actively insured new loans until 1968, when the Section 236 program replaced it as a vehicle for affordable housing development. (The Section 221 (d)(3) program is codified at 12 U.S.C. § 1715). Like Section 236, units created under this program are offered for below-market rents and units may also receive rental assistance.

Table 3. Appropriations for Section 202 and Section 811,
FY1999-FY2008 ($ in millions).

FY	Section 202[a]	Section 811
1999	660	194
2000	610	201
2001	677	216
2002	683	240
2003	678	249
2004	698	249
2005	648	238
2006	635	231
2007	639	236
2008	629	237

Source: HUD Budget Justifications from FY2001 through FY2009.

a. The amounts appropriated for Section 202 include funds for new capital grants, new project rental assistance, and renewals of or amendments to project rental assistance contracts. These figures do not include funds for Service Coordinators or the Assisted Living Conversion Program.

Rural Rental Housing (Section 515) and Rental Assistance (Section 521)

Title V of the Housing Act of 1949 authorized the U.S. Department of Agriculture (USDA) to make loans to farmers to enable them to construct, improve, repair, or replace dwellings and other farm buildings to provide decent, safe, and sanitary living conditions for themselves, their tenants, lessees, sharecroppers, and laborers. USDA was authorized to make grants, or combinations of loans and grants to those farmers who could not qualify to repay the full amount of a loan, but who needed the funds to make their dwellings sanitary or to remove health hazards to the occupants or the community. Although the act was initially targeted to farmers, over time the act has been amended to enable USDA to make housing loans and grants to rural residents in general.

The USDA housing programs are generally referred to by the section number under which they are authorized in the Housing Act of 1949, as amended. Under the Section 515 program, the Rural Housing Service of the USDA is authorized to make direct loans for the construction of rural rental and cooperative housing. (The program is codified at 42 U.S.C. § 1485.) The loans are made at a 1% interest rate and are repayable in 50 years. Except for public agencies, all borrowers must demonstrate that financial assistance from other sources is not enough to enable the borrower to provide the housing at terms that are affordable to the target population. Under the Section 521 program, rental assistance payments, which are made directly to owners of rental properties, make up the difference between the tenants' rent payments and the USDA-approved rent for the Section 515 units. (The program is codified at 42 U.S.C. § 1490a.) Owners must agree to operate the property on a limited profit or nonprofit basis. For more information, see CRS Report RL33421, *USDA Rural Housing Programs: An Overview*, by Bruce E. Foote.

Table 4. Appropriations for the USDA Section 515 and Section 521 Programs, FY1999 - FY2008 ($ in millions).

FY	Section 515	Section 521 Rental Assistance
1999	114	583
2000	114	640
2001	114	686
2002	118	701
2003	115	724
2004	116	581
2005	99	592
2006	98	647
2007	90	329
2008	70	482

Source: U.S. Department of Agriculture Budget Justifications and Appropriations Acts.

Funding for States and Localities

Low Income Housing Tax Credit

The LIHTC was enacted as part of the Tax Reform Act of 1986 (P.L. 99-514) and provides incentives for the development of affordable rental housing through federal tax credits administered through the Internal Revenue Service. (The program is codified at 26 U.S.C. §42.) The tax credits are disbursed to state housing finance agencies (HFAs) based on population. HFAs, in turn, award the credits to housing developers that agree to build or rehabilitate housing where a certain percentage of units will be affordable to low income households. Housing developers then sell the credits to investors and use the proceeds from sale of the credits to help finance the housing developments. The benefit of the tax credits to the purchasing investors is that they reduce the investor's federal income tax liability annually over a ten year period.

Because tax credits reduce the amount of private financing required to build or rehabilitate housing, the owners of developments financed through tax credits are able to charge lower rents. In order to qualify for the tax credits, at least 20% of units in a development must be occupied by households with incomes at or below 50% of area median income, or at least 40% of units must be occupied by households with incomes at or below 60% of area median income. Rent charged for the rent restricted units in a development may not exceed 30% of an imputed income limitation—calculated based on area median incomes. Units financed with tax credits must remain affordable for at least 15 years. As of 2005, over 1.5 million units had been created using LIHTCs.[21] In 2007, the Joint Committee on Taxation estimated that the LIHTC would result in a $5.1 billion tax expenditure.[22] For more information, see CRS Report RS22389, *An Introduction to the Design of the Low-Income Housing Tax Credit,* by Mark P. Keightley.

Mortgage Revenue Bonds

The federal government authorizes state and local governments to issue private activity bonds, up to a certain limit, which are exempt from federal taxes. One form of a private activity bond is a mortgage revenue bond (MRB). State or local governments—or their authorized agencies, such as housing finance agencies—sell MRBs to investors. Because the interest earned by bondholders is exempt from federal (and sometimes state) taxation, the bonds can be marketed at lower interest rates than would be required for similar taxable instruments. The proceeds of the bond sale, less issuance costs and reserves, are used to finance home mortgages to eligible (generally first-time) homebuyers. In effect, the tax exemption on the bonds provides an interest rate subsidy to homebuyers.

In order to qualify for the benefit, a borrower must not have been a homeowner in the past three years, the mortgage must be for the principal residence of the borrower, the purchase price may not exceed 90% (110% in targeted areas) of the average purchase price in the area, and the income of the borrower may not exceed 110% (140% in targeted areas) of the median income for the area. In 2007, the Joint Committee on Taxation estimated that MRBs would result in a $1.4 billion tax expenditure.[23]

Table 5. Appropriations for the Community Development Fund and CDBG, FY1999- FY2008 ($ in millions).

FY	CDBG Formula Grants	Set-Asides	Community Development Fund Account Total
1999	4,218	532	4,750
2000	4,236	545	4,781
2001	4,399	647	5,046
2002	4,341	659	5,000
2003	4,340	565	4,905
2004	4,331	603	4,934
2005	4,117	585	4,702
2006	3,711	467	4,178
2007	3,711	61	3,772
2008	3,593	273	3,866

Source: HUD Congressional Budget Justifications; for FY2004-FY2007, HUD's website http://www.hud.gov/ offices/cpd/about/budget/ HUD Budget Justifications, FY2000-FY2008 (enacted funding levels FY1 998-FY2006), P.L. 110-5 (enacted funding levels for FY2007), P.L. 110-161 (enacted funding levels for FY2008), and FY2009 President's budget.

Note: The CDBG program is funded in an account called the Community Development Fund. That account also funds set-asides including funding for Economic Development Initiatives and Neighborhood Initiatives. This table excludes emergency funding provided to CDBG in response to disasters.

Community Development Block Grants

The Community Development Block Grant (CDBG) program was enacted as part of the Housing and Community Development Act of 1974 (P.L. 93-383), and is administered by HUD. (The program is codified at 42 U.S.C. §§5301-5321.)

The purpose of the CDBG program is to develop viable urban communities by providing decent housing, a suitable living environment, and expanding economic opportunities primarily for low- and moderate-income persons. The CDBG program distributes 70% of total funds through formula grants to entitlement communities—central cities of metropolitan areas, cities with populations of 50,000 or more, and urban counties—and the remaining 30% goes to states for use in small, non-entitlement communities.

Recipient communities may use CDBG funds for a variety of activities, although at least 70% of funds must be used to benefit low- and moderate-income persons. Eligible activities include the acquisition and rehabilitation of property for purposes such as public works, urban beautification, historic preservation; the demolition of blighted properties; services such as crime prevention, child care, drug abuse counseling, education, or recreation; neighborhood economic development projects; and the rehabilitation or development of housing as well as housing counseling services.

HOME Block Grants

The HOME Investment Partnerships program is a housing block grant program administered by HUD designed to expand the supply of decent, safe, sanitary, and affordable housing. (The program is codified at 42 USC § § 12741 et seq.) HOME funds are provided via formula allocation; 60% of funds are awarded to participating jurisdictions (which have populations above a certain threshold) and 40% are awarded to states to use in areas not served by participating jurisdictions. HOME grantees must match 25% of their HOME grants (with some exceptions) and submit a plan to HUD detailing their community needs and priorities.

HOME funds can be used for four main purposes: homeowner rehabilitation, homebuyer assistance, rental construction and rehabilitation, and the provision of tenant-based rental assistance. In 2003, Congress added a special set-aside of funding, called the American Dream Downpayment Initiative (ADDI) program, which can be used only for downpayment and closing cost assistance for eligible first time homebuyers. All HOME funds must be used to benefit low- income families (those with incomes at or below 80% of the area median income) and at least 90% of funds must be used to benefit families with incomes at or below 60% of area median income. (For more information about HOME, see CRS Report R40 118, *An Overview of the HOME Investment Partnerships Program*, by Katie Jones.)

Homeless Assistance Grants

HUD administers four homeless assistance grants, three of which were enacted in 1987 as part of the McKinney-Vento Homeless Assistance Act (P.L. 100-77). (The Homeless Assistance Grants are codified at Title 42, Chapter 119, Subchapter IV of the United States Code.) The four homeless assistance grants are (1) the Emergency Shelter Grants (ESG) program,[24] (2) the Supportive Housing Program (SHP), (3) the Single Room Occupancy (SRO) program, and (4) the Shelter Plus Care (S+C) program.[25] The four grants are distributed to local communities through both formula allocations and a competitive grant process. Depending on the program under which funds are awarded, grantees may use their awards to provide permanent supportive housing, transitional housing, and supportive services for homeless individuals.

Table 6. Appropriations for HOME, FY1999-FY2007 ($ in millions).

FY	HOME Formula Grants	Set-Asides	HOME Account Total
1999	1,550	50	**1,600**
2000	1,553	47	**1,600**
2001	1,734	62	**1,796**
2002	1,743	53	**1,796**
2003	1,850	137	**1,987**
2004	1,855	150	**2,006**
2005	1,785	115	**1,900**
2006	1,677	81	**1,757**
2007	1,677	81	**1,757**
2008	1,625	79	**1,704**

Source: FY1999-FY2005 data provided by HUD to CRS; FY2006-FY2007 data available from HUD's website http://www.hud.gov/offices/cpd/about/budget/; FY2008 data taken from HUD FY2009 Congressional Budget Justifications.

Note: In addition to funding HOME block grants, the HOME account is also used to fund the American Dream Downpayment Initiative and other set-asides, including housing counseling assistance and funding for insular areas.

The ESG program funds are distributed by formula to both local communities and states, and may be used by grantees to address the emergency requirements of persons experiencing homelessness. The other three homeless assistance grants—SHP, SRO, and S+C—focus on the longer term needs of persons experiencing homelessness—transitional and permanent housing together with supportive services. Funds for each of the three grants are distributed through a competition in which local communities (usually cities, counties, or combinations of both) collaborate and apply for funds through HUD's "Continuum of Care" process. SHP funds may be used for transitional housing for homeless individuals and families for up to 24 months, permanent housing for disabled homeless individuals, and supportive services. The SRO program provides permanent housing to homeless individuals in efficiency units where bathroom and kitchen facilities are shared. The S+C program provides permanent supportive housing for disabled homeless individuals and their families. (For more information about the Homeless Assistance Grants, see CRS Report RL33764, *The HUD Homeless Assistance Grants: Distribution of Funds*, by Libby Perl.)

Housing Opportunities for Persons with AIDS

The Housing Opportunities for Persons with AIDS (HOPWA) program is the only federal program that provides funding specifically for housing for persons with acquired immunodeficiency syndrome (AIDS) and related illnesses. Congress established the HOP WA program as part of the National Affordable Housing Act (P.L. 101-625) in 1990. (The program is codified at 42 U.S.C. § § 12901-12912.) HOP WA program funding is distributed both by formula allocations and competitive grants. HUD awards 90% of appropriated funds by formula to states and eligible metropolitan statistical areas (MSAs) that meet thresholds regarding population, AIDS cases, and AIDS incidence. Recipient states and MSAs may allocate grants to nonprofit organizations or administer the funds through government agencies. HOPWA grantees may use funds for a wide range of housing, social services, program planning, and development costs. (For more information about HOPWA, see CRS Report RL343 18, *Housing for Persons Living with HIV/AIDS*, by Libby Perl.)

Table 7. Appropriations for the Homeless Assistance Grants and HOPWA, FY1999- FY2008 ($ in millions).

FY	Homeless Assistance Grants	HOPWA
1999	975	225
2000	1,020	232
2001	1,123	257
2002	1,123	277
2003	1,217	290
2004	1,260	295
2005	1,229	282
2006	1,327	286
2007	1,442	286
2008	1,586	300

Source: HUD Budget Justifications, FY200 1 through FY2009.

Table 8. Appropriations for NAHASDA, FY1999-FY2008 ($ in millions).

FY	NAHASDA
1999	620
2000	620
2001	650
2002	649
2003	645
2004	650
2005	622
2006	624
2007	624
2008	630

Source: HUD Budget Justifications, FY200 1-FY2009, and Appropriations Acts.

NAHASDA

The Native American Housing Assistance and Self-Determination Act of 1996 (NAHASDA, P.L. 104-330), reorganized the system of federal housing assistance to Native Americans by separating Native American programs from the public housing program, and by eliminating several separate programs of assistance and replacing them with a single block grant program. In addition to simplifying the process of providing housing assistance, the purpose of NAHASDA was to provide federal assistance for Indian tribes in a manner that recognizes the right of Indian self- determination and tribal self-governance.

The act provides block grants to Indian tribes or their tribally designated housing entities (TDHE) for affordable housing activities. The tribe must submit an Indian housing plan (IHP), with long- and short-term goals and proposed activities, which is reviewed by HUD for compliance with statutory and regulatory requirements. Funding is provided under a needs-based formula, which was developed pursuant to negotiated rule-making. Tribes and TDHEs can leverage funds, within certain limits, by using future grants as collateral to issue obligations under a guaranteed loan program.

Homeownership Assistance

Federal Housing Administration

The Federal Housing Administration (FHA) is an agency within HUD that insures mortgages made by private lenders. Since lenders are insured against loss if borrowers default, they are willing to make loans to borrowers who might not otherwise be served by the private market, particularly those with low downpayments or little credit history. FHA-insured borrowers pay an insurance premium to FHA and are subject to limits on the size of loan that they can obtain.

The FHA administers a variety of mortgage insurance products, including insurance for home purchase and home improvement loans, reverse mortgages to allow the elderly to remain in their homes, as well as loans for the purchase, repair, or construction of apartments, hospitals, and nursing homes. The programs are administered through two program accounts—the Mutual Mortgage Insurance/Cooperative Management Housing Insurance fund account (MMI) and the General Insurance/Special Risk Insurance fund account (GI/SRI). The MMI fund provides insurance for home mortgages. The GI/SRI fund provides insurance for more risky home mortgages, for multifamily rental housing, and for an assortment of special purpose loans such as hospitals and nursing homes.

Table 10 presents the FHA share of the home mortgage market for FY1998 - FY2007. The share of home purchases financed with an FHA-insured mortgage each year was about 14% for FY1999 through FY2001 and then it began to decline to a low of 4% in FY2006. The FHA share of loans doubled between FY2006 and FY2007, as FHA obtained a higher share of a smaller mortgage market. For more information on FHA, see CRS Report RS20530, *FHA-Insured Home Loans: An Overview*, by Bruce E. Foote and Katie Jones.

Table 9. FHA Share of Mortgage Market, FY1998 - FY2007.

FY	Number of FHA-Insured Mortgages Originated (000)	FHA-Insured Mortgages as a % of All Home Sales
1998	790	13
1999	911	14
2000	858	14
2001	872	14
2002	808	12
2003	657	9
2004	506	6
2005	346	4
2006	302	4
2007	289	8

Source: HUD, http://www.hud.gov/offices/hsg/comp/rpts/fhamktsh/fhamktcurrent.pdf.

Table 10. VA Share of Mortgage Market, FY1998 - FY2007.

FY	Number of VA-Insured Mortgages Originated (000)	VA-Insured Mortgages as a % of All Home Sales
1998	344	6
1999	486	8
2000	199	3
2001	250	4
2002	317	5
2003	489	7
2004	336	4
2005	166	2
2006	143	2
2007	133	2

Source: VA loan data provided to CRS by U.S. Department of Veterans Affairs. Total market data taken from HUD's website at http://www.hud.gov/offices/hsg/comp/rpts/fhamktsh/fhamktcurrent. pdf. Percentages calculated by CRS.

Department of Veterans Affairs Loan Guarantees

The Servicemen's Readjustment Act of 1944 (P.L. 78-346) established the home loan guaranty program, which is now administered by the Department of Veterans Affairs (VA). The VA loan guaranty program was an alternative to cash bonuses for the millions of men and women who served in the Armed Forces during World War II.

Under this program, an eligible veteran may purchase a home through a private lender and the VA guarantees to pay the lender a portion of the losses if the veteran defaults on the loan, similar to FHA. While initially established to benefit veterans who had served during war times, the program has been amended to extend eligibility to all parties who are on active duty or honorably discharged from the services. The main objective of the current VA home loan guaranty program is to help veterans finance the purchase of homes on favorable loan terms.

Table 11 presents the VA-insured share of the home mortgage market for FY1998 to FY2007. The total number of VA-insured loans originated per year as a share of all home sales declined from 8% in FY1999 to 2% in FY2005 through FY2007. For more information on VA home loans, see CRS Report RS20533, *VA-Home Loan Guaranty Program: An Overview*, by Bruce E. Foote.

Federal Home Loan Banks

The Federal Home Loan Banks (FHLB; the Banks) were created in 1932 by the Federal Home Loan Bank Act (P.L. 72-304) to serve as lenders to savings and loan associations, which at the time made the majority of home mortgage loans. The Banks were established to ensure the liquidity of these lenders, and today lend money to commercial banks, credit unions, and insurance companies in addition to savings and loans. The FHLB System includes twelve regional wholesale Banks and an Office of Finance. Each Bank is a separate legal entity, cooperatively owned by its member financial institutions, and has its own management, employees, and board of directors. Each Bank is assigned a distinct geographic area.

Although the Federal Home Loan Banks are not subject to federal income tax, they do pay 20% of their net earnings to fund a portion of the interest on the Resolution Funding Corporation (REFCorp) debt, which was issued for the resolution of insolvent savings and loans association during the 1980s. In addition, the Federal Home Loan Banks contribute the greater of 10% of their net income or $100 million toward an Affordable Housing Program, the purpose of which is to extend grants and subsidized housing loans to very low- to moderate-income families and individuals. The Affordable Housing Program includes a First-time Homebuyer Program which enables up to $10,000 to be awarded to eligible homebuyers for downpayment and closing cost assistance. For more information, see CRS Report RL328 15, *Federal Home Loan Bank System: Policy Issues*, by Edward V. Murphy.

Department of Agriculture Rural Housing Loans

Through the Section 502 Guaranteed Rural Housing Loan program, USDA is authorized to make both direct loans and to guarantee private loans to very low- to moderate-income rural residents for the purchase or repair of new or existing single-family homes. (The program is codified at 42 U.S.C. § 1472.) The direct loans have a 33-year term and interest rates may be as low as 1%. Borrowers with incomes at or below 80% of area median income qualify for the direct loans. The guaranteed loans have 30-year terms, and borrowers with incomes at or below 115% of the area median qualify. Priority for both direct and guaranteed loans is given to first-time homebuyers, and USDA may require that borrowers complete a homeownership counseling program.

Through the Section 504 program, the USDA makes loans and grants to very low-income homeowners (those with incomes at or below 50% of area median income) for home repairs or improvements, or to remove health and safety hazards. (The program is codified at 42 U.S.C. § 1474.) The Section 504 grants may be available to homeowners who are age 62 or older. To qualify for the grants, the elderly homeowners must lack the ability to repay the full cost of the repairs. Depending on the cost of the repairs and the income of the elderly homeowner, the owner may be eligible either for a grant that will cover the full cost of the repairs, or for some combination of loan and grant. For more information, see CRS Report RL3 3421, *USDA Rural Housing Programs: An Overview*, by Bruce E. Foote.

Section 235

The Section 235 program, enacted as part of the Housing and Urban Development Act of 1968 (P.L. 90-448), helped to subsidize the home purchases of individual borrowers. Through the program, FHA provided a monthly subsidy payment to lenders in order to reduce the interest liability of loans made to eligible borrowers. As originally enacted and administered, homebuyers were required to pay at least 20% of their income toward debt service on their mortgages, and FHA paid the lenders the lesser of (1) balance of the monthly payment due after the borrowers paid 20% of their income or (2) the difference between the required payments at the FHA interest rate and the payments that would be due on a loan with a 1% interest rate. As a result, the subsidy to homeowners varied depending upon their income, the amount of the mortgage, and the market interest rate.

The Section 235 program had a two-tiered eligibility component. At least 80% of program funds were made available for homebuyers with incomes that did not exceed 135% of the maximum income for admission to public housing. Applicants in this group could purchase homes with downpayments as low as $200. The remaining 20% of program funds were available for a higher income group. Applicants in this group had to make downpayments of at least 3% of the sales price. New commitments under the Section 235 program were halted by the 1973 Nixon moratorium; a revised version of the program was reactivated in 1976. The Section 235 program was terminated as of October 1, 1989 by the Housing and Community Development Act of 1987 (P.L. 100-242); however, roughly 4,000 families continue to be assisted by the program.[26]

Mortgage Interest Deduction

Homeownership promotion has generally taken two forms: government assistance in the financing of home purchases, and tax preferences favoring homeowners. One of the tax incentives that promotes homeownership is the mortgage interest deduction. The mortgage interest deduction allows homeowners to deduct any interest paid on their mortgage from their taxable income, thus reducing their tax liability. The deduction benefits those households that own homes, that have a mortgage on which they pay interest, that have federal income tax liability, and for whom itemized deductions exceed the standard deduction (approximately 75% of taxpayers take the standard deduction). It is not targeted to lower-income households.

Although the mortgage interest deduction was not initially created to promote homeownership,[27] today, the mortgage interest deduction could be considered the federal government's largest housing program. According to the Joint Committee on Taxation (JCT), in FY2007, the mortgage interest deduction resulted in a $73.7 billion tax expenditure.[28]

ISSUES AND TRENDS IN HOUSING ASSISTANCE PROGRAMS

Incidence of Housing Problems

When the federal housing assistance programs began in the 1930s, the nation was considered to be ill-housed. The Housing Act of 1937 identified an "acute shortage of decent, safe, and sanitary dwellings." Thanks in part to stricter building codes and standards, most housing in the United States today is decent, safe, and sanitary. Although some units are still considered substandard, today the greatest perceived housing problem is affordabililty. Housing is considered "affordable" if it costs no more than 30% of a household's income. Households that pay half or more of their income toward their housing costs are considered severely cost burdened; households that pay between 30% and 50% of their income toward their housing costs are considered moderately cost burdened. According to data from the Census Bureau's American Community Survey, 20 million households were moderately cost burdened and 17 million households were severely cost burdened in 2005.[29]

HUD is directed to report to Congress periodically on the incidence of "worst case" housing needs. Worst case housing needs are defined as unassisted renters with very low incomes (at or below 50% of area median income) who pay more than half of their income for housing costs or live in severely substandard housing. In a report to Congress on worst case housing needs, HUD found that roughly 6 million households had worst case housing needs in 2005, accounting for 5.5% of all households.[30] This was a statistically significant increase from 2003, when 5.2 million households had worst case housing needs (4.9% of all households). Prior to the increase in 2005, the percentage of households having worst case housing needs had remained relatively steady— roughly 5%—since HUD began reporting on worst case housing needs in 1991. The vast majority of households with worst case housing needs (91%) were severely cost burdened, but lived in standard housing; only about 4% of households had worst case housing needs solely because they lived in substandard housing. In other words, their worst case housing needs were a function of the cost of their housing to a much greater extent than the condition of their housing.

Characteristics of Families Receiving Assistance

Public housing, Section 8 vouchers, and the project-based rental assistance programs (including project-based Section 8, Section 202 and Section 811) combined serve roughly 4 million households and can be considered the primary housing assistance programs for low-income families. These three forms of assistance are similar in many ways. They all target assistance to extremely low-income families, require families to pay 30% of their incomes toward rent, and generally have long waiting lists for assistance. However, the three vary significantly in terms of their evolution, the structure of their benefit (a portable voucher versus a housing unit), and their administration (PHA versus private owner).

The similarities and differences in the programs themselves result in similarities and differences in the characteristics of the households they serve. **Table 11** provides household characteristics data for participants in the Section 8 tenant-based voucher program, the public housing program, and the project-based rental assistance programs (including project-based Section 8, housing for the elderly and disabled, and the rental assistance payment programs).

Table 11. Characteristics of Households Served in Selected Housing Assistance Programs.

	Tenant-Based	Public Housing	Project-Based
Household Characteristics			
Elderly Head of Household	16%	32%	48%
Disabled Head of Household	25%	20%	15%
All Households with Children	59%	42%	29%
Non-Married Female Head of Household With Children	54%	38%	26%
Race and Ethnicity (Head of Household)			
White	54%	50%	63%
Black	43%	47%	32%
Hispanic (any race)	16%	21%	11%
Household Income (2004)			
Median Annual Income	$9,500	$8,400	$9,300
Zero Income	4%	5%	5%
Source of Income (All Households)			
Any Wages	37%	31%	22%
Any Welfare	24%	17%	9%
Any Social Security, Pension, or Disability Income	28%	39%	65%
Source of Income (Non-elderly, Non-disabled)			
Any Wages	55%	54%	49%
Any Welfare	29%	25%	17%
Any Social Security, Pension, or Disability Income	6%	6%	10%
Tenure (in years)			
25th Percentile	1.8	1.9	1.7
Median	3.4	5.3	3.8
75th Percentile	6.6	12.1	8.6
Location			
Suburb	32%	17%	28%
Central City	47%	54%	50%
Non-Metro Area	21%	29%	21%

Source: Calculated by CRS, based on data provided by HUD.
Note: Data reflect participating households in December 2004.

The Section 8 (tenant-based) voucher program serves more single, female-headed households with children than do the public housing program or project-based programs. In 2004, over half of voucher households were households with children headed by unmarried females, compared to less than 40% of public housing households and less than 30% of project-based households. The project-based programs primarily serve elderly and disabled households, who account for nearly two-thirds of all households served in those programs. This is not surprising given that owners of project-based housing may designate entire properties for elderly or disabled households. Public housing is more evenly divided, with about half of all households being elderly or disabled.

In all three programs, the majority of households served have heads of household who identify their race as white, although all three serve a substantial number of households whose heads identify their race as black. Public housing serves the highest proportion of black households, 47% compared to 43% in the voucher program and 32% in the project-based programs. Between 10% and 20% of households served across the three programs have heads of household who identify their ethnicity as Hispanic, with public housing again having the largest share. Public housing is also more concentrated in central cities than are vouchers or project-based units.

The rules governing the three main housing assistance programs require that they serve low- income households. In 2004, the median household income across the three programs ranged from $8,400 in the public housing program to $9,500 in the voucher program. The median income of the households served in the HUD programs was less than one-fifth of national median income. (In FY2004, national median income for a family of four was $57,500.[31]) Across all three programs, roughly 5% of households reported having zero income.

Given the differences in characteristics of households served by each program, it is not surprising that the source of tenant income varies significantly by program. Among households receiving project-based rental assistance, nearly two-thirds reported receiving pension income, Social Security income, or disability-related fixed income. In the voucher program, which serves fewer elderly and disabled households than the project-based programs, nearly as many households reported receiving some income from welfare as receiving income from pension, Social Security, or disability-related payments. In the public housing program, a little over a third of households reported receiving income from Social Security, pension, or disability payments and a little under a third reported income from work.

Unlike the Temporary Assistance for Needy Families (TANF) program, the housing assistance programs do not contain a requirement that recipients obtain employment, with the exception of an 8-hour per month community service requirement for non-working, non-elderly, non-disabled public housing residents. There have been proposals offered in Congress to institute a work requirement for recipients of assisted housing, and some public housing authorities have experimented with instituting such requirements. Looking at non-elderly, non-disabled households across the three programs, half or more of all households have at least some income from work.

Concern has been raised that perhaps the income-based rent structure in the assisted housing programs acts as a disincentive for households to increase their earnings; for every new dollar a family earns, thirty-cents must go toward rent.[32] There have been some efforts to mitigate this perceived work disincentive, including the adoption of an earned income disregard in the public housing program and an earned income disregard for disabled families in the voucher program. Congress also developed the Family Self Sufficiency (FSS) program in an effort to promote work. Families in the FSS program enter into contracts with their PHAs in which they agree to take steps toward becoming self sufficient within five years. The PHA, in turn, agrees to deposit any increased rent collected as a result of the family's increased earnings into an escrow account that the family will receive at the end of the five years, or from which they can make interim withdrawals for approved purposes. FSS is voluntary for PHAs to administer and voluntary for families to join.

Also unlike TANF, the housing assistance programs do not have time limits. Once a household begins receiving housing assistance, that household can continue to receive assistance for as long as they wish to participate in the program and continue to comply with program rules. Families whose incomes increase above the initial eligibility thresholds can continue to receive assistance until 30% of their income is equal to their rent. At that point, they no longer qualify for rental assistance under the voucher program, and in the case of the public housing program, they can continue to live in their apartments and pay market rate rent. Among the households receiving assistance in December 2004, the median length of time that households had lived in assisted housing (tenure) was greatest in the public housing program, at just over five years, and shortest in the voucher program, at just under three and a half years.[33]

The Federal Government's Role in Housing

Beginning in the 1980s, the federal government took on a lesser role in the creation of assisted housing. This occurred in several ways. Congress ceased funding new construction under the Section 8 project-based program, which from its enactment in 1974, had subsidized hundreds of thousands of units of assisted housing. This left very few active programs in which HUD supported the development of physical housing units. Between 1976 and 1982, the federal housing programs produced more than one million units of subsidized housing.[34] In the following years, however, annual production was around 25,000 new subsidized units.[35] Around the time that housing production was declining, Congress created two programs that gave a good deal of control over decisions regarding housing policy and development to state and local governments—these included the Low Income Housing Tax Credit (LIHTC) program and the HOME Investment Partnerships program. These programs, particularly the LIHTC, have been used by states and localities to create hundreds of thousands of units of affordable housing.

The federal government's decision to take a lesser role in the development of housing has had several consequences. First, state and local governments have taken on an increased role in providing affordable housing and establishing priorities in their communities.[36] Second, due to a reduction in the number of new affordable housing units that are created each year, the need to preserve existing affordable housing units has taken on a new importance. A third consequence is the need for multiple streams of funding other than federal grants in order both to support the creation of new affordable housing units and to preserve existing units. Those three consequences are discussed more fully below.

First, with the advent of both the LIHTC program and the HOME program, states and localities were able to exercise discretion in determining how to prioritize and develop housing using a larger pool of federal funds. Until that point, even though states, through their Housing Finance Agencies, helped finance mortgage loans and affordable rental housing, their role was limited by the amount of funds available.

In the Low Income Housing Tax Credit program, states develop plans in which they may set aside a certain percentage of tax credits for populations such as homeless individuals or persons with disabilities. They may also decide to use tax credits to preserve existing housing as well as to build new housing. Funds that states receive from the HOME program may be used for the construction of new rental housing and rental assistance for low-income households. A potential drawback of these programs is their inability, on their own, to reach the neediest households.[37] For example, in a LIHTC development, at least 20% of units must be affordable to households at or below 50% of area median income, or 40% of units must be affordable to households at or below 60% of area median income. Many of the older HUD programs constructed housing that was affordable to households at or below 30% of area median income—those considered extremely low-income. Often these households cannot afford units in LIHTC properties without rental subsidies, such as Section 8 vouchers.[38]

Another way some states and local governments support affordable housing is outside of the assistance of the federal government, through establishment of their own housing trust funds. These trust funds use dedicated funding sources such as document recording fees or real estate transfer taxes to create a pool of funds for affordable housing. By using a dedicated source of financing, trust funds may not be as subject to the vicissitudes of state budgets as are other means of funding housing development. States and local communities also support affordable housing through inclusionary zoning. Through this method, housing developers are expected to dedicate a percentage of units they build as affordable housing. In exchange, states or local communities give developers incentives that allow them to expand or speed up the pace of development. Some of the incentives include density bonuses or zoning variances that allow developers to build larger facilities than they would be able to under existing zoning regulations, as well as expedited approval of building permits.

A second consequence of the decreased role of the federal government in the creation of affordable housing units is the increased pressure to maintain the affordability of existing units. Many HUD subsidized units that were developed in the 1960s and 1970s through programs such as Section 236 and Section 221(d)(3), as well as those units that received Section 8 project-based rental assistance, are no longer available to low-income households. At the time the properties were developed, building owners entered into contracts with HUD in which they agreed to maintain affordability for a certain number of years. The duration of these contracts varied; depending on the federal program, these contracts, or "use restrictions" may last between 15 years (the Low Income Housing Tax Credit program) and 50 years (early Section 202 developments). In recent years, these contracts have begun to expire or, in some cases, property owners have chosen to pay off their mortgages early and end the use restrictions. Contracts for rental assistance, including project-based Section 8 rental assistance, have also begun to expire. When any of these events occur, owners may charge market-rate rents for the units, and the affordable units are lost. The term used to refer to efforts to maintain the affordability of these housing units is "affordable housing preservation." In coming years, more and more property owners will be in a position to opt out of affordability restrictions and thousands of units could be lost.[39]

Congress has attempted to enact laws that would preserve affordable housing units; however, due to the temporary nature of some of the measures, preservation remains a concern. Congress first enacted legislation to help preserve affordable rental housing in 1987. The Emergency Low- Income Housing Preservation Act (ELIHPA), enacted as part of the Housing and Community Development Act of 1987 (P.L. 100-242), was a temporary measure that prevented owners of Section 236 and Section 221(d)(3) properties from prepaying their mortgages. In 1990, the Low- Income Housing Preservation and Resident Homeownership Act (LIHPRHA), enacted as part of the Cranston-Gonzalez National Affordable Housing Act (P.L. 101-625), offered incentives to owners to keep them from prepaying their mortgages. However, six years after LIHPRHA was enacted, Congress reinstated the right of owners to prepay their mortgages. (See P.L. 104-134.) Another effort to preserve affordable housing was enacted as part of the Multifamily Assisted Housing Reform and Accountability Act (MAHRA, P.L. 105-65). Through this effort, called Mark-to-Market, HUD restructures the debt of building owners while at the same time renegotiating their rental assistance contracts. Unlike ELIHPA and LIHPRHA, the Mark-to-Market program is still in effect.

A third consequence of decreased federal funding for the construction of affordable housing is the need for low-income housing developers to bring together multiple funding streams in order to build a development. When the federal government first began to subsidize the production of affordable housing, in many cases the funds appropriated for housing programs were sufficient to construct or rehabilitate the affordable units without the need for funds from the private financial markets. Over the years, however, federal programs that provide grants for the construction of multifamily housing for low-income households have become a smaller portion of the government's housing portfolio. At the same time, the grants themselves have become a smaller portion of the total amount needed to support the development of affordable housing. As a result, it has become necessary for developers to turn to multiple sources of financing, including Low Income Housing Tax Credits, tax exempt bonds, and state or local housing trust funds. In addition, it is often necessary for building owners to seek rent subsidies through programs like Section 8, HOME, and Shelter Plus Care to make renting to very low- or extremely low-income households feasible.

The interactions among these various financing streams can be complex, and putting together a development plan may require the expertise of housing finance professionals.

Shift to Tenant-Based Assistance

Over time, the number of Section 8 vouchers provided and funded by the federal government has grown, while the number of federally-subsidized housing units—through project-based Section 8 rental assistance and public housing—has declined. From 1998 to 2007, the number of vouchers has increased by more than half a million;[40] over the same time period, the number of public housing units declined by over 140,000 units[41] and the number of project-based Section 8 units declined by about 120,000 units.[42]

This change from project-based assistance to tenant-based assistance is due, in part, to Congress' decision to increase the voucher program by creating new vouchers after new construction in the project-based Section 8 program and public housing program had been halted.[43] Between FY1998 and FY2007, Congress authorized and funded 276,981 new vouchers—referred to as incremental vouchers.[44] Some of these vouchers were general purpose vouchers, available to any eligible family, and some were special purpose vouchers, targeted to special populations, such as families transitioning from welfare to work.

This shift is also due, in part, to declines in the number of project-based assistance and public housing units. As previously noted in this report, the project-based rental assistance contracts between private landlords and HUD began expiring in the 1980s. When these contracts expire, private property owners can either renew their contracts with HUD (typically on an annual or five-year basis) or leave the program. When property owners leave the program, their tenants typically receive Section 8 vouchers—referred to as tenant protection vouchers. As also noted earlier in this report, since the mid-1990s, when public housing units are demolished or sold, PHAs are not required to replace each lost unit with a new public housing unit. Instead, displaced families who are not relocated to other public housing units are provided with tenant-protection vouchers. From FY1998 to FY2007, HUD awarded 280,784 tenant protection vouchers.[45][46]

The shift from project-based assistance to tenant-based assistance has several implications for families. Vouchers offer portability, which, for some residents of public or other assisted housing, may mean the ability to move out of a troubled community to a community with new opportunities. However, there is debate over whether vouchers' portability leads to economic or social mobility. Early research on mobility showed promise that families—particularly, low- income black families—that moved from heavily poverty- and minority-concentrated public housing neighborhoods to more economically- and racially-integrated neighborhoods using vouchers could see improved employment and child outcomes.[47] However, more recent mobility research has shown mixed results.[48] There is also some evidence that, for families accustomed to living in public housing, the transition to the private market rental market with a voucher can be difficult without counseling and other supports, which may not be consistently provided.[49]

Promoting Homeownership

Historian James Truslow Adams is generally credited with coining the term "the American Dream" when he wrote a book titled "The Epic of America." Adams defined the American Dream as "That dream of a land in which life should be better and richer and fuller for every man, with opportunity for each according to his ability or achievement."[50] Over time, the meaning of the American Dream has often been truncated and associated with becoming a homeowner.

For the First Quarter of 2008, the Census Bureau reported a U.S. homeownership rate of 67.8%.[51] The distribution of homeownership is not even, however. The rate is highest in the Midwest (72%) and lowest in the West (62.8%). It is highest for those age 65 years or more (79.9%), and lowest for those under 35 years old (41.3%). It is higher for whites (75%) than it is for blacks (47.1%). Hispanics, who can be of any race, had a homeownership rate of 48.9%. The homeownership rate is higher for those with income greater than the median (82.8%) and lower for those with incomes less than the median (51.2%).

Homeownership has been promoted by favorable treatment in the tax code (mortgage interest and property tax deductions); by the creation and favorable treatment of lending institutions that make home loans (federal home loan banks); by the establishment of federal programs that insure lenders against losses on home loans (FHA, VA, and USDA); by establishing institutions that create a secondary market for mortgages and enable funds for mortgages to be available throughout the U.S. (Fannie Mae, Freddie Mac, and Ginnie Mae); by establishing counseling programs, within HUD and USDA, that fund agencies that counsel prospective homebuyers on obtaining and maintaining homeownership; and by funding grant programs that provide downpayment and closing cost assistance to some homebuyers.

Since the 1940s nearly every U.S. president has expressed support for the concept of increased homeownership. For example, there has been the "Blueprint for the American Dream" by the George H.W. Bush Administration, the "National Homeownership Strategy" of the Clinton Administration, and the "Homeownership Initiative" of George W. Bush Administration. Generally, the proposals have involved little new federal funding, but have sought to rally the private sector to use existing programs to reach some specified target.

The primary focus of recent proposals has been to increase homeownership among those who have been traditionally left out of the homeownership dream, such as low-income families and minorities. The success of these proposals will likely depend on the success of such families in maintaining homeownership once obtained.

DATA

The following tables present data on federal spending (outlays) on selected housing assistance programs as well as data on the number of assisted units, since 1980.

Table 12 presents outlays for selected programs, in both real and nominal dollars. It is important to note that this table does not include any spending information related to loan commitments or obligations.

As can be seen in **Table 12**, outlays for the selected programs have increased, in both real and nominal dollars, over the nearly three decades presented (a 363% increase in nominal dollars, a 105% increase in real dollars). The growth in outlays was greatest from the late-1980s to mid- 1990s (from 1988 to 1995 outlays grew by over 98% in nominal terms, over 62% in real terms), but has slowed in recent years (from 2000 to 2007, outlays grew by 29% in nominal terms, 8% in real terms).

Another trend that can be seen in **Table 12** is the increase in outlays for the rental assistance programs in recent years, while outlays in the public housing and other housing assistance programs are declining. This is consistent with the shift from project-based assistance to tenant- based assistance (or vouchers) discussed earlier in this report.

Table 13 presents the number of units eligible for payment across several programs. Units eligible for payment is a measure of the number of housing units under rental assistance contracts with HUD (project-based Section 8, Section 202 and Section 811 units, and rental assistance payment and rent supplement units) as well as the number of Section 8 vouchers. Generally, over the course of a year, each unit will be available for one household, although given turnover, properties are rarely at 100% occupancy and vouchers are rarely 100% utilized. As a result, fewer households receive assistance in a year than there are units eligible for payment in a year.

Table 12. Outlays, Selected Housing Programs, FY1980-FY2007
(nominal dollars in millions, unless otherwise noted).

Fiscal Year	Rental Assistance[a]	Public Housing[b]	Other Housing Assistance[c]	Block Grants[d]	Homeless and HOPWA[e]	Total Nominal Dollars	Total 2007 Dollars
1980	2104	2,185	924	3910		9,123	20,539
1981	3115	2,401	1,011	4048		10,575	21,685
1982	4085	2,574	1,074	3795		11,528	22,126
1983	4995	3,206	1,003	3557		12,761	23,456
1984	6030	2,821	910	3823		13,585	24,081
1985	6818	3,408	861	3820		14,907	25,595
1986	7430	2,882	785	3329		14,426	24,205
1987	8125	2,161	758	2970	2	14,016	22,918
1988	9133	2,526	752	3054	37	15,501	24,574
1989	9918	3,043	690	2,951	70	16,673	25,444
1990	10581	3,918	679	2,821	82	18,081	26,605
1991	11400	4,544	687	2981	120	19,732	27,983
1992	12307	5,045	610	3,099	145	21,205	29,335
1993	13289	6,296	627	3,416	172	23,799	32,192
1994	14576	6,771	607	4,439	189	26,583	35,201
1995	16948	7,414	603	5519	270	30,754	39,886
1996	15779	7,605	600	5761	453	30,199	38,427
1997	16393	7,687	629	5,731	718	31,158	38,968
1998[f]	16114	7,534	576	6,360	916	31,499	38,922
1999	15652	6,560	547	6,748	1,032	30,539	37,247
2000	16692	7,193	667	7,077	1,100	32,729	39,128
2001	17494	7,483	659	7,047	1,208	33,892	39,584
2002[g]	19394	8,193	644	7,349	1,358	36,937	42,330
2003	21941	7,837	630	7,229	1,376	39,013	43,822
2004	23498	7,490	620	7,113	1,492	40,213	44,024
2005	24495	7,426	603	7225	1,562	41,312	43,823
2006	24756	7,560	569	7,086	1,655	41,626	42,742
2007	25674	7,295	559	7,011	1,664	42,202	42,202

Source: Table prepared by CRS based on data from the Department of Housing and Urban Development Annotated Tables for the 2001 Budget, Congressional Budget Justifications, and the Office of Management and Budget's Public Budget Database.

Note: Earlier versions of this table contained an error; the total columns added some figures more than once.

a. Rental Assistance includes Section 8, Section 202 and Section 811.

b. Public Housing includes Public Housing Capital Fund, Public Housing Operating Fund, Public Housing Drug Elimination Program, and HOPE VI.

c. Other Housing Assistance includes Section 235, Section 236, and Rent Supplement.

d. Block Grants includes Community Development Fund (CDBG), HOME Investment Partnerships, Native American Housing Block Grants and Housing Counseling Assistance.

e. Homeless includes HOPWA, Homeless Assistance Grants, Emergency Shelter Grants, Shelter Plus Care (including renewals), Section 8 SRO, Supportive Housing, Innovative Homeless Demonstration Program, Supplemental Assistance for Facilities to Assist the Homeless.

f. Prior to FY1 998, funding for the Native American housing programs that were consolidated by NAHASDA was included in other accounts.

g. Congress periodically provides emergency funding through the CDBG program following disasters, generally in amounts less than $1 billion per year. However, Congress provided substantially more funding following the September 11, 2001 terrorist attacks ($3 billion) and following the 2005 hurricanes (over $16 billion). The amounts shown in **Table 12** include spending of emergency funds, except for FY2002-FY2007, when spending of emergency CDBG funding was excluded.

As shown in **Table 13**, the total number of units eligible for payment under the selected housing programs has grown by over 50% over the nearly three decades presented. However, most of that growth happened in the 1980s. Since the early 1990s, the number of units eligible for payment has gone up and down from year to year, with an overall decline in units from FY2001 to FY2007.

Table 13 also helps to illustrate the trend away from public housing and other housing assistance to rental assistance (Section 8 vouchers) discussed earlier in this report. The number of units assisted under the other housing assistance programs has been on the decline since the Nixon Moratorium in the 1970s. For many of those units, once the family leaves the program, they receive a voucher. In the case of public housing, the number of units continued to increase until the mid-1990s, as contracted units became available. Since the mid-1990s, through the HOPE VI program and other authority, PHAs have been demolishing and disposing of many of their public housing developments. In their place, some replacement public housing units have been built, but many of the units were replaced with Section 8 vouchers.

KEY CRS HOUSING POLICY EXPERTS

Area of Expertise	Name	Telephone and E-Mail
Assisted rental housing, including Section 8, public and assisted housing, HOME	Maggie McCarty	7-2163 mmccarty@crs.loc.gov
Community and economic development, including Community Development Block Grants, Brownfields, empowerment zones	Eugene Boyd and Oscar R. Gonzales	7-8689 eboyd@crs.loc.gov 7-0764 ogonzales@crs.loc.gov
Consumer law and mortgage lending, housing law, including fair housing, consumer issues of bankruptcy	David H. Carpenter	7-9118 dcarpenter@crs.loc.gov
Emergency management policy, including post-disaster FEMA temporary housing issues.	Francis X. McCarthy	7-9533 fmccarthy@crs.loc.gov
Fannie Mae, Freddie Mac, and SBA disaster loans	N. Eric Weiss	7-6209 eweiss@crs.loc.gov
Homeownership, including FHA, predatory lending, rural housing, RESPA	Bruce E. Foote	7-7805 bfoote@crs.loc.gov
Affordable Housing Trust Fund, HOME, NAHASDA	Katie Jones	7-4162 kmjones@crs.loc.gov
Housing finance issues, including mortgage underwriting and FHA lending criteria	Darryl E. Getter	7-2834 dgetter@crs.loc.gov
Housing for special populations, including the elderly, disabled, homeless, HOPWA	Libby Perl	7-7806 eperl@crs.loc.gov
Housing tax policy, including the Low-Income Housing Tax Credit, mortgage revenue bonds, and other incentives for rental housing and owner-occupied housing	Mark Patrick Keightley	7-1049 mkeightley@crs.loc.gov
Non-traditional mortgages, including lending oversight by the OCC, OTS, FDIC, and Federal Reserve, and Federal Home Loan Banks	Edward Vincent Murphy	7-4972 tmurphy@crs.loc.gov

Table 13. Units Eligible for Payment, Selected Housing Programs, FY1980-FY2007.

Fiscal Year	Rental Assistance[a]	Public Housing	Other Housing Assistance[b,c]	Annual Total
1980	1153311	1,192,000	761,759	3,107,070
1981	1318927	1,204,000	774524	3,297,451
1982	1526683	1,224,000	757,213	3,507,896
1983	1749904	1,250,000	663,424	3,663,328
1984	1909812	1,331,908	617,956	3,859,676
1985	2010306	1,355,152	577,780	3,943,238
1986	2143339	1,379,679	553,765	4,076,783
1987[d]	2239503	1390098	521,651	4,151,252
1 988[d]	2332462	1,397,907	496,961	4,227,330
1989[d]	2419866	1,403,816	491,635	4,315,317
1990	2500462	1,404,870	481,033	4,386,365
1991	2547995	1410137	473,945	4,432,077
1992	2796613	1,409,191	428,986	4,634,790
1993	2812008	1,407,923	434,498	4,654,429
1994	2925959	1,409,455	413,999	4,749,413
1995	2911692	1,397,205	415,165	4,724,062
1996	2958162	1,388,746	404,498	4,751,406
1997	2943634	1,372,260	385,651	4,701,545
1998[e]	3000935	1,295,437	359,884	4,656,256
1999[f]	2985339	1,273,500	337856	4,596,695
2000	3196225	1,266,980	302,898	4,766,103
2001	3396289	1219238	262,343	4,877,870
2002	3420669	1,208,730	233,736	4,863,135
2003	3476451	1,206,721	179,952	4,863,124
2004	3508091	1,188,649	155,289	4,852,029
2005	3483511	1162808	128,771	4,775,090
2006[g]	3498363	1172204	123,503	4,794,070
2007	3532079	1155377	100,595	4,788,051

Source: Table prepared by CRS based on data from the Department of Housing and Urban Development Annotated Tables for the 2001 Budget and Congressional Budget Justifications.

Note: Earlier versions of this table contained an error; the totals in some years were incorrect.

a. Rental Assistance includes Section 8, Section 202, Section 811.

b. Other Housing Assistance includes Section 235, Section 236, Rent Supplement.

c. Total is adjusted for units receiving multiple subsidies.

d. Voucher counts for FY1987-FY1989 reflect vouchers leased, rather than reserved (contracted) vouchers.

e. Prior to FY1998, Native American public housing units were included in the count of public housing units. Beginning in 1998, those units are not included in the public housing unit count.

f. The voucher count in FY1999 reflects obligated vouchers, rather than reserved (contracted) vouchers.

g. Beginning in FY2006, HUD reported the total number of "funded" vouchers, which is HUD's estimate of how many vouchers the amount of funding provided by Congress would sustain, given the distribution of that funding.

End Notes

[1] For more information on the history of public housing, see Fisher, Robert Moore, 20 Years of Public Housing, Harper and Brothers, 1959 and Wood, Elizabeth *The Beautiful Beginnings, the Failure to Learn: Fifty Years of Public Housing in America*, The National Center for Housing Management, October 1982.

[2] Peter Dreir, Labor's Love Lost? Rebuilding Unions' Involvement in Federal Housing Policy, Housing Policy Debate, vol. 2, issue 2, p. 327.

[3] President Harry S. Truman, State of the Union Address, January 5, 1949.

[4] See, for example, Committee on Banking and Currency, report to accompany S. 1922, the Housing Act of 1961, 87th Cong., 1st sess., S.Rept. 281, May 19, 1961 ("The largest unfilled demand in the housing market is that of moderate- income families.").

[5] S.Rept. 281. "Perhaps the most significant reason that previous proposals to establish a moderate-income housing program have not been favorably received by the Congress is that the majority of those proposals would have placed sole responsibility for such a program on the Federal Government."

[6] U.S. Department of Housing and Urban Development, *Multifamily Properties: Opting In, Opting Out and Remaining Affordable*, January 2006, p. 1, available at http://www.huduser.org/Publications/pdf/opting_in.pdf.

[7] U.S. Department of Housing and Urban Development, *Housing for the Elderly and Handicapped: The Experience of the Section 202 Program from 1959 to 1977*, January 1979, p. 17.

[8] U.S. Congress, Senate Committee on Banking, Housing and Urban Affairs, Subcommittee on Housing and Urban Affairs, *An Analysis of the Section 235 and 236 Programs*, committee print, 93rd Cong., 1st sess., May 24, 1973, p. 9, available at http://www.congress.gov/crsx/products-nd/73.1142.doc.pdf.

[9] U.S. Department of Housing and Urban Development FY1974 Budget Summary, Housing Production and Mortgage Credit, p. 7.

[10] HUD, "Annotated Tables for 2001 Budget," p. 86.

[11] President Richard Nixon, Presidential Message to Congress on Housing Policy, September 19, 1973.

[12] The National Housing Task Force, *A Decent Place to Live*, March 1988, available from S.Hrg. 100-689. See p. 142.

[13] See *A Decent Place to Live*, available at S.Hrg. 100-689, p. 142.

[14] Ibid., pp. 154-155. See also Michael A. Stegman and J. David Holden, *Non-federal Housing Programs: How States and Localities Are Responding to Federal Cutbacks in Low-Income Housing* (Washington, DC: The Urban Land Institute, 1987).

[15] Ibid. See also Charles J. Orlebeke, "The Evolution of Low-Income Housing Policy, 1949 to 1999," *Housing Policy Debate*, vol. 11, no. 2 (2000), pp. 509-510, available at http://www.mi.vt.edu/data/files/hpd%2011(2)/ hpd%201 1(2)_orlebeke.pdf.

[16] Karl E. Case, "Investors, Developers, and Supply-Side Subsidies: How Much is Enough?" *Housing Policy Debate*, vol. 2, no. 2 (April 1990), pp. 349-351, available at http://www.mi.vt.edu/data/files/hpd%202(2)/ hpd%202(2)%20case.pdf.

[17] For more information, see the final report of the National Commission on Severely Distressed Public Housing, 1992.

[18] "Handicapped" families were added to the definition of "elderly" families in P.L. 88-560, the Housing Act of 1964. In 1990, the Cranston-Gonzalez National Affordable Housing Act (P.L. 10 1-625) separated housing for disabled persons from housing for elderly persons with the creation of the Section 811 Housing for Persons with Disabilities program.

[19] A disability is defined as (1) having a physical, mental, or emotional impairment that is expected to be of long-continued or indefinite duration, substantially impedes the ability to live independently, and could improved by suitable housing, (2) a developmental disability. 42 U.S.C. §8013(k)(2).

[20] HUD, Congressional Justifications for FY2009, p. K-1.

[21] Data taken from U.S. Department of Housing and Urban Development's LIHTC Database.

[22] Joint Committee on Taxation, *Estimates of Federal Tax Expenditures for Fiscal Years 2007-2011*, committee print, 110th Cong., September 27, 2007. The Joint Committee on Taxation (JCT) measures a tax expenditure as the difference between tax liability under present law and tax liability computed without the tax expenditure provision. The JCT assumes all other tax expenditures remain in the tax code and that taxpayer behavior is unchanged. The tax expenditure estimate for the LIHTC includes tax credits taken by individuals and corporations.

[23] Joint Committee on Taxation, *Estimates of Federal Tax Expenditures for Fiscal Years 2007-2011*, committee print, 110th Cong., September 27, 2007. The Joint Committee on Taxation (JCT) measures a tax expenditure as the difference between tax liability under present law and tax liability computed without the tax expenditure provision. The JCT assumes all other tax expenditures remain in the tax code and that taxpayer behavior is unchanged. The tax expenditure estimate for MRBs includes tax credits taken by individuals and corporations.

[24] ESG was enacted one year prior to McKinney-Vento as part of the Continuing Appropriations Act for FY1987 (P.L. 99-59 1). However, it was made part of McKinney-Vento.

[25] The S+C program was authorized in 1990 by the Stewart B. McKinney Homeless Act Amendments (P.L. 10 1-645).

[26] HUD, Congressional Justifications for FY2009, p. K-1.

[27] As described in CRS Report RL33025, *Fundamental Tax Reform: Options for the Mortgage Interest Deduction*, by Pamela J. Jackson, when the federal income tax was instituted in 1913, all interest payments were deductible. Over time, mortgage interest became distinguishable from other interest, and the deductibility of mortgage interest was separated and maintained (although changes have been made over time), while the deductibility of personal interest payments was eliminated.

[28] Joint Committee on Taxation, *Estimates of Federal Tax Expenditures for Fiscal Years 2007-2011*, committee print, 110th Cong., September 27, 2007. The Joint Committee on Taxation (JCT) measures a tax expenditure as the difference between tax liability under present law and tax liability computed without the tax expenditure provision. The JCT assumes all other tax expenditures remain in the tax code and that taxpayer behavior is unchanged.

[29] Harvard Joint Center for Housing Studies, "State of the Nation's Housing, 2007," Table A-6.

[30] Department of Housing and Urban Development, "Affordable Housing Needs 2005: Report to Congress," May 2007.

[31] See http://www.huduser.org/Datasets/IL/IL04/BRIEFING-MATERIALs.pdf.

[32] Olsen, Edgar, et al., Effects of Different Types of Housing Assistance on Earnings and Employment Cityscape: A Journal of Policy Development and Research, vol. 8, no. 2, 2005.

[33] Median length of stays taken from point-in-time data cannot predict how long a household entering a housing program is likely to stay.

[34] The National Housing Task Force, *A Decent Place to Live*, March 1988. See S.Hrg. 100-689, p. 142.

[35] Ibid.

[36] Michael A. Stegman, *State and Local Affordable Housing Programs: A Rich Tapestry* (Washington, DC: Urban Land Institute, 1999).

[37] See, for example, Recapitalization Advisors, Inc., *The Low Income Housing Tax Credit Effectiveness and Efficiency: A Presentation of the Issues*, March 4, 2002, p. 11, available at http://www.affordablehousing institute.org/resources/ library/MHC_LIHT.pdf.

[38] Ethan Handelman, Jeffrey Oakman, and David A. Smith, *The Interaction of LIHTC and Section 8 Rents*, Recapitalization Advisors, Inc., January 30, 2007, p. 4, available at http://www.recapadvisors.com/pdf/Wu%2061.pdf.

[39] For example, according to HUD's database of Section 236 properties with active loans, at least 1,200 loans representing 137,000 units will have mortgages that mature over a five-year period between 2008 and 2013.

[40] From roughly 1.6 million vouchers in FY1998 to 2.1 million vouchers in FY2007. The 1998 estimate of Section 8 vouchers is taken from the Government Accountability Office Report, GAO-06-405, *Rental Housing Assistance: Policy Decisions and Market Factors Explain Changes in the Costs of the Section 8 Programs*, April 28, 2006; the 2007 estimate was taken from the FY2009 HUD Congressional Budget Justifications. Note that the methodology for counting Section 8 vouchers has changed over time, therefore, the 2007 count may underestimate the number of vouchers.

[41] From just under 1.3 million units in FY1998 to just under 1.16 million units in FY2007. Data on public housing units are taken from HUD Congressional Budget Justifications.

[42] From just under 1.4 million units in CY1998 to just under 1.29 million units in FY2007. Data on project-based Section 8 units are taken from Econometrica, et al., *Multifamily Properties: Opting In, Opting Out and Remaining Affordable*, January 2006 (CY1998 data, Table 2.2) and HUD Congressional Budget Justifications (FY2007 data). Note that for project-based figures, a calendar year figure is compared to a fiscal year figure.

[43] The authority to enter into new project-based Section 8 contracts was repealed in 1983 and the 1998 public housing reform law prohibited PHAs from increasing the number of public housing units under contract.

[44] Estimates of incremental vouchers from FY1998-FY2004 are taken from Government Accountability Office Report, GAO-06-405, *Rental Housing Assistance: Policy Decisions and Market Factors Explain Changes in the Costs of the Section 8 Programs*, April 28, 2006. Between FY2004 and FY2007, no new incremental vouchers were funded or awarded.

[45] Estimates of tenant protection vouchers from FY1998-FY2004 are taken from Government Accountability Office Report, GAO-06-405, *Rental Housing Assistance: Policy Decisions and Market Factors Explain Changes in the Costs of the Section 8 Programs*, April 28, 2006. Estimates of tenant protection vouchers from FY2005-FY2007 are taken from Notices published by HUD in the *Federal Register*.

[46] Note that the number of tenant protection vouchers awarded exceeds the decline in the number of public housing and project-based Section 8 units. This may be partly due to the awarding of tenant-protection vouchers to other project- based rental assisted units and partly due to differences in timing between the award of the vouchers and the units leaving the inventory.

[47] J.E. Rosenbaum, *Changing the Geography of Opportunity by Expanding Residential Choice: Lessons from the Gautreaux*, Housing Policy Debate, vol. 6 no. 1, Fannie Mae Foundation, 1995.

[48] Larry Orr, et al., *Moving to Opportunity for Fair Housing Demonstration : Interim Impacts Evaluation*, Abt Associates, September 2003.

[49] Popkin, Susan, et al., *A Decade of HOPE VI: Research Findings and Policy Challenges,* Urban Institute, May 18, 2004.

[50] Youngro Lee, "To Dream or Not to Dream: A Cost-Benefit Analysis of the Development, Relief, and Education for Alien Minors (DREAM) Act," *Cornell Journal of Law and Public Policy*, Fall 2006.

[51] Department of Commerce, U.S. Census Bureau News, Census Bureau Reports on Residential Vacancies and Homeownership, April 28, 2008, p. 4, available at http://www.census.gov/hhes/www/housing/hvs/qtr108/q108press.pdf.

In: An Overview of Federal Housing Assistance Programs   ISBN: 978-1-61122-419-1
Editor: Brandon C. Sherman   © 2011 Nova Science Publishers, Inc.

Chapter 2

SECTION 202 AND OTHER HUD RENTAL HOUSING PROGRAMS FOR LOW-INCOME ELDERLY RESIDENTS

Libby Perl

SUMMARY

The population of persons age 65 and older in the United States is expected to grow both in numbers and as a percentage of the total population over the next 25 years, through 2030. In 2002, a bipartisan commission created by Congress issued a report, *A Quiet Crisis in America*, that detailed the need for affordable assisted housing and supportive services for elderly persons and the shortage the country will likely face as the population ages. The Department of Housing and Urban Development (HUD) operates a number of programs that provide assisted housing and supportive services for low-income elderly persons (defined by HUD as households where one or more persons are age 62 or older) to ensure that elderly residents in HUD-assisted housing can remain in their apartments as they age. This report describes those programs, along with current developments in the area of housing for elderly households.

HUD operates five programs that designate assisted housing developments for either low-income elderly residents alone, or low-income elderly residents and residents with disabilities. The primary HUD program that provides housing for low-income elderly households is the Section 202 Supportive Housing for the Elderly program. Established in 1959, it is the only HUD program that currently provides housing exclusively for elderly residents. The Section 221(d)(3) Below Market Interest Rate and Section 236 programs are mortgage subsidy programs that provide housing for all age levels, but have properties specifically dedicated to elderly households. The Public Housing and project-based Section 8 housing programs also have projects dedicated to elderly households.

In addition to providing housing, HUD operates four supportive services programs for elderly persons residing in HUD-assisted properties. The Congregate Housing program, Service Coordinator program, and Resident Opportunity and Self-Sufficiency (ROSS) Service Coordinator program each provide services such as meals and assistance with activities of daily living to help residents remain independent. The Assisted Living Conversion program gives grants to HUD-assisted developments so that they can convert units or entire buildings into assisted living facilities.

Among current issues involving HUD-assisted housing for elderly residents is housing preservation. In its report *A Quiet Crisis in America*, the Commission on Affordable Housing and Health Facility Needs for Seniors in the 21st Century noted that units of affordable housing for low-income elderly households could be converted to market-rate housing in the coming years due to mortgage maturity and prepayment. Another concern is the deterioration of existing housing developments.

In the 111th Congress, language in both the FY2009 Omnibus Appropriations Act (P.L. 111-8) and the FY2010 Consolidated Appropriations Act (P.L. 111-117) made changes to current law regarding the refinancing of Section 202 loans. The change is meant to make it feasible for owners of older Section 202 developments (generally those funded prior to 1974) to refinance their loans and use proceeds to improve the properties. However, HUD has not released guidance yet on how the provisions would be implemented. The change is similar to provisions in the Section 202 Supportive Housing for the Elderly Act (S. 118), a bill that was introduced on January 6, 2009.

INTRODUCTION

In 1999, Congress created a bipartisan commission to study the housing needs of the senior population as it ages. The commission's final report, entitled *A Quiet Crisis in America*, warned of the nation's growing senior population and the lack of affordable housing and supportive services programs to meet future demand.[1] The percentage of individuals age 65 and older is beginning to make up a larger percentage of the total U. S. population, and is expected to continue to grow through 2030.[2] Between 2000 and 2030, the number of persons age 65 and older is expected to grow from 35.0 million to 71.5 million, and from 12.4% of the population to 19.6%.[3] In particular, the "oldest old," those individuals aged 85 and older, are becoming a larger share of the elderly population, raising concerns about the availability of supportive services in addition to affordable housing. The bipartisan housing commission estimated that the aging of the population will result in the need for an additional 730,000 units of affordable housing by 2020.[4]

The Department of Housing and Urban Development (HUD) operates a number of programs that provide both housing and supportive services for elderly households.[5] HUD defines "elderly person" as a household composed of one or more persons in which at least one person is age 62 or older at the time of initial occupancy.[6] Five HUD programs provide affordable rental housing that is designated for low-income elderly households. Of these five, only one, the Section 202 Supportive Housing for the Elderly program, provides housing exclusively for elderly persons. The other four programs provide housing for all age groups, but allow some properties to be devoted primarily to housing elderly residents. The Section 236 and Section 221(d)(3) programs extended subsidized loans to private developers during the 1960s and early 1970s so that they could build low-income housing, some of which included buildings dedicated to elderly residents (neither program makes new loans, although some buildings still have active mortgages). The Public Housing and project-based Section 8 programs also dedicate some buildings primarily for use by elderly households.

In addition to housing, HUD funds four supportive services programs for elderly residents in its subsidized properties. These programs are the Congregate Housing program, the Service Coordinator program, the Resident Opportunity and Self-Sufficiency (ROSS) Service Coordinator program, and the Assisted Living Conversion program. Each program works to allow elderly persons living in HUD-eligible properties to remain in their apartments through assistance and services.

This report provides a summary of the HUD programs that provide multi-family rental housing for low-income elderly households and their related supportive services programs. It also discusses funding and current issues in the area of assisted housing for low-income elderly persons. However, the report does not include a comprehensive look at all housing programs that serve elderly households. Major sources of assistance that are not discussed include HUD's Section 8 voucher program,[7] HUD's mortgage insurance and reverse mortgage programs,[8] and the Department of Agriculture's rural housing programs that provide assistance to elderly households.[9]

HUD HOUSING PROGRAMS

The Section 202 Supportive Housing for the Elderly Program

The Section 202 Supportive Housing for the Elderly program is the only HUD program that currently provides housing exclusively for elderly households, with approximately 263,000 units available for elderly households (this does not include Section 202 units for persons with disabilities).[10] Established as part of the Housing Act of 1959 (P.L. 86-372) and last authorized in FY2003 (P.L. 106-569), the current version of the Section 202 program makes capital grants and project rental assistance available to developers so that they can build housing that is affordable to very low-income elderly households. The program was not always structured this way, however, and it has changed several times since its inception. During the nearly 50 years that the Section 202 program has existed, the system of providing financing for developments has changed from loans to grants, the tenant population it targets has moved from moderate-income elderly households to very low-income elderly households, and the program has gone from serving only elderly households to serving elderly and disabled households, and then back to serving elderly households exclusively. The history of Section 202 is important because many projects developed in the early years of the program continue to operate under the rules in place at the time they were built.

The history of the Section 202 program can be divided into three distinct phases based primarily on changes to its financing structure and the income eligibility of tenants. From 1959 to 1974, the program provided housing units affordable to moderate-income elderly households and households with an adult member with a disability by extending low-interest construction loans to nonprofit developers. Between 1974 and 1990, the program continued to extend loans to developers, but added project-based Section 8 rental assistance to subsidize tenant rents so that developers could afford to rent units to low-income elderly and disabled households (those with incomes at or below 80% of area median income) or, beginning in

1981, very low-income households (those with incomes at or below 50% of area median income).[11] Finally, beginning in 1990, HUD replaced the Section 202 loan program with capital grants and a different form of rental assistance referred to as PRAC (project rental assistance contracts). These units are available to very low-income elderly households.

History of the Section 202 Program: 1959 to 1974

When the Section 202 program was established in 1959, its purpose was to provide housing for moderate-income elderly tenants—those with too much income for Public Housing but insufficient income for market-rate housing.[12] Through the program, the government loaned funds to private nonprofit developers so that they could build housing for elderly families and individuals. Unlike most of its loan programs, HUD made the Section 202 loans directly to developers rather than insuring loans from private lenders.[13] The interest rates on the loans were low—approximately 3%—and had a duration of up to 50 years.[14] The developers, assisted by low-interest mortgage payments, could set rents in their buildings at levels that were affordable to elderly households with moderate incomes. At the time, there were no income eligibility restrictions on the properties. Between 1959 and 1968, developers constructed 45,257 Section 202 units in 335 projects, with an average of 135 units per building, most of which were efficiency apartments.[15]

In 1962, HUD began setting rents for Section 202 properties on a community-by-community basis. The new rents were meant to be affordable for lower-middle-income elderly households, and they varied across the country.[16] In 1968, HUD set income eligibility limits for all Section 202 developments at the higher of 135% of Public Housing limits or 80% of area median income.[17] To make units affordable for low-income elderly tenants (those with incomes at or below 80% of area median income), Congress enacted a rental subsidy program called the Rent Supplement program (described later in this report) as part of the Housing and Urban Development Act of 1965 (P.L. 89-117).[18] Those tenants receiving rent subsidies made up a relatively small percentage of total tenants during the early years of the Section 202 program, however. [19]

The eligible tenant population for the Section 202 program changed in 1964 when non-elderly "handicapped" individuals and families were added to the definition of "elderly families" as part of the Housing Act of 1964 (P.L. 88-560).[20] Yet very few tenants who were considered non- elderly handicapped participated in the Section 202 program between 1964 and 1974. Although data were not kept, HUD surveyed property owners and estimated that through 1977, less than 1% of tenants were non-elderly handicapped.[21]

In FY1970, the Section 202 program was not funded for the first time since its enactment. The Nixon Administration did not propose any new funds for the program and Congress did not appropriate them. The Administration's rationale was, at least in part, that the large size of the Section 202 loans had a negative effect on the size of the federal budget.[22] This was due to the fact that the program showed only expenditures and not the offsets made when developers paid back the Section 202 loans.[23] Between 1970 and 1974, the Section 202 program did not fund any new construction projects. Instead, housing for elderly households was constructed using the Section 236 mortgage subsidy program, established as part of the Housing and Civil Rights Act of 1968 (P.L. 90-448, discussed later in this report).

Of the Section 202 properties funded prior to 1974, there are approximately 250 buildings, representing more than 35,000 units, that still have active loans.[24] These properties continue to accept tenants according to the rules in place at the time they were developed.

Section 202 developments that applied for HUD funds prior to 1962 are not subject to income limits, while those constructed after 1962 but prior to July 1972 are subject to the income limits approved by HUD at the time.[25] In addition, in the years since many pre-1974 Section 202 developments were constructed, HUD has provided rental assistance for approximately 38% of the units, primarily through the Loan Management Set Aside (LMSA) program. LMSA was a special allocation of project-based Section 8 assistance contracts available for units in troubled FHA-insured properties.

History of the Section 202 Program: 1974 to 1990

In 1974, the Housing and Community Development Act of 1974 (P.L. 93-383) both reactivated the Section 202 program and instituted a number of changes. The primary change was to make project-based Section 8 rental assistance available to building owners. Project-based Section 8 rental assistance is a rent subsidy that, at the time, made up the difference between 25% of tenant income and market rate rent as established by HUD (tenant payments were later raised to 30% of income), and was available only to low-income tenants. Although the law did not restrict Section 202 units only to those households that qualified for project-based Section 8 rental assistance, the availability to owners of the rental subsidy meant that more low-income tenants began to live in Section 202 projects, a change from the program's previous tendency to serve mostly moderate- income elderly families.[26] Contracts for project-based Section 8 rental assistance payments between HUD and Section 202 owners were initially set for up to 20 years and were renewable.[27]

Loans for the construction of Section 202 housing continued to be available to developers when the program was reactivated; however, P.L. 93-3 83 changed the interest rate, raising it from 3% to the U.S. Treasury's cost of borrowing, while the duration of the loan term dropped from 50 years to 40 years. Another change was in the distribution of Section 202 loan funds. Prior to 1974, Section 202 developments were largely concentrated in urban areas.[28] However, the Housing and Community Development Act directed that 20% to 25% of funds go to nonmetropolitan areas.[29] By 1988, the share of Section 202 units located in cities with populations less than 10,000 rose to 11.5%, compared to 2.7% through 1974.[30] A final change to the Section 202 program in P.L. 93- 383 was the requirement that Section 202 developments support state and local plans to provide services such as transportation, homemaker services, and counseling and referral services to elderly tenants.

In 1981, the tenant income guidelines for Section 202 units that receive project-based Section 8 rental assistance were changed as part of the Omnibus Budget Reconciliation Act of 1981 (P.L. 97-35).[31] The law required that HUD units receiving project-based Section 8 rental assistance, including Section 202 projects, be made available primarily to very low-income households— those with incomes at or below 50% of area median income. The law specified that, of the units receiving project-based Section 8 rental assistance prior to 1981, 10% could be occupied by households with incomes between 50% and 80% of the area median income (those households considered low income), while only 5% of new units could be occupied by families earning between 50% and 80% of the area median. These percentages were later changed to 25% and 15%, respectively.[32]

Between 1974 and 1988, an estimated 128,636 additional units of Section 202 housing were built using construction loans and project-based Section 8 rental assistance.[33] The average size of developments declined from 153 units in developments built between 1959 and 1974 to 92 units in developments built between 1975 and 1984, and then to 56 units in developments built between 1985 and 1 988.[34] Only 5.4% of the units built between 1974 and 1985 were efficiencies, compared to more than 60% prior to 1974; however, between 1985 and 1988 the percentage of efficiencies rose again, to 18.9%.[35]

History of the Section 202 Program: 1990 to the Present

In 1990, the Cranston-Gonzalez National Affordable Housing Act (P.L. 10 1-625) again changed the financing scheme of the Section 202 program. The law replaced loans to developers with capital advances. The capital advances do not accrue interest, and developers need not pay them back as long as the properties are made available to very low-income elderly households for at least 40 years.

The change in financing was prompted by concern about the costs involved in paying back Section 202 loans. Under the Section 202 loan program, developers often used project-based Section 8 rental assistance to service their loan debt in addition to using it to supplement tenant rents—its intended purpose.[36] At the time P.L. 101-625 was enacted, it was estimated that approximately 75% of Section 8 project rental assistance was used by developers to service their loan debt, leaving only 25% for operating expenses and improvements.[37] Under the new program of capital grants, it was thought that developers would no longer need to use rental assistance to make loan payments, allowing HUD to make lower project rental assistance payments, requiring less budget authority.[38]

Both the method of providing project-based rental assistance and the way in which development cost limitations for Section 202 projects are determined also changed as a result of P.L. 101-625. Rental subsidies are no longer provided through the Section 8 program, meaning that rents are not based on Section 8 fair market rents (FMRs).[39] The new project rental assistance—referred to as PRAC—is meant to ensure that owners have the capacity to determine the needs of residents for supportive services, coordinate those services, and identify sources of funding to deliver the services.[40] Although the duration of the new project rental assistance contracts was initially 20 years, HUD's current practice is to extend new rental assistance contracts for three years. In addition, P.L. 101-625 provided that project development costs be calculated on the basis of factors specific to constructing Section 202 projects rather than using FMR standards, as had been the case. These new factors include the prevailing costs of construction, rehabilitation, and acquisition of property; the costs of special design features for elderly residents; and the costs of adding congregate space.[41] The new system is meant to ensure that all areas of the country have adequate funds to develop and maintain Section 202 housing; under the old system of FMRs, those areas of the country with low FMRs often could not afford to develop Section 202 projects.[42]

Another significant change in P.L. 101-625 was the removal of housing for persons with disabilities from the Section 202 program. Congress began to initiate the split between housing for elderly and disabled households in 1978 when the Housing and Community Development Amendments (P.L. 95-557) required that, beginning in FY1979, at least $50 million of the amounts available for loans under the Section 202 program be devoted to housing for non-elderly "handicapped" individuals.[43] Later, as part of the Housing and Community Development Act of 1987 (P.L. 100-242), Congress further specified that 15% of total Section 202 funds should be devoted to housing for persons with disabilities. In P.L. 101-625, Congress directed that beginning in 1992, housing for persons with disabilities be provided through a completely separate program called the Section 811 Supportive Housing for Persons with Disabilities program.[44] As with the Section 202 program, developers of

Section 811 housing receive capital grants and project rental assistance to construct, rehabilitate, or acquire housing for very low- income individuals with disabilities. The advent of Section 811 has not completely eliminated Section 202's role in serving disabled households; however, Section 202 developments constructed before 1992 continue to provide housing for persons with disabilities according to the rules that existed at the time of construction.

Between 1993 and 1998, the Section 202 program created approximately 27,632 units of housing for elderly households,[45] and between 2000 and 2006, another 35,281 units were constructed.[46] In this phase of the Section 202 program, developments have become smaller, with an average of 50 units per project through 1998, and 42 units per site in those developed between 2000 and 2006.[47] These newer Section 202 developments have virtually no efficiency units.[48]

The Section 202 Program's Grant Process

HUD awards Section 202 grants to private nonprofit groups and to for-profit general partnerships where the sole general partner is a nonprofit organization. The grant process consists of two parts, one of which involves a formula and the other a competitive process. In the first step, HUD uses a need-based formula to allocate the total amount of Section 202 funds available for capital grants and project rental assistance in a fiscal year to each of the 18 HUD multifamily hubs.[49] Of the funds available, HUD allocates 85% to metropolitan areas and 15% to non-metropolitan areas.

The formula for allocating Section 202 funds to the HUD field offices looks at "relevant characteristics of the elderly population" in each field office's jurisdiction, including the population of elderly renters.[50] HUD also considers the number of one-person elderly renter households that have incomes at or below 50% of the area median income, together with one of three "housing conditions." These three housing conditions are paying more than 30% of income toward rent, occupying a unit without a kitchen or plumbing, or occupying an overcrowded unit (defined as accommodating 1.01 or more persons per room).[51]

In the second step in the grant process, applicants apply directly to their field offices for the funds that have been allocated to their areas. HUD then evaluates grantee applications and uses a point system to assign up to 102 points per application.[52] Points are awarded in the following categories:

- up to 25 points are awarded for the applicant's capacity to provide housing, including experience in providing housing to minorities;
- up to 13 points are awarded for the need for funding in the applicant's target area;
- up to 45 points are awarded for the approach to providing housing, including the quality and effectiveness of the proposal, the involvement of elderly persons in designing the proposal, and the proximity and accessibility of the site to transportation and services;
- up to 5 points are awarded for the applicant's ability to secure funding from other sources; and
- up to 12 points are awarded for development of an evaluation plan to measure performance of the project.

In FY2008, $526 million was distributed to grant recipients in 39 states to construct or convert more than 3,700 units of housing for elderly households.[53]

Section 202 and Low-Income Housing Tax Credits

Financing affordable housing, including housing for elderly residents, may require multiple streams of funding in order to support the design, construction, and ongoing operating costs of a project. In addition to federal funds provided through HUD programs, affordable housing developers may use mortgage revenue bonds, tax credits, and local housing trust fund resources, among other sources, to develop housing for low-income and special-needs populations. While HUD funds might once have been sufficient on their own to develop an affordable housing project, that is not always the case today. This is true for Section 202 developers, who may bring together multiple sources of funding to develop a project. One of the primary sources of funding available for developing affordable housing is the Low-Income Housing Tax Credit (LIHTC). The LIHTC was enacted as part of the Tax Reform Act of 1986 (P.L. 99-514) and provides incentives for the development of affordable rental housing through federal tax credits administered by the Internal Revenue Service (IRS). The IRS allocates tax credits to states based on population, and states award the credits to developers to use as a source of financing for the development of affordable rental housing.[54]

In 2000, in order to help Section 202 (and Section 811) developers bring together multiple financing sources, Congress enacted a law that makes the interaction of Section 202 funds and LIHTCs more feasible by changing the way in which federal funds are treated. The value of LIHTCs are determined, in part, based on the cost of developing a property—referred to as the qualified basis.[55] The costs of constructing, acquiring, and rehabilitating a property (among other costs[56]) are included in calculating the qualified basis, but the amount must then be reduced by any federal grants received by the developer, which in turn reduces the value of the tax credits. Therefore, if a nonprofit developer were to receive a Section 202 capital grant, its value would be subtracted in calculating the qualified basis, which could result in minimal LIHTCs. The Homeownership and Economic Opportunity Act (P.L. 106-569), enacted in 2000, allowed for- profit limited partnerships, where a nonprofit organization is the sole general partner, to be eligible Section 202 owners. The changed law allows a nonprofit Section 202 grantee to loan the Section 202 capital grant to the limited partnership. Under this arrangement, the Section 202 funds are no longer a "federal grant" to be subtracted in calculating the qualified basis, potentially increasing the value of LIHTCs.

The change in the law to allow for-profit limited partnerships to own Section 202 housing developments has not immediately made mixed financing arrangements common, however. The transactions are complicated and may require extensive expertise in housing finance to make them work. HUD acknowledges that "most developers seek to avoid the use of federal grant financing in most LIHTC projects."[57] In addition, the treatment of Section 202 PRAC in tax credit transactions has been unclear. Although the IRS has created exceptions to the rule that federal grants do not count toward the qualified basis of a property for certain categories of rental assistance, Section 202 PRAC has not been among the exceptions. The programs that have been exempted from the requirement include project-based Section 8 rental assistance payments and public housing capital and operating funds,[58] the Native American Housing Block Grant Program,[59] Rent Supplement and Rental Assistance Payments programs,[60] and the Shelter Plus Care and Single Room Occupancy programs.[61] Despite language in the Homeownership and Economic Opportunity Act of 2000 indicating that

Congress intended Section 202 (and Section 811) assistance to be included in calculating qualified basis (rather than subtracted from it), the IRS has not issued a ruling that would be necessary to make this possible.[62]

Another possible limitation in developing mixed finance projects using federal grants, such as Section 202 together with the LIHTC, was removed with passage of the Housing and Economic Recovery Act of 2008 (P.L. 110-289). Under LIHTC law, developers may qualify for tax credits worth roughly 9% or 4%.[63] Under previous LIHTC law, the higher 9% credit was available for new construction that was *not* federally subsidized, while the 4% credit was available for either federally subsidized new construction or existing buildings. The statutory definition of "federally subsidized" included below market federal loans (the structure used by limited partnerships to loan Section 202 capital grants).[64] The fact that developers of federally subsidized buildings did not qualify for the higher tax credit made financing projects with the LIHTC less lucrative. Developers either had to accept the lower 4% credit or set up a system through which federal grants were loaned to the project at a market rate of interest.[65]

However, P.L. 110-289 removed the phrase "below market federal loans" from the definition of federal subsidy in the LIHTC statute. This makes all federally subsidized new construction placed in service after the effective date of P.L. 110-289 eligible for 9% tax credits. The 9% credits are very competitive,[66] however, and it may still be difficult for Section 202 developers to obtain them.

Section 221(d)(3) below Market Interest Rate Program

In 1961, Congress enacted the Section 221 (d)(3) Below Market Interest Rate (BMIR) program (P.L. 87-70) to help public agencies, cooperatives, limited dividend corporations, and nonprofit sponsors create housing for low- and moderate-income families.[67] The BMIR program has not provided funds for new developments since 1968, but properties with active mortgages continue to operate. The program, like the Section 202 program at the time it was created, was meant to serve those families with incomes too high for Public Housing, but too low for market-rate rents.[68] The program was, and continues to be, run by the Federal Housing Administration (FHA). Through the program, private lenders extended FHA-insured loans with interest rates of 3% and durations of up to 40 years to developers of multi-family rental housing projects of at least five units.[69] Lenders then sold the mortgages to the Federal National Mortgage Association (Fannie Mae).[70] The program continued until 1968, when the Section 236 program replaced it as a vehicle for producing multi-family housing for low-income families. Section 221 (d)(3) BMIR properties are still active, providing approximately 1,154 units in projects dedicated to the elderly.[71] Units are open to households with incomes of up to 95% of the area median income.[72]

The Rent Supplement program was enacted as part of the Housing and Urban Development Act of 1965 (P.L. 89-117) to subsidize the rent payments of low-income households living in Section 221(d)(3) BMIR housing developments. FHA entered into contracts with building owners to make up the difference between 25% of tenant income (later raised to 30%) and the fair market rent as determined by HUD.[73] Generally, up to 20% of units in a building were eligible for Rent Supplement payments, although the Housing and Urban Development Act of 1969 (P.L. 91-152) made up to 40% of units eligible for subsidy payments if the HUD Secretary determined it was necessary.[74] Most, but not all, of these contracts have been converted to project-based Section 8 rental assistance.[75]

The Section 236 Program

In 1968, Congress determined that the Section 221(d)(3) program and the Section 202 program were of limited usefulness in developing large numbers of assisted housing units. The Section 221(d)(3) program depended on Fannie Mae to purchase loans, and only limited funds were available for this purpose.[76] And the Section 202 program's system of direct loans had a large negative effect on the budget. As a result, the Housing and Urban Development Act of 1968 (P.L. 90-448) established the Section 236 program to provide housing for low- and moderate-income families, including facilities dedicated to elderly persons and persons with disabilities. The program was intended to replace the Section 221(d)(3) and Section 202 programs,[77] and for a time it did. The program produced approximately 400,000 new units in 3,601 developments by 1976.[78] But after January 1973, when President Nixon imposed a moratorium on the new construction of subsidized housing, the program did not receive new funds, although it has continued to subsidize existing developments.

The Section 236 program assisted both private and nonprofit owners of rental housing projects for low-income and moderate-income households by insuring mortgages for construction or substantial rehabilitation of buildings, and by subsidizing the mortgage payments. Under the program, project owners borrowed funds from private lenders at the market interest rate, and the government then made (and continues to make) subsidy payments to the owners, called Interest Reduction Payments (IRPs), so that owners effectively pay an interest rate of only 1% on their mortgages. By paying the low 1% interest rate, owners are expected to be able to charge tenants affordable rents. Each Section 236 unit has both a basic rent and a market rent: the basic rent is the payment amount needed to operate the project at a 1% mortgage interest rate, and the market rent is the amount needed to operate the project at the actual mortgage interest rate.[79] Tenants pay the higher of the basic rent or 30% of their income (initially, tenants paid 25%), but rent cannot exceed the fair market rent amount.[80] Households with low incomes—at or below 80% of area median income—are eligible for Section 236 housing. Approximately 66,000 units, 23% of all Section 236 units, are reserved for elderly residents.[81]

In order to help make Section 236 housing more affordable to low-income households, some projects receive rent subsidies through a program called Rental Assistance Payments (RAP). Congress enacted the program in 1974 (P.L. 93-383) to ensure that tenants did not have to pay more than 25% of their income toward rent. Building owners were able to receive RAP for up to 20% of the units in a project (subject to increase or decrease at the discretion of the Secretary). In addition, Section 236 owners were eligible to receive Rent Supplement payments, originally developed for the Section 221(d)(3) BMIR program and made available to the Section 236 program in the Housing and Urban Development Act of 1968 (P.L. 90-448). Both RAP and Rent Supplement payments have largely been converted to project-based Section 8 rental assistance.[82]

Public Housing

Public Housing is the original federally assisted housing program for low-income families, created as part of the Housing Act of 1937 (P.L. 75-412). The program provides housing for very low-income households (those with incomes at or below 50% of the area median income) and requires tenants to pay 30% of their income toward rent. Public Housing projects have long dedicated buildings to elderly tenants. The Housing Act of 1956 (P.L. 84-1020) authorized the Public Housing Administration (a predecessor to HUD) to provide units specifically for low- income elderly individuals (prior to this, HUD's definition of elderly families did not include single individuals), which increased the number of elderly households living in Public Housing.

Congress did not intend to separate elderly residents from younger tenants.[83] Rather, units for elderly residents were to be integrated with those of non-elderly families. Despite this desire not to segregate elderly tenants, by 1960 the first elderly-only Public Housing development had been created.[84] Today, approximately 76,000 Public Housing units are designated exclusively for elderly residents.[85]

Beginning in 1961, persons with disabilities were included in the definition of "elderly families" for purposes of the Public Housing program. Combining elderly residents and residents with disabilities in Public Housing has been controversial. During the early years of Public Housing for elderly persons, residents with disabilities made up only a small proportion of residents. However, the number of residents with disabilities in Public Housing for the elderly began to increase in the 1980s and early 1990s for at least two reasons. First, individuals with mental illnesses were less likely to be institutionalized as a result of the availability of outpatient mental health care, and were therefore in need of affordable housing.[86] A second factor was passage of the 1988 Fair Housing Act Amendments (P.L. 100-430). The amendments added "handicapped" individuals to the class of individuals protected from discrimination in the provision of housing. The definition of "handicapped" included individuals with alcohol and drug addictions.[87] As a result of the increase of younger residents with disabilities in Public Housing, often with mental illnesses and addictions, Public Housing Authorities faced a greater number of incidents of disruptive behavior, and many elderly residents reported feeling unsafe.[88]

Due to the conflicts between tenants with disabilities and elderly residents, Congress in 1992 allowed Public Housing Authorities (PHAs) to designate buildings as elderly only, disabled only, or elderly and disabled only.[89] In 1996, The Public Housing Opportunity Extension Act of 1996 (P.L. 104-120) streamlined the process for designating buildings as elderly-only. If a PHA wants to change the composition of a building to only elderly residents, it must submit a plan to HUD to ask for approval. If the plan is approved, PHAs cannot evict non-elderly residents with disabilities, although PHAs may help residents relocate if they want to move. The law also requires that, if a PHA is unable to rent an available unit to an elderly household within 60 days, it must make the unit available to near-elderly tenants (where the head of household or spouse is age 50 or older). If the unit cannot be rented to near-elderly families, then it must be made available to all families.

Table 1. HUD Rental Housing Programs for Low-Income Elderly Households.

Program	Income Eligibility[a]	Tenant Rent	Units Designated for Elderly Households Only[b]
Section 202			262,704
1959 to 1962	No income limits.	Set by owner based on funds required to support building operation.	
1962 to 1968	Income limits set on a community-by-community basis.	Set by owner.	
1968 to 1974	Higher of 80% of area median income or 135% of Public Housing income limits.	Set by owner.	
1974 to 1981	80% of area median income.[c]	For units with project-based Section 8 rental assistance, the greater of 30% of adjusted income or 10% of gross income.	
1981 to present	50% of area median income.[d]	The greater of 30% of adjusted income or 10% of gross income	
Section 221(d)(3) BMIR	95% of area median income.	Rent is set building-by-building and approved by HUD.	1,154
Section 236	80% of area median income.	The greater of 30% of adjusted income or "basic rent" as calculated by HUD.	65,877
Public Housing	80% of area median income.	The greater of 30% of adjusted income or 10% of gross income.	76,638
Project-based Section 8 Rental Assistance	50% of area median income.[d]	The greater of 30% of adjusted income or 10% of gross income.	200,455

Source: Prepared by CRS based on HUD Handbook 4350.3, chapter 3, paragraph 3-6, and chapter 5, paragraphs 5-25 through 5-30; *Federal Housing Programs that Offer Assistance for the Elderly*, Government Accountability Office, February 2005, p. 11; and Barbara A. Haley and Robert W. Gray, *Section 202 Supportive Housing for the Elderly: Program Status and Performance Measurement*, U.S. Department of Housing and Urban Development, Office of Policy Development and Research, June 2008, p. 38.

a. Income limits are subject to exceptions. This table provides information on the majority of housing units for each program.

b. The units are those in use as of 2005. The number of units does not include units for non-elderly residents with disabilities and includes only those units specifically designated for elderly residents (elderly residents may also reside in units not specifically designated for their use).

c. Although it was not mandated that Section 202 projects serve tenants with low incomes beginning in 1974, the availability of project-based Section 8 rental assistance for low-income tenants meant that eligibility for most Section 202 units was the same as that for the Section 8 program—80% of area median income.

d. In 1981, P.L. 97-35 required that the majority of units receiving project-based Section 8 rental assistance must be made available to very low-income households.

Project-Based Section 8 Housing

Between 1974 and 1983, the Section 8 new construction and substantial rehabilitation programs made rental assistance available to developers that were creating new and rehabilitated rental housing for low-income families.[90] From the inception of the program, owners were able to develop properties dedicated for use by elderly households and households with an adult member who has a disability. Today, elderly residents and residents with disabilities continue to live together in project-based Section 8 housing. Although owners may give a preference to elderly families (P.L. 102-550),[91] unlike Public Housing, most Section 8 properties may not completely exclude residents with disabilities. The statute requires that owners continue to reserve some units for tenants with disabilities; the number is either the number of units occupied by residents with disabilities in 1992 or 10%, whichever is lower. If owners are unable to rent units to elderly families, they may give preference to near-elderly families with an adult member who has a disability. After the Section 202 program, project-based Section 8 housing provides the most housing dedicated specifically to elderly households. Of the number of units that continue to receive project-based rental assistance, approximately 200,000 are dedicated to elderly households.[92]

SUPPORTIVE SERVICES AND ASSISTED LIVING PROGRAMS

Four programs are available to provide services for elderly residents who live in HUD-subsidized buildings. The programs are the Congregate Housing program, the Service Coordinator program, the Resident Opportunity and Self Sufficiency (ROSS) Service Coordinator program, and the Assisted Living Conversion program. Three of the four programs—Congregate Housing, Service Coordinator, and Assisted Living Conversion—base their services on whether residents are considered to be either frail elderly or at-risk elderly. In the ROSS program, services are available whether residents are frail or not. Whether individuals are frail elderly or at-risk elderly depends on their ability to engage in activities of daily living (ADLs). ADLs consist of five or six categories of activities considered necessary for an individual to maintain independent functioning and their own personal care; the number of categories of activities varies slightly by program. The five common categories of activities included in all three programs are

- eating, which includes cooking and serving food;
- dressing;
- bathing, which includes getting in and out of a tub or shower;
- grooming; and
- home management, which includes housework, shopping, and laundry.[93]

The Congregate Housing program contains one additional ADL focused on an individual's ability to move, and includes getting in and out of chairs, walking, going outdoors, and using the toilet.

Residents who are age 62 or older and unable to perform at least three ADLs to some degree are considered frail, while those who are unable to perform one or two ADLs are considered at risk.[94] However, each of the three programs specifies that residents must be able to participate in ADLs at some minimal level. For example, residents must be able to feed, dress, and wash themselves; be able take care of their personal appearance; and be mobile (including use of a wheelchair). In the Congregate Housing and Assisted Living Conversion programs, residents qualify for assistance on an individual basis, while in the Service Coordinator program, entire buildings are eligible for services if a high enough percentage of residents is frail or at risk.

Congregate Housing

The Congregate Housing Services program, enacted as part of the Housing and Community Development Amendments of 1978 (P.L. 95-557), was the first program to make funds available so that HUD housing facilities could provide services for elderly residents. The purpose of the program was to prevent senior residents of Section 202 and Public Housing developments from moving to nursing homes by providing meals and other supports like housekeeping, case management, personal care, and transportation. In 1990, the Cranston-Gonzalez National Affordable Housing Act (P.L. 101-625) expanded eligible developments to include those assisted under project-based Section 8 rental assistance contracts, and those assisted through the Section 221(d)(3) and Section 236 programs. Cranston-Gonzalez also specified that Congregate Housing funds could be used to renovate properties to make them accessible to elderly residents with mobility problems, and to hire service coordinators to assist residents.

Since 1995, no new Congregate Housing contracts have been awarded, but HUD continues to fund contracts that were already in existence through funds appropriated to the Service Coordinator program (described below).[95] Current regulations provide that HUD will pay up to 40% of Congregate Housing costs, grant recipients must pay 50% of costs, and elderly participants must make payments that total at least 10% of total program costs.[96] Not all project residents are eligible for Congregate Housing services. They must be frail: defined as deficient in at least three ADLs.[97] Eligible project residents are identified by a committee appointed by grantees and made up of three individuals, at least one of whom is a medical professional, who are competent to determine the abilities of elderly residents.[98]

Multi-Family Housing Service Coordinators

Service coordinators in HUD developments for elderly persons and persons with disabilities work with residents to provide a wide range of services. These include the arrangement of transportation; meal services; housekeeping; medication management; visits from nurses, dentists, and massage therapists; haircuts; and social activities. Service coordinators became eligible for funding through the Section 202 program starting in 1990 (P.L. 101-625). HUD developments funded through the Section 221(d)(3) and Section 236 programs were made eligible for service coordinator funding in the Housing and Community Development Act of 1992 (P.L. 102-550).[99] In 2000, the law was further amended to allow service coordinators to assist those elderly residents and residents with disabilities living in the vicinity of the HUD-subsidized buildings in which the service coordinators work (P.L. 106-569).

Funding for the Service Coordinator program is awarded on a competitive basis. Owners of eligible properties may apply for funds on an annual basis through HUD's grant process.[100] To qualify, at least 25% of residents in a development must be considered frail elderly, at-risk elderly, or disabled non-elderly.[101] Applicants must also show that they have no other funds available to pay for a service coordinator. Grants are made for three years and are renewable.

Resident Opportunity and Self-Sufficiency (ROSS) Service Coordinators Program

The ROSS program was established in the FY1999 HUD Appropriations Act (P.L. 105-276) to assist Public Housing residents making the transition from welfare to work, and to provide service coordinators and supportive services for elderly residents and residents with disabilities living in designated Public Housing developments.[102] The ROSS program for those making the transition from welfare to work was referred to as the ROSS Family Self-Sufficiency program, whereas the program for elderly residents was referred to as the ROSS Elderly/Persons with Disabilities program.[103] In the FY2008 grant year, HUD combined the ROSS Elderly/Persons with Disabilities program with the ROSS Family and Homeownership Program to become one grant program: ROSS Service Coordinators.[104]

The ROSS program is much like the Service Coordinator program. Its service coordinators may arrange for meals, transportation, housekeeping, health and nutrition programs, case management, job training, and assistance with personal care.[105] ROSS funds are made available annually to PHAs, tribes, and nonprofit organizations through a competitive grant process. Awards are based on factors that include (1) the applicant's capacity and resources to implement services using a service coordinator; (2) the need for service coordinators and supportive services in the community, together with identification of service providers to meet the need; (3) the applicant's ability to leverage additional resources; and (4) the development of a system to measure the grantee's performance.[106] The ROSS program requires grant recipients to provide a 25% cash or in-kind match to the federal grant, and initial grants are made for three years. Beginning in FY2008, unlike previous grant years, recipient grantees may only use funds to pay for service coordinators, not for the services themselves.

Assisted Living Conversion

The HUD Appropriations Act of FY2000 (P.L. 106-74) created the Assisted Living Conversion program to allow HUD-subsidized facilities for elderly residents to modify their apartments and common areas to accommodate elderly persons and persons with disabilities who need additional assistance in order to remain in their units.[107] HUD-funded buildings developed under the Section 202 program, Section 236 program, and Section 221(d)(3) program, or units supported by project- based Section 8 rental assistance, are eligible to apply for funds. Owners may use funds to convert some or all units in a building for use as assisted living units.

HUD's definition of an assisted living facility contains three parts: (1) the facility is licensed and regulated by the state in which it is located, (2) it provides supportive services to assist residents in carrying out activities of daily living, and (3) it has separate housing units for residents, together with common rooms.[108] There is no uniform state definition for what constitutes an assisted living facility, and the level of care required by state law varies.[109] Requirements for physical standards such as unit size and the presence of a kitchen also vary from state to state. Recipients of assisted living conversion grants must comply with state or HUD requirements regarding physical standards, whichever are more stringent. To be eligible for Assisted Living Conversion funds, HUD requires that facilities contain a central kitchen and lounge and/or recreational areas available to all residents.[110] HUD also requires that assisted living facilities meet certain program requirements and construction requirements. Program requirements include staff ability to respond to a crisis 24 hours a day, supervision of nutrition and medication for dependent residents, and the availability of three meals per day.[111] Construction requirements include bathrooms that are accessible to persons with disabilities and a 24-hour emergency response system in each unit.[112]

Owners of eligible properties may apply for assisted living conversion funds through HUD's annual NOFA process. Grant recipients may use the funds to make units accessible by installing grab bars, widening doors, installing accessible appliances and counters, and adding emergency alert systems, among other modifications.[113] Grant recipients may also use funds to renovate common spaces for kitchen, dining, or recreational use, and to provide furniture, appliances, and equipment for those areas.

Table 2. Supportive Services and Assisted Living Programs.

Programs	Developments that Qualify for Services	Eligibility
Congregate Housing	Section 202 Section 221(d)(3) Section 236 Project-based Section 8 Rental Assistance	Frail elderly and non-elderly persons with disabilities.
Service Coordinator	Section 202 Section 221(d)(3) Section 236	All residents if at least 25% of residents are frail elderly, at-risk elderly, or non-elderly persons with disabilities.
ROSS	Public Housing	All residents.
Assisted Living Conversion	Section 202 Section 221(d)(3) Section 236 Project-based Section 8 Rental Assistance	Frail elderly and non-elderly persons with disabilities.

Source: Prepared by CRS on the basis of 42 U.S.C. § 8011 (k)(6) and (7); Notice of Funding
    Availability for Service Coordinators, *Federal Register*, vol. 72, no. 48, March 13, 2007, pp.
    11691; P.L. 105-276; 12 U.S.C. § 1701 q-2.

FUNDING AND CURRENT ISSUES

Funding

From FY2007 through FY2009, the Bush Administration proposed to reduce the combined funding level for the programs that provide housing and services for elderly households (primarily the Section 202 program)—by 26% in FY2007, by 22% in FY2008, and by nearly 27% in FY2009. However, in each of these fiscal years Congress did not reduce funding for the program. For FY20 10, President Obama proposed to maintain the same funding level as in FY2009—$765 million for Section 202 and related programs. Congress appropriated approximately $60 million more than was requested by the President, a combined $825 million for Section 202, the Assisted Living Conversion Program, Service Coordinators, and related expenses. See **Table 3** for Section 202 funding levels, as well as funding for supportive services programs. For more information about current year appropriations, see CRS Report R40727, *The Department of Housing and Urban Development: FY2010 Appropriations*, coordinated by Maggie McCarty.

Table 3. Funding for Selected Programs, FY2001-FY2010(dollars in millions).

Fiscal Year	Section 202[a]	Service Coordinators	ROSS	Assisted Living Conversion
2001	677.0	49.9	—[b]	49.9
2002	682.6	50.0	—[b]	50.0
2003	678.5	49.6	9.3	24.8
2004	698.7	29.8	11.4	24.8
2005	648.3	49.6	16.3	24.8
2006	634.7	51.1	8.8	24.6
2007	638.7	51.1	16.7	24.6
2008	628.7	59.8	—[d]	24.8
2009	626.4	90.0	—[e]	25.0
2010	—[c]	90.0	—[e]	40.0

Source: Prepared by CRS on the basis of FY2000 to FY2010 HUD Budget Justifications, P.L. 111-8, P.L. 111-1 17, and HUD Funding Notices (ROSS).

a. Includes funds for new capital grants, new project rental assistance, and renewals of project rental assistance contracts.

b. From FY2000 through FY2002, HUD split ROSS grants between non-elderly families and elderly residents/residents with disabilities. In FY2000 and FY200 1, $24 million was distributed; in FY2002, $22.9 million was distributed.

c. P.L. 111-117 did not specify an amount for Section 202 in FY2010.

d. Beginning in FY2008, the ROSS Service Coordinator program was created to serve both non-elderly families as well as elderly residents/residents with disabilities. In FY2008, $28 million was awarded to ROSS Service Coordinator grantees, but the amount of funds used to serve elderly residents specifically is not broken out of the total.

e. ROSS funding for FY2009 and FY2010 has not yet been awarded.

Legislation

Refinancing Provisions in the FY2009 and FY2010 Appropriations Acts

The statute governing the Section 202 program allows building owners to refinance their mortgages under certain circumstances in order to take advantage of lower interest rates and to use funds freed up as a result of the refinancing to improve conditions for tenants. Specifically, the law allows refinancing if an owner agrees to continue to operate the project under terms at least as advantageous to tenants as the terms of the existing loan *and* if the refinancing results in a lower interest rate and reduced debt service (i.e., reduced principal and interest payments).[114] However, for older Section 202 properties with interest rates as low as 3% (those funded prior to 1974), obtaining a loan with a lower interest rate and reduced debt service is not necessarily possible.

To make refinancing available to owners of Section 202 projects developed prior to 1974, the FY2009 Omnibus Appropriations Act (P.L. 111-8) and the FY2010 Consolidated Appropriations Act (P.L. 111-117) included language that broadened the refinancing provisions of the Section 202 program.[115] However, the refinancing provisions do not specifically amend existing law, so they are in effect only for the duration of the fiscal year that the appropriations law is in effect. During FY2009, HUD did not release guidance regarding the new provisions, so no properties were refinanced pursuant to P.L. 111-8.

Under P.L. 111-117, owners are to be able to refinance mortgages with interest rates at or below 6% in order to address a property's physical needs (and would not necessarily be required to refinance into a loan with a lower interest rate and reduced debt service). These refinancing transactions for loans with interest rates at or below 6% also have several other requirements:

- the transactions have to meet a cost benefit analysis to be established by HUD;
- the transactions cannot result in increased costs for project-based Section 8 rental assistance except under certain circumstances;
- with the approval of HUD, owners can raise tenant rents in order to meet increased debt service and operating costs if insufficient project-based Section 8 rental assistance is available to meet these costs. However, HUD's approval of increased tenant rents would be "the basis for the owner to agree to terminate the project-based rental assistance contract," triggering tenant eligibility for enhanced Section 8 vouchers;
- when tenants who receive enhanced vouchers as a result of refinancing terminate their occupancy, those units would become eligible for project-based Section 8 rental assistance; and
- owners have to enter into a use agreement to maintain affordability of units for 20 years beyond the maturity date of the original Section 202 loan.

The Section 202 Supportive Housing for the Elderly Act (S. 118)

A bill that would make some changes and additions to current law governing the Section 202 program has been introduced in the 111th Congress. The Section 202 Supportive Housing for the Elderly Act of 2009 (S. 118) is similar to two bills that were introduced in the 110th Congress— H.R. 2930 (which was passed by the House) and S. 2736. The version of the bill introduced in the 111th Congress would address the financing of new Section 202 projects as well as how existing properties are refinanced. S. 118 would also change the definition of assisted living facilities in the Assisted Living Conversion Program.

In the area of financing for new Section 202 developments, S. 118 would provide that, upon expiration of a contract for Section 202 rental assistance, HUD will adjust the contract to account for reasonable project costs as well as the increased costs of project reserves, service coordinators, and supportive services. The bill would also make a change to the definition of "private nonprofit organization." Under current law, nonprofits must have governing boards that are responsible for operation of the Section 202 project. S. 118 would allow national nonprofit sponsors to form local advisory boards to fulfill this requirement. Another provision in S. 118 would give Section 202 project owners the authority to give a preference to homeless elderly applicants by either requesting the preference in their initial application for HUD funds or making their request after funds have been awarded.

S. 118 would also address the refinancing of existing Section 202 properties. A similar proposal for refinancing Section 202 mortgages was included in the FY2009 and FY2010 appropriations acts, described in the previous section, "Refinancing Provisions in the FY2009 and FY2010 Appropriations Acts." The change would allow owners of older Section 202 developments (those funded prior to 1974) to refinance in order to address the property's physical needs. Under current law, owners may refinance their Section 202 mortgages if the refinancing "results in a lower interest rate on the principal of the loan for the project and in reductions in debt service" (i.e. reduced principal and interest payments).[116] Owners that refinance are required to maintain affordability through the term of the original Section 202 mortgage. S. 118 would extend the term of affordability to 20 years beyond the term of the original Section 202 loan. Unlike the FY2010 Consolidated Appropriations Act (P.L. 111-117), in which only those owners with loans that have interest rates at or below 6% must extend the affordability term by 20 years, S. 118 would extend the term for all owners that refinance.

The bill also outlines the ways in which owners would be able to use proceeds from a refinancing. Current law describes how savings that result from a refinancing can be used for various purposes and requires that at least 50% be used in a manner that is advantageous to tenants.[117] S. 118 would amend this section of the law. While S. 118 would allow owners to use proceeds from a refinancing in a manner that is advantageous to tenants, it would also allow owners to use proceeds to provide affordable rental housing and social services for elderly persons generally, without a requirement that they be tenants of the property being refinanced. Examples of the ways in which owners could use refinancing proceeds that are listed in S. 118 include supportive services without limitation (the current law limit is 15% of savings resulting from refinancing), payment of developers' fees, and payment of equity to the owner. Additionally, a provision in S. 118 would limit HUD's ability to put conditions on the amount of proceeds that Section 202 owners may realize from a sale or refinancing, or the way in which owners use the proceeds. HUD would only be able to impose conditions on the amount or use of proceeds if there was an existing contract between HUD and the project owner that authorized the conditions.

Another change to existing law contained in S. 118 would be a new "preservation project rental assistance" program for owners with Section 202 units that were built prior to 1974, when most units did not receive rental assistance.[118] The rental assistance would be available if owners chose to refinance in order to prevent displacement of tenants. This differs from provisions in the FY2010 Consolidated Appropriations Act, where tenants are to receive enhanced Section 8 vouchers when owners refinance.

The bill would also create a mortgage sale demonstration program in which up to five states could participate. HUD would sell portfolios of Section 202 mortgages to state Housing Finance Agencies (HFAs) in participating states. The purpose of the program would be to demonstrate the "efficiency, effectiveness, quality, and timeliness of asset management and regulatory oversight ..." by state HFAs. S. 118 would require the HUD Secretary to conduct a study of the demonstration program and release a report with findings and recommendations.

S. 118 would also change the definition of "assisted living facility" in the Assisted Living Conversion Program. Under current law, an assisted living facility is owned by a private nonprofit organization, is licensed by the state (or locality), makes available certain supportive services, and provides separate dwelling units for residents. The bill would change the definition so that private nonprofit organizations may meet the requirements *either* through state or local licensure *or* by providing certain supportive services through "recognized and experienced third party service providers" at the request of residents. The new definition would continue to require nonprofit ownership and provision of separate dwelling units.

Another section of S. 118 would create a National Senior Housing Clearinghouse within HUD to disseminate information about available rental units for elderly tenants and characteristics of those rental units. The Clearinghouse would include not only units in Section 202 facilities, but also units subsidized through the Section 8 program, the Low-Income Housing Tax Credit, the Assisted Living Conversion program, and other programs that subsidize units dedicated for use by elderly households. Information would be made available to prospective residents through a website and a toll-free number.

Legislation Enacted in the 110th Congress

The Housing and Economic Recovery Act of 2008 (P.L. 110-289), which was enacted on July 30, 2008, included a provision to direct HUD to delegate to state housing finance agencies (HFAs) the ability to process Section 202 capital grants. Under this provision, those grantee organizations that are awarded Section 202 capital grants, and that also intend to use Low Income Housing Tax Credits to develop their properties, may have their state HFA review and process the capital grant instead of HUD. Because HFAs are the agencies that administer tax credits, delegating the processing of the Section 202 capital grant to the HFA, together with the tax credit, is thought to be more efficient. As part of the delegated processing, HFAs may recommend project rental assistance in excess of the amount awarded by HUD, though an increase is subject to HUD approval.

Preservation of Federally Assisted Housing

A growing concern exists that the market will lose assisted housing units for elderly tenants because private for-profit and nonprofit owners of Section 202, 221(d)(3), and 236 developments have no obligation to continue providing subsidized housing beyond their contract terms. Therefore, owners may eventually convert these units to market-rate rental housing, jeopardizing the availability of affordable housing for their tenants. Affordable housing units may be converted under several circumstances. First, when HUD-subsidized mortgages reach maturity or when owners decide to prepay their mortgages, they may decide to convert the units to market-rate rentals. A second possibility is that owners receiving project-based Section 8 rental assistance could lose or terminate their contracts. A third concern is that owners of older buildings will not have enough funds to modernize or renovate deteriorating facilities, and units will be unavailable because they are not habitable. Congress has enacted several laws that have attempted to prevent the loss of affordable housing units due to these factors.

Section 202 Program

Most owners of Section 202 properties may prepay their loans with HUD approval, however, in general, they must maintain the affordability of the units.[119] Congress initially addressed the prepayment of Section 202 mortgage loans in 1984 (P.L. 98-181) by allowing prepayment only if property owners continue to operate their properties on terms at least as favorable to tenants as the terms under the original loan agreement up through the original date of loan maturity. In 2000, the American Homeownership and Economic Opportunity Act (P.L. 106-569) added provisions that allow owners to refinance as part of the prepayment if the terms of the new loan result in a lower interest rate and reduced debt service payments. HUD will then make at least 50% of its savings from reduced rental assistance payments available to owners to assist tenants either through supportive services, facility improvements, or rent reductions for unassisted tenants. In the 111th Congress, legislation has been introduced that would make some changes to the way in which Section 202 loans are refinanced (see the previous section for a discussion of S. 118).

Section 221(d)(3) and Section 236 Programs

Although the initial mortgage subsidy contracts between HUD and property owners in the Section 221(d)(3) and Section 236 programs had a duration of 40 years,[120] in order to attract developers to the program, HUD gave owners the right to prepay their mortgages (and potentially leave the program) after 20 years.[121] By the late 1980s, many Section 236 and 221(d)(3) project owners were in the position to prepay their mortgages and charge market rate rents, displacing the low- income tenants who lived in their developments. Recognizing that HUD could lose thousands of affordable housing units in the coming years,[122] Congress in 1990 enacted Title VI of the Cranston-Gonzalez National Affordable Housing Act (P.L. 101-625), the Low-Income Housing Preservation and Resident Homeownership Act (LIHPRHA). The act created incentives for building owners to continue offering affordable housing through the Section 221(d)(3) and Section 236 programs.[123]

LIHPRHA continued to allow owners to prepay their mortgages after 20 years, but only as long as the change did not create economic hardship for current tenants or reduce the availability of low-income housing, housing near jobs, or housing for minorities.[124] To convince owners to maintain affordable properties, HUD could ensure that owners receive rent subsidies sufficient to guarantee an 8% return after mortgage payments and operating expenses were paid and adequate reserves were established.

If building owners still chose to prepay their mortgages and begin charging market-rate rents, HUD protected tenants by issuing enhanced Section 8 vouchers. Enhanced vouchers require building owners in low-vacancy areas, or with elderly tenants and tenants with disabilities, to accept the vouchers, allowing tenants to remain in the building at the lower rental amount for up to three years.[125] The law also required owners to pay 50% of tenant moving expenses. LIHPRHA has not been funded since FY1997 (P.L. 104-204), but during the 1990s it is estimated to have preserved 110,000 units of Section 221(d)(3) and Section 236 housing.[126] Current law requires that owners give Section 221(d)(3) and Section 236 tenants at least 150 days' notice when they plan to prepay their mortgages.[127]

Project-Based Section 8 Rental Assistance

A large number of assisted housing units for elderly households are supported with project-based Section 8 rental assistance contracts. When Section 8 rental assistance contracts began to expire in the 1 990s, many owners began to opt out of the program. In its FY1 998 HUD Appropriations Act (P.L. 105-65), Congress responded to the opt-outs by providing that contracts for rental assistance with HUD could be renewed at rental rates up to the rate prevailing in the market whenever market rate rents exceed the contract rent. (Market rent is based on either the rent levels of comparable unassisted properties in a building's area or on area fair market rent levels as determined by HUD.) This provision is sometimes called "mark up to market," and it attempts to give incentives to owners to stay in the Section 8 program even if they could otherwise make more money in the private market. If owners decide to opt out of the rental assistance program, tenants may qualify for enhanced Section 8 vouchers that they may use to either remain in the building or move elsewhere. [128] P.L. 105-65 also created the "mark-to-market" program for cases in which Section 8 payments exceed market-rate rents. Mark-to-market allows those owners with above-market rents to renew their rental assistance contracts with HUD, although at a lower rate, while also restructuring their outstanding debt on the property. The program is designed both to ensure that HUD pays reasonable market rents for subsidized properties and to provide incentives for owners of assisted properties to renew their contracts with HUD.

Children Living in Housing Developments for Elderly Residents

The most recent Census estimated that 2.4 million grandparents were raising grandchildren, and that of this number, approximately 19% of grandparents were poor. [129] The HUD guidelines governing the Section 202, Section 221(d)(3), Section 236, and certain project-based Section 8 assistance programs specifically prohibit the exclusion of children from these developments ("owners may not exclude otherwise eligible elderly families with children from elderly properties ...").[130] Guidelines governing Public Housing developments are less specific, although the guidance states that "there is nothing in the definition of elderly family that excludes children. Many elderly families today consist of grandparents with custody of grandchildren. This is an elderly family."[131]

Even if developments designed for elderly residents do allow children, however, they might not be equipped to serve families with both elderly members and young children. For example, most units in elderly housing developments are either efficiencies or have only one bedroom, and may not have the space to accommodate family members. In addition, elderly developments might lack common spaces where children might play, or the after-school programs that are often a part of HUD-subsidized complexes for families.

In order to address the growing number of grandparents raising grandchildren, Congress enacted the Living Equitably—Grandparents Aiding Children and Youth (LEGACY) Act in 2003 as part of the American Dream Downpayment Act (P.L. 108-186). The LEGACY Act provides for the funding of housing units in the Section 202 program for elderly residents raising grandchildren or other relatives age 19 or younger. Congress did not fund the LEGACY Act until FY2006, when it appropriated $3.96 million for an Intergenerational Families Demonstration Project. On April 25, 2008, HUD released a Notice of Funding Availability (NOFA) to solicit grant applications for LEGACY Act funds.[132] In December 2008, HUD announced two awardees, both of which will receive capital grants and rental assistance: one project consisting of 10 units will be located in Chicago, while the other, consisting of nine units, will be in Smithville, TN.[133]

The LEGACY Act also called for HUD, together with the Census Bureau, to produce a study of the affordable housing needs of grandparents raising grandchildren. In April 2008, HUD released a *Report to Congress on Intergenerational Housing Needs and HUD Programs*.[134] The report describes the number, characteristics, and housing conditions of grandparent-headed households and households with other relatives raising related children. The report estimated that 265,000 grandparent-headed households and 225,000 households headed by other relatives would qualify for assistance under the LEGACY Act.[135]

End Notes

[1] The report by the Commission on Affordable Housing and Health Facility Needs for Seniors in the 21st Century was released to four congressional committees on June 30, 2002: the House and Senate Appropriations Committees, the House Financial Services Committee, and the Senate Banking, Housing and Urban Affairs Committee. The report is available at http://govinfo.library.unt.edu/seniorscommission/pages/final_report/finalreport.pdf.

[2] Wan He, Manisha Sengupta, Victoria A. Velkoff, and Kimberly A. DeBarros, *65+ In the United States: 2005*, U.S. Census Bureau, December 2005, http://www.census.gov/prod/2006pubs/p23-209.pdf.

[3] Ibid., pp. 12-13.

[4] *A Quiet Crisis in America*, p. 22.

[5] Although other terms such as "Older Americans" may be preferred, this report uses the term "elderly" to refer to those individuals eligible for HUD-assisted housing for persons age 62 or older because it is the term used by HUD and has a meaning specific to HUD's housing programs.

[6] 12 U.S.C. § 1701q(k)(1).

[7] For more information on Section 8 vouchers, see CRS Report RL32284, *An Overview of the Section 8 Housing Programs*, by Maggie McCarty.

[8] For more information on reverse mortgages, see CRS Report RL33843, *Reverse Mortgages: Background and Issues*, by Bruce E. Foote.

[9] For more information on the Department of Agriculture's rural housing programs, see CRS Report RL33421, *USDA Rural Housing Programs: An Overview*, by Bruce E. Foote.

[10] Barbara A. Haley and Robert W. Gray, *Section 202 Supportive Housing for the Elderly: Program Status and Performance Measurement*, U.S. Department of Housing and Urban Development, Office of Policy Development and Research, June 2008, p. 22, http://www.huduser.org/Publications/pdf/sec_202_1.pdf (hereinafter, *Section 202 Supportive Housing for the Elderly: Program Status and Performance Measurement*). Although the Section 202 program no longer provides housing for persons with disabilities, between 1965 and 1992, Section 202 housing was developed for both elderly and disabled households. The total number of Section 202 units available for both elderly households and households with an adult member who has a disability is around 303,000 units. Ibid.

[11] In 1981, the Housing and Community Development Amendments (P.L. 97-35) required that Section 202 units be made available primarily to very low-income households.

[12] U.S. Department of Housing and Urban Development, *Housing for the Elderly and Handicapped: The Experience of the Section 202 Program from 1959 to 1977*, January 1979, p. 29 (hereinafter, *Housing for the Elderly and Handicapped*).

[13] Barry G. Jacobs, Kenneth R. Harney, Charles L. Edson, and Bruce S. Lane, *Guide to Federal Housing Programs* (Washington, DC: Bureau of National Affairs, 1982), p. 77.

[14] *Housing for the Elderly and Handicapped*, p. 18.

[15] Ibid., p. 17. See also United States Senate Special Committee on Aging, *Section 202 Housing for the Elderly: A National Survey*, committee print 98-257, 98th Cong., 2nd sess., (Washington, DC: GPO, 1984), p. 7.

[16] *Housing for the Elderly and Handicapped*, p. 29.

[17] Ibid., p. 18.

[18] The Rent Supplement program primarily provided rent subsidies for tenants living in Section 221(d)(3) housing, but Section 202 residents were eligible as well.

[19] *Housing for the Elderly and Handicapped*, p. 97.

[20] For more information about housing for persons with disabilities, see CRS Report RL34728, *Section 811 and Other HUD Housing Programs for Persons with Disabilities*, by Libby Perl.

[21] Ibid., p. 36.

[22] Senate Committee on Aging, Subcommittee on Housing for the Elderly, *Examination of Proposed Section 202 Housing Regulations*, hearing before the 94th Cong., 1st sess., June 6, 1975, p. 2.

[23] M. Powell Lawton, *Planning and Managing Housing for the Elderly* (New York: John Wiley & Sons, 1975), p. 38.

[24] CRS analysis of HUD data downloaded in September 2009.

[25] HUD Handbook 4350.3: Occupancy Requirements of Subsidized Multifamily Housing Programs, June 2007, chapter 3, paragraph 3-23, http://www.hud.gov/offices/adm/hudclips/handbooks/hsgh/4350.3/index.cfm (hereinafter, "HUD Handbook 4350.3").

[26] *Housing for the Elderly and Handicapped*, pp. 105-106.

[27] An exception for contracts up to 40 years was made for developments built or rehabilitated by loans from state or local agencies.

[28] *Housing for the Elderly and Handicapped*, p. 38.

[29] P.L. 93-383, section 213(d).

[30] House Committee on Aging, Subcommittee on Housing and Consumer Interests, *The 1988 National Survey of Section 202 Housing for the Elderly and Handicapped*, 101st Cong., 1st sess., December 1, 1989, p. 29.

[31] See Section 323.

[32] The Supplemental Appropriations Act of 1984 (P.L. 98-18 1) changed the requirement for units assisted prior to 1981 from 10% to 25%, and the Housing and Community Development Act of 1987 (P.L. 100-242) changed the requirement for units assisted after 1981 from 5% to 15%. See 42 U.S.C. § 1437n(c).

[33] Leonard F. Heumann, Karen Winter-Nelson, and James R. Anderson, *The 1999 National Survey of Section 202 Elderly Housing*, American Association of Retired Persons, January 2001, p. 9, http://assets.aarp.org/rgcenter/il/ 200 1_02_housing.pdf (hereinafter, *The 1999 National Survey of Section 202 Elderly Housing*).

[34] *The 1988 National Survey of Section 202 Housing for the Elderly and Handicapped*, p. 27.

[35] Ibid.

[36] Senate Committee on Banking, Housing, and Urban Affairs, *The National Housing Act*, Senate report to accompany S. 566, 101st Cong., 2nd sess., S.Rept. 101-3 16, June 8, 1990, p. 133.

[37] Ibid.

[38] Ibid., p. 34.

[39] FMRs are generally set at the 40th percentile of rents paid in an area, although in some high-cost areas, FMRs are set at the 50th percentile.

[40] S.Rept. 101-316, Report of the Senate Committee on Banking, Housing, and Urban Affairs, to accompany S. 566, the National Affordable Housing Act, 101st Cong., 2nd sess., June 8, 1990, pp. 133-134. The provisions in S. 566 regarding Section 202 were adopted in P.L. 101-625. See H.Rept. 101-943.

[41] *Cranston-Gonzalez National Affordable Housing Act*, conference report to accompany S. 566, 101st Cong., 2nd sess., H.Rept. 101-943, October 25, 1990, p. 484.

[42] S.Rept. 101-316, p. 134.

[43] Housing provided for persons with disabilities through the Section 202 program is sometimes referred to as "Section 202(h)" housing, referring to the subparagraph that was added to the Section 202 statute by P.L. 95-557.

[44] For more information about the Section 811 program, see CRS Report RL34728, *Section 811 and Other HUD Housing Programs for Persons with Disabilities*, by Libby Perl.

[45] *The 1999 National Survey of Section 202 Elderly Housing*, p. 9.

[46] *Section 202 Supportive Housing for the Elderly: Program Status and Performance Measurement*, p. 20.

[47] Ibid.

[48] Ibid., p. 29.

[49] HUD lists the multifamily hubs in its annual Notice of Funding Availability (NOFA). They are Atlanta, GA, Baltimore, MD, Boston, MA, Buffalo, NY, Chicago, IL, Columbus, OH, Denver, CO, Detroit, MI, Fort Worth, TX, Greensboro, NC, Jacksonville, FL, Kansas City, MO, Los Angeles, CA, Minneapolis, MN, New

York, NY, Philadelphia, PA, San Francisco, CA, and Northwest/Alaska. The FY2009 NOFA is available on HUD's website, http://www.hud.gov/offices/adm/grants/nofa09/sec202esec.pdf (hereinafter, FY2009 Section 202 NOFA).

[50] 24 CFR § 79 1.402(c).

[51] FY2009 Section 202 NOFA, p. 6.

[52] Ibid., p. 62. Two of the points are bonus points awarded for projects that are part of renewal communities, empowerment zones, or enterprise communities.

[53] The list of grantees is available at http://www.hud.gov/utilities/intercept.cfm?/content/releases/pr09-007.pdf.

[54] For more information on the LIHTC, see CRS Report RS22389, *An Introduction to the Design of the Low-Income Housing Tax Credit*, by Mark P. Keightley.

[55] Specifically, a property's qualified basis is determined as follows: (1) the cost of constructing, acquiring, or rehabilitating the property is calculated, (2) this amount is reduced by federal grants received by the developer, and (3) the resulting value is then multiplied by the percentage of space in the housing development that is devoted to low- income use. This percentage is the lower of either the "unit fraction"—the ratio of low-income units to all units in the building—or the "floor space fraction"—the ratio of square footage in low-income units to total square footage. 26 U.S.C. § 42(c). The qualified basis is then multiplied by the value of the tax credits—these are roughly either 9% or 4%—to determine the total annual value of the tax credits.

[56] In addition to the costs of materials, construction, and/or rehabilitation, among the costs included in determining qualified basis are contractor fees, developer fees, engineering fees, and the cost of drawing up architectural specifications. Among the costs that are not included are the cost of land and fees associated with long-term financing. See Joseph Guggenheim, *Tax Credits for Low Income Housing* (Glen Echo, MD: Simon Publications, 1996) p. 37.

[57] See HUD website, "Calculating the Qualified Basis," http://www.hud.gov/offices/cpd/affordablehousing/training/web/lihtc/calculating/qualifiedbasis.cfm.

[58] 26 C.F.R. § 1.42-16.

[59] Rev. Rul. 2008-6.

[60] Rev. Rul. 2002-65.

[61] Rev. Rul. 98-49.

[62] P.L. 106-569 amended the Section 202 statute to state that "[n]otwithstanding any other provision of law, assistance amounts provided under this section may be treated as amounts not derived from a Federal grant." See Section 832. On September 17, 2003, the IRS issued a letter stating that it was reviewing the applicability of the LIHTC section of federal grants to PRAC under the Section 202 program. The letter is available at http://www.irs.gov/pub/irs-wd/04- 0061.pdf.

[63] These credit rates are not set exactly at 9% and 4%—they vary depending on the current interest rate used in the Department of the Treasury credit rate formula. For more information about this issue, see CRS Report RS22917, *The Low-Income Housing Tax Credit Program: The Fixed Subsidy and Variable Rate*, by Mark P. Keightley.

[64] The statute also specifically exempted funds received under CDBG, HOME, and Native American Housing and Self Determination Act programs from the definition of federally subsidized, so those projects have been eligible for the 9% credit all along.

[65] See U.S. Department of Housing and Urban Development, "Mixed Finance Development for Supportive Housing for the Elderly or Persons with Disabilities: Final Rule," *Federal Register,* vol. 70, no. 176, September 13, 2005, p. 54202.

[66] See, for example, Liz Enochs, "Affordable Housing Equity: Developers Share Tips for Converting Projects That Fail to Win 9% LIHTCs into 4% Deals," *Affordable Housing Finance,* July 2007, http://www.housingfinance.com/ahf/ articles/2007/jul/AFFORDABLE0707.htm.

[67] The Section 221(d)(3) program also contained a market interest rate component, but unlike the BMIR program, it was not designed to ensure affordability. John R. Gallagher, *Nonprofit Housing Rent Supplement Program Under Section 221(d) (3) of the National Housing Act* (Washington, DC: Urban America, Inc., 1968), p. 4.

[68] Senate Committee on Banking and Currency, *Housing Act of 1961,* Senate report to accompany S. 1922, 87th Cong., 1st sess., S.Rept. 281, May 19, 1961.

[69] Leonard Garland Gaston, "The 221(d)(3) Below Market Interest Rate and Rent Supplement Housing Program" (Ph.D. dissertation, Ohio State University, 1969), p. 120.

[70] John R. Gallagher and John J. O'Donnell, *Nonprofit Housing Under Section 221(d)(3) of the National Housing Act* (Washington, DC: Urban America, Inc., 1966), p. 20.

[71] U.S. Government Accountability Office, *Federal Housing Programs That Offer Assistance to the Elderly,* GAO-05- 174, February 2005, p. 11, http://www.gao.gov/new.items/d05174.pdf (hereinafter, *Federal Housing Programs that Offer Assistance to the Elderly*).

[72] HUD Handbook 4350.3, chapter 3, paragraph 3-6.

[73] 12 U.S.C. § 1701s(d).

[74] 12 U.S.C. § 1701s(j)(1)(d).

[75] HUD FY20 10 Budget Justifications, p. N-1, http://www.hud.gov/offices/cfo/reports/2010/cjs/hsg2010.pdf.

[76] House Committee on Banking and Currency, *Housing and Urban Development Act of 1968*, House report to accompany H.R. 17989, 90th Cong., 2nd sess., H.Rept. 1585, June 25, 1968.

[77] Ibid.

[78] General Accounting Office (now the Government Accountability Office), *Little Accomplished in Insuring that Proper Rents Are Charged Under the Section 236 Rental Assistance Housing Program*, CED-76-146, October 5, 1976, p. 2, http://archive.gao.gov/f0402/100542.pdf.

[79] 12 U.S.C. § 1715z-1(f)(1). The Section 236 market rent is different from Section 8 fair market rent.

[80] Charles L. Edson, "Sections 235 and 236—The First Year," *Urban Lawyer* 2, No. 14 (1970), p. 22.

[81] *Federal Housing Programs that Offer Assistance to the Elderly*, p. 11.

[82] HUD FY2009 Budget Justifications, p. K-3, http://www.hud.gov/offices/cfo/reports/2009/cjs/hsg1.pdf. The exceptions in the RAP program are state-aided, uninsured projects.

[83] House Committee on Banking and Currency, *Housing Act of 1956*, House report to accompany H.R. 11742, 84th Cong., 2nd sess., H.Rept. 2363, July 15, 1956.

[84] Frances Merchant Carp, *A Future for the Aged, Victoria Plaza and Its Residents* (Austin: University of Texas Press, 1966).

[85] *Federal Housing Programs That Offer Assistance to the Elderly*, p. 11.

[86] See General Accounting Office (now the Government Accountability Office), *Housing Persons with Mental Disabilities with the Elderly*, GAO/RCED-92-81, August 1992, pp. 10-11, http://archive.gao.gov/d33t10/147294.pdf.

[87] Congress intended the definition of handicap to be interpreted consistently with the Rehabilitation Act of 1973 (P.L. 93-112), which includes drug addiction and alcoholism as physical or mental impairments. 28 CFR § 41.31.

[88] *Housing Persons with Mental Disabilities with the Elderly*, p. 17. See, also, remarks of Representative Peter Blute, *Congressional Record*, daily edition, vol. 142 (February 27, 1996), p. H1274.

[89] The Housing and Community Development Act of 1992, P.L. 102-550. The provisions are codified at 42 U.S.C. § 1437e; the regulations are at 24 CFR §§ 945.101-945.303.

[90] The new construction and substantial rehabilitation programs were created in P.L. 93-3 83 and abolished in P.L. 98- 181. For more information on Section 8 housing, see CRS Report RL32284, *An Overview of the Section 8 Housing Programs*, by Maggie McCarty.

[91] 42 U.S.C. §§ 13611-13620.

[92] *Federal Housing Programs that Offer Assistance to the Elderly*, p. 11.

[93] For the Service Coordinator and Assisted Living Conversion programs, ADLs are listed at 24 CFR § 89 1.205. For the Congregate Housing program, they are listed at 24 CFR § 700.105.

[94] The at-risk category applies only to the Service Coordinator program.

[95] Although the President's budget for FY1996 did not propose funds for the Congregate Housing program, it did propose that projects similar to the Congregate Housing program would be funded through a new initiative called the Housing Certificates for Families and Individuals Performance Funds program. Congress did not appropriate funds for the program.

[96] 24 CFR § 700. 145.

[97] 24 CFR § 700.135.

[98] HUD Handbook 4640.1: Congregate Housing Services Program Operating Procedures, November 6, 1996, chapter 2, paragraph 2-8, http://www.hud.gov/offices/adm/hudclips/handbooks/hsgh/4640.1/46401c2HSGH.pdf.

[99] See Section 676.

[100] Note that Section 202 developments that receive project-based Section 8 rental assistance are not eligible for service coordinator funds. Instead, they may request an increase in their rental assistance payments to support a service coordinator.

[101] This requirement is present in HUD's Notice of Funding Availability for Service Coordinators. The most recent NOFA can be found on HUD's website, http://www.hud.gov/offices/adm/grants/nofa09/scmhsec.pdf.

[102] See the program's first Notice of Funding Availability, *Federal Register*, vol. 64, no. 153, August 10, 1999, p. 43543.

[103] Prior to the ROSS program, grants were available from HUD to Public Housing Authorities to fund service coordinators beginning in FY1994 (P.L. 103-124), and congregate housing and supportive services beginning in FY1996 (P.L. 104-134).

[104] See FY2008 Resident Opportunity and Self-Sufficiency Programs Webcast Presentation, May 13, 2008, http://www.hud.gov/offices/adm/grants/nofa08/grpross.cfm.

[105] HUD FY2009 Notice of Funding Availability for ROSS, pp. 15-20, http://www.hud.gov/offices/adm/grants/nofa09/ rossscsec.pdf.

[106] Ibid., pp 20-30.

[107] The statute governing the Assisted Living Conversion program is at 12 U.S.C. § 1701q-2.

[108] 12 U.S.C. §1715w(b)(6).

[109] For more information on state requirements, see Robert Mollica and Heather Johnson-LeMarche, *State Residential Care and Assisted-Living Policy: 2004*, Department of Health and Human Services, March 31, 2005, http://aspe.hhs.gov/daltcp/reports/04alcom.htm.

[110] See FY2009 Notice of Funding Availability for the Assisted Living Conversion Program, p. 3, http://www.hud.gov/offices/adm/grants/nofa09/alcpsec.pdf.

[111] Ibid., pp. 11-15.

[112] HUD Handbook 4600.1: Residential Care Facilities—Nursing Homes, Board and Care Homes, and Assisted Living Facilities, January 17, 1995, chapter 13, paragraph 13-7.

[113] Ibid., p. 27283.

[114] 12 U.S.C. § 1701q note.

[115] See Section 234 of "General Provisions—Department of Housing and Urban Development" in Division I of the FY2009 Omnibus Appropriations Act and Section 229 of the FY20 10 Consolidated Appropriations Act.

[116] 12 U.S.C. § 1701q, note.

[117] Ibid.

[118] However, some pre-1974 properties later received rental assistance through the Rent Supplement program and the Loan Management Set Aside program.

[119] Some Section 202 loans made during the late 1970s and early 1980s may be prepaid without HUD approval.

[120] See Senate Subcommittee on Housing for the Elderly of the Special Committee on Aging, *Adequacy of Federal Response to Housing Needs of Older Americans*, hearing, 92nd Cong., 1st sess., August 2, 1971, p. 130.

[121] House Subcommittee on Housing and Community Development of the Committee on Banking, Finance and Urban Affairs, *Preventing the Disappearance of Low-Income Housing*, hearing, 100th Cong., 2nd sess., June 8, 1988, p. 4. See, also, *Cranston-Gonzalez National Affordable Housing Act*, conference report to accompany S. 566, 101st Cong., 2nd sess., H.Rept. 101-943, October 25, 1990, p. 457.

[122] In 1990, Congress noted that over the next 12 years, more than 360,000 units of federally assisted housing could be lost. H.Rept. 10 1-943, p. 457.

[123] The act is codified at 12 U.S.C. §§ 4101-4125.

[124] 12 U.S.C. § 4108.

[125] 12 U.S.C. § 4113.

[126] The National Housing Law Project, *HUD Housing Programs: Tenants' Rights* (Oakland, CA: The National Housing Law Project, 2004), 15/37.

[127] P.L. 105-276.

[128] 42 U.S.C. § 143 7f(t).

[129] Tavia Simmons and Jane Lawler Dye, *Grandparents Living with Grandchildren: 2000*, U.S. Census Bureau, October 2003, pp. 1, 9, http://www.census.gov/prod/2003pubs/c2kbr-31.pdf.

[130] HUD Handbook 4350.3, chapter 3, paragraph 3-23, http://www.hud.gov/offices/adm/hudclips/handbooks/hsgh/4350.3/43503c3HSGH.pdf.

[131] HUD Public Housing Occupancy Guidebook, June 2003, Section 2.2, p. 25, http://www.hud.gov/offices/pih/programs/ph/rhiip/phguidebooknew.pdf.

[132] See Notice of Funding Availability for FY2007 Demonstration Program for Elderly Housing for Intergenerational Families, *Federal Register*, vol. 73, no. 81, April 25, 2008, pp. 22759-22776.

[133] See HUD's funding announcement, http://www.hud.gov/offices/hsg/mfh/eldfam/announcement.pdf.

[134] The report is available at http://www.huduser.org/Publications/pdf/intergenerational.pdf, and the data tables are at http://www.huduser.org/Publications/pdf/intergenerational_tables.pdf.

[135] Ibid., p. 6.

In: An Overview of Federal Housing Assistance Programs   ISBN: 978-1-61122-419-1
Editor: Brandon C. Sherman   © 2011 Nova Science Publishers, Inc.

Chapter 3

AN OVERVIEW OF THE HOME INVESTMENT PARTNERSHIPS PROGRAM

Katie Jones

SUMMARY

The HOME Investment Partnerships Program was authorized by the Cranston-Gonzalez National Affordable Housing Act of 1990 (P.L. 101-625). HOME is a federal block grant program that provides funding to states and localities to be used exclusively for affordable housing activities to benefit low-income households.

Funds for HOME are appropriated annually to the Department of Housing and Urban Development (HUD), which in turn distributes funding to states and certain localities by formula. Sixty percent of HOME funds are allocated to localities, and 40% of HOME funds are allocated to states. The formula takes into account six factors, including the number of units in a jurisdiction that are substandard or unaffordable, the age of a jurisdiction's housing, and the number of families living below the poverty line in the jurisdiction. States and localities that receive HOME funds are known as participating jurisdictions. As part of the process of becoming a participating jurisdiction, states and localities must submit a Consolidated Plan to HUD that identifies the community's housing needs and describes in detail how HOME and other HUD block grant funds will be used to meet those needs. Participating jurisdictions can undertake projects themselves, or they can distribute funds to qualified organizations to undertake projects on their behalf.

HOME funds can be used to finance a wide variety of affordable housing activities that generally fall into four categories: rehabilitation of owner-occupied housing, assistance to home buyers, rental housing activities, and tenant-based rental assistance. Projects that use HOME funding must meet certain income targeting and affordability requirements. Specifically, all HOME funds must go to projects that benefit households with incomes at or below 80% of area median income, and 90% of the funds that are used for rental units or tenant-based rental assistance must benefit households with incomes at or below 60% of area median income. Additionally, all housing that uses HOME funds must remain affordable for a set period of time that varies according to the type of activity for which funds are used and the amount of HOME funding contributed to the project. Participating jurisdictions must also match the HOME funds they receive with their own 25% permanent contribution to affordable housing activities.

Funding for HOME has been between $1.5 and $2 billion for each of the last several years. In FY2008, all fifty states and 591 localities received HOME formula grants, along with the District of Columbia, Puerto Rico, and four insular areas. The median state grant amount was about $9.9 million, and the median locality grant amount was about $831,000. Since the program's inception, over half of HOME funding has been used for rental housing or tenant-based rental assistance. Furthermore, a larger percentage of HOME funding has been used for housing rehabilitation activities than for new construction or acquisition.

This report will be updated as events warrant.

MOST RECENT DEVELOPMENTS

American Recovery and Reinvestment Act of 2009

On February 17, 2009, President Obama signed the American Recovery and Reinvestment Act of 2009 (P.L. 111-5), or ARRA, into law. ARRA provides supplemental appropriations to a number of programs with the intention of stimulating the economy. The HOME account received $2.25 billion under ARRA, which is in addition to its regular FY2009 appropriation. However, this funding is not actually to be used for the conventional HOME program. Rather than being used for traditional HOME program activities, the HOME funding appropriated under ARRA is to be used solely to provide gap financing to stalled Low-Income Housing Tax Credit (LIHTC) projects. (HUD is referring to this funding as the Tax Credit Assistance Program.) This additional funding is to be distributed to states only, based on the percentage of funding that states and their participating localities received for HOME formula grants in FY2008.[1] State housing credit agencies, rather than HOME allocating agencies or subrecipients, will distribute the funding to qualified LIHTC projects.

Under the Tax Credit Assistance Program, state housing credit agencies will competitively award funds to projects that received low-income housing tax credit allocations between FY2007 and FY2009, giving priority to projects that are expected to be completed by 2012. The state housing credit agencies must commit 75% of the available funds by February 2010, and project owners must use 75% of the committed funds by February 2011 and 100% of the committed funds by February 2012. Projects generally must comply with the requirements of the LIHTC program rather than the HOME program, although there are some exceptions; for example, projects must follow the HOME environmental review requirements. Only the fifty states, the District of Columbia, and Puerto Rico are eligible to receive Tax Credit Assistance Program funds.

American Dream Downpayment Initiative

The American Dream Downpayment Initiative (ADDI) has been funded within the HOME account since FY2003. Although President Bush's budget requested $50 million in FY2009 funding for the program, Congress chose not to fund ADDI in FY2009.

Housing Counseling

The Department of Housing and Urban Development's housing counseling program has been funded as a set-aside within the HOME account since FY1997. For the past several years, President Bush has requested that housing counseling be funded through its own account, but until recently Congress has chosen to continue funding the program as a set-aside within HOME. In FY2009, Congress appropriated funding for housing counseling under its own account rather than as a set-aside within HOME.

INTRODUCTION

The HOME Investment Partnerships Program was created by the Cranston-Gonzalez National Affordable Housing Act of 1990. HOME is a federal block grant program that provides dedicated funding for affordable housing activities to states and localities through formula grants. States and localities that receive HOME grants can choose to fund a wide range of affordable rental and homeownership housing activities that benefit low-income households in order to best meet local needs. This report provides an introduction to the HOME program, including its history, funding mechanism, eligible activities, and program requirements. It also provides information on recent trends in the appropriation and use of HOME funds. This report will be updated as events warrant.

BACKGROUND AND CONTEXT

In the late 1980s, some Members of Congress expressed concern about the state of the nation's housing. This concern stemmed from an increasing awareness of a variety of problems related to housing, including homelessness, families living in sub-standard housing, and decreasing opportunities for homeownership.[2] The concern over these issues led to a number of efforts to focus attention on housing policy, including the creation of a National Housing Task Force comprised of housing policy experts and industry leaders. In March 1988, the Task Force produced a report on its findings.[3] Among the housing issues that the Task Force report identified was a diminishing supply of rental and homeownership housing that was affordable to low- income households.[4]

In a 1988 hearing on the Task Force report, some members of the Senate Committee on Banking, Housing, and Urban Affairs suggested that the federal funding for housing programs was inadequate to meet the affordable housing needs identified in the report.[5] Most federal housing assistance distributed to states and localities at the time was restricted to specific uses, such as Section 8 vouchers or Public Housing projects. Furthermore, programs that did give communities flexibility to choose how to use their funds, such as the Community Development Block Grant (CDBG) program,[6] were primarily meant to fund economic development and community revitalization activities and restricted the ways in which funding could be used for affordable housing (for example, CDBG funds could be used for some housing rehabilitation but could not generally be used to construct new housing units).[7] Concerned that existing programs were not meeting the nation's affordable housing needs, members of the Housing Task Force argued to the Subcommittee that the level of federal funding specifically dedicated to affordable housing should be increased in order to fully address affordable housing issues. At the same time, Task Force members argued that local jurisdictions should be allowed more control over the ways in which they used any such dedicated federal affordable housing funding.[8]

In 1990, Congress passed a major housing bill that responded to some of the issues raised by the Housing Task Force and other experts.[9] The Cranston-Gonzalez National Affordable Housing Act (P.L. 10 1-625), or NAHA, stated that the nation's housing policy was not meeting the goal of providing "decent, safe, sanitary, and affordable living environments for all Americans" that was first set out in the Housing Act of 1949.[10] The law revised and amended several existing housing programs and authorized a number of new programs, including the HOME Investment Partnerships Program.[11]

The HOME Investment Partnerships Program is authorized by Title II of NAHA.[12] In creating HOME, the law consolidated several smaller housing programs into the largest federal block grant program that provides funding dedicated exclusively to increasing adequate, affordable housing opportunities for low-and very low-income households.[13] The program places a particular emphasis on giving states and localities flexibility in how they achieve their affordable housing goals. HOME is also designed to expand the capacity of states and localities to meet their long-term affordable housing needs by leveraging federal funding to attract state, local, and private investment in affordable housing and by strengthening the ability of government and nonprofit organizations to meet local housing needs.[14]

DISTRIBUTION AND USES OF HOME FUNDS

The Funding Process

Each fiscal year, Congress appropriates funding to the Department of Housing and Urban Development (HUD) for the HOME program during the annual appropriations process. HUD then uses a formula to allocate 40% of the funds to states and the remaining 60% to localities. (The allocation formula is discussed in detail later in this report.) For the purposes of the HOME program, the District of Columbia and Puerto Rico are considered to be states.

Before distributing funds to states and localities, HUD sets aside the greater of $750,000 or 0.2% of total HOME appropriations for insular areas. Insular areas eligible for HOME funds are Guam, the Northern Mariana Islands, the United States Virgin Islands, and American Samoa.

Allocation by HUD to Participating Jurisdictions

In order to receive HOME funds from HUD, states and localities must first become participating jurisdictions (PJs). Participating jurisdictions can be states, localities, or multiple contiguous localities that join together to form consortia. States are automatically eligible to become PJs and receive the greater of their formula grant amount or $3 million annually. Localities can only become PJs if they are metropolitan cities or urban counties,[15] and if they meet two funding thresholds. First, localities must be eligible for a minimum amount of funding under the formula, usually $500,000.[16] Once localities meet this threshold, they must also meet a second threshold: localities must dedicate a total of at least $750,000 to affordable housing activities, either by having a HOME formula grant of at least $750,000 or by making up the difference between their grant amount and the $750,000 threshold with their own funds or state HOME funds.[17]

Localities that do not meet the requirements to become participating jurisdictions may join with other contiguous localities to form consortia in order to reach the minimum funding thresholds. Localities that are not PJs can also participate in the HOME program by applying to their home state to receive a portion of the state's allocation of HOME funds. States in which no locality receives its own allocation of HOME funding have their grant amounts increased by $500,000.

Once a state or locality is informed of how much funding it is eligible to receive according to the formula, the entity must (1) notify HUD of its intention to participate in the program, and (2) submit a Consolidated Plan for HUD's approval before it can become a PJ. (The Consolidated Plan is described later in this report.) Once a state or locality has been designated a PJ, it remains one unless its designation is revoked by the Secretary of HUD. The Secretary has the authority to revoke a jurisdiction's designation if he finds that the jurisdiction is not complying with program requirements, or if a locality's formula grant or contribution to affordable housing falls below certain thresholds over a specified period of time, although he or she is not required to do so.[18]

The Home Formula

HUD allocates HOME funds to states and localities based on a formula that takes into account six factors.[19] Four of these factors are weighted 20%:

- The number of occupied rental units in a jurisdiction that have at least one of four problems: (1) overcrowding, defined as more than one occupant per room; (2) incomplete kitchen facilities, defined as the lack of a sink with running water, a range, or a refrigerator; (3) incomplete plumbing, defined as the lack of hot and cold piped water, a flush toilet, or a bathtub or shower that is inside the unit and used solely by the unit's occupants; or (4) high rent costs, defined as rent that costs more than 30% of the household's income.
- The number of rental units in a jurisdiction that were built before 1950 and are occupied by poor households.
- The number of occupied rental units in a jurisdiction that have at least one of the four problems discussed above (overcrowding, incomplete kitchen facilities, incomplete plumbing, or high rent costs) multiplied by the ratio of the cost of producing housing within the jurisdiction to the cost of producing housing nationally.

- The number of families at or below the poverty level in a jurisdiction.

The remaining two factors are weighted 10%:

- The number of rental units in a jurisdiction, adjusted for vacancies, where the head of household's income is at or below the poverty line. This number is multiplied by the ratio of the national rental unit vacancy rate over the jurisdiction's rental unit vacancy rate.
- The jurisdiction's population multiplied by its net per capita income.[20]

Allocation by Participating Jurisdictions

Once a participating jurisdiction receives its formula allocation, it has 24 months to commit HOME funds to specific projects and five years to expend the funds. If a PJ does not commit its funds within the time allotted, the funds will revert to HUD and be reallocated to other PJs. A participating jurisdiction can administer HOME funds itself, or it can designate a public agency or non-profit organization to administer all or part of the HOME program on its behalf. Such an organization is referred to as a subrecipient. Participating jurisdictions or their subrecipients can distribute funds to a variety of organizations to undertake specific projects. These organizations can include developers, owners, and sponsors of affordable housing, Community Housing Development Organizations (CHDOs),[21] private lenders, faith-based organizations, and third- party contractors. Participating jurisdictions can also disburse HOME funds in a variety of ways. Forms of disbursement may include, but are not limited to, grants, various types of loans, or loan guarantees to lending organizations.

The Consolidated Plan

As mentioned earlier, a state or locality must submit a Consolidated Plan to HUD before it can be designated a participating jurisdiction. The Consolidated Plan serves as a jurisdiction's application for HOME funding and funding from HUD's three other block grant programs.[22] While many activities are eligible uses of HOME dollars, participating jurisdictions must specify which activities they intend to fund in their Consolidated Plans in order to use HOME funds to finance those activities.

The Consolidated Plan includes a detailed description of the jurisdiction's housing needs and an explanation of how it will use HOME and other HUD block grant funds to meet those needs over a five-year period. The Consolidated Plan also describes how the jurisdiction will leverage HOME funds to attract local, private, non-profit, or other non-federal sources of funds for affordable housing, and it prioritizes projects by type and geographic location.

The Consolidated Plan is meant to be the product of "a participatory process among citizens, organizations, businesses, and other stakeholders" in a community.[23] The HOME regulations stress community participation, especially by low- and moderate-income persons, in developing the Consolidated Plan. Although a jurisdiction's Consolidated Plan covers a five-year period, it must be updated annually, and each year the jurisdiction must submit to HUD an update on its progress and a "citizen participation plan" that describes how citizens have been included and consulted in the process.

Eligible HOME Activities

In the years leading up to NAHA's passage, some experts argued that local affordable housing needs varied, and that localities should be free to develop solutions that fit local conditions.[24] HUD describes one of the purposes of the HOME program as reinforcing the principle that states and localities should have flexibility and control over how to best meet their affordable housing needs.[25] Accordingly, a wide range of activities qualifies for HOME funding, including both homeownership and rental housing activities. The law requires participating jurisdictions to give rehabilitation of existing rental and owner-occupied units priority. However, a PJ can undertake other activities if it certifies that rehabilitation is not the most cost-effective way for it to increase its supply of affordable housing or that rehabilitation is inadequate to meet its affordable housing needs.

The eligible uses of HOME funds fall into four broad categories:

- *Rehabilitation of Owner-Occupied Housing.* Funds may be used to help existing homeowners repair, rehabilitate, or reconstruct owner-occupied housing.
- *Assistance to Home Buyers.* Funds may be used to help home buyers acquire; acquire and rehabilitate; or, in certain circumstances, construct new homes.
- *Rental Housing Activities.* Funds may be used to help developers or other housing organizations acquire; rehabilitate; or, in certain circumstances, construct affordable rental housing.
- *Tenant-Based Rental Assistance.* Funds may be used to help renters with costs related to renting, such as security deposits; rent; and, under certain circumstances, utility payments.

There are certain activities which are not eligible for funding under the HOME program. Ineligible uses of HOME funds include modernizing public housing, providing tenant-based rental assistance under the Section 8 program, supporting ongoing operational costs of rental housing, paying back taxes or fees on properties that are or will be assisted with HOME funds, and providing non-federal matching funds for any other federal program. Other uses not authorized in statute or regulation are also prohibited.[26]

HOME Requirements

While PJs have much flexibility in choosing which eligible activities they will fund with HOME dollars, any projects funded through HOME must meet certain requirements in keeping with the program's stated objectives. This section describes some of the key requirements with which PJs must comply.

Income Targeting

A stated purpose of the HOME program, according to the authorizing statute, is to increase the supply of decent, affordable housing for people with low incomes and very low incomes.[27] Accordingly, all HOME funds must be used to assist low-income households, which are households with annual incomes at or below 80% of area median income.

Additional income targeting requirements apply to rental housing and tenant-based rental assistance.

   Homeownership Housing. All HOME funds that are used for existing owner-occupied housing or to assist home buyers must benefit units that are occupied by households with incomes at or below 80% of area median income.

   Rental Housing and Tenant-Based Rental Assistance. Ninety percent of the funds used for rental housing and tenant-based rental assistance must benefit households whose incomes are at or below 60% of area median income. The remaining 10% must be used to benefit households with incomes at or below 80% of area median income.

Long-Term Affordability and other Requirements
   The income targeting requirements described above ensure that HOME-assisted units benefit low-income households. Additionally, HOME-assisted units must continue to be occupied by low-income households and remain affordable to such households over the long term. In order to achieve this goal, HOME-assisted units must meet a number of requirements. Some of these requirements govern the value of HOME-assisted units or the amounts that a household can pay to rent or purchase a unit. HOME-assisted units must also meet additional requirements, separate from the value of the home, to ensure affordability. As with income targeting, the precise requirements that must be met depend on whether HOME funding is used for assistance to home buyers, owner-occupied housing rehabilitation, or rental housing activities.

   Assistance to Home Buyers. Housing bought by home buyers with the assistance of HOME funds must meet the following requirements:

- The home buyer must belong to a low-income family, and the family must use the home as a principal residence.
- The initial purchase price or value after rehabilitation must be no more than 95% of the median purchase price of homes in the area, as determined by the Secretary of HUD and adjusted as the Secretary deems necessary for different types of structures and the age of the housing.[28]
- Home buyer units must continue to meet the definition of affordability described above for between five and fifteen years, depending on the per-unit amount of HOME funds expended on a project.
- The housing must be single-family housing.[29]
- If the housing is newly constructed, it must meet energy-efficiency standards.
- Participating jurisdictions must impose resale or recapture restrictions on units in which they have assisted the home buyer using HOME funds. These restrictions specify that if a homeowner sells his or her home during the affordability period, he or she is required to sell it to another qualified low-income buyer (resale) or to return some of the proceeds of the sale to the PJ in order to cover the HOME funds that were invested in the home (recapture).

Resale and recapture restrictions are set by the jurisdiction and approved by the Secretary. Resale restrictions must ensure that, upon resale, (1) the housing remains affordable to low-income home buyers, and (2) the owner receives a fair return on investment. Recapture restrictions must ensure that the investment in the housing is recaptured in order to assist other persons who qualify for HOME-assisted housing.

Owner-Occupied Housing Rehabilitation. Owner-occupied housing that is rehabilitated using HOME funds must meet the following requirements:

- The owner must belong to a low-income family at the time HOME funds are committed to the project, and the family must use the housing as a principal residence.
- The value of the housing after rehabilitation must be no more than 95% of the median purchase price of homes in the area, as determined by the Secretary of HUD and adjusted as the Secretary deems necessary for different types of structures and the age of the housing.[30]
- There are no statutory long-term affordability requirements for owner-occupied units that are rehabilitated using HOME funds. However, the PJ can choose to impose an affordability period.

Rental Housing. Rental housing that benefits from the use of HOME funds must meet the following requirements:

- Units must be occupied only by low-income households.
- Rents must not exceed HUD's published maximum rents for the HOME program. The maximum rent for a HOME-assisted rental unit is the lesser of (1) the fair market rent[31] for comparable units in the jurisdiction, or (2) 30% of the adjusted income of a household whose income is 65% percent of area median income.[32]
- If a project includes five or more HOME-assisted units, at least 20% of the units must be occupied by families with incomes at or below 50% of area median income. Additionally, those families must have rents that meet *one* of the following requirements:
  - Rents are no higher than 1) the fair market rent for a comparable unit in the jurisdiction, or 2) 30% of 50% of area median income, whichever is lower.
  - Rents are no higher than 30% of the household's adjusted income.[33]
- Rental units must continue to meet these requirements for between five and twenty years, depending on the per-unit amount of HOME funds expended on a project and the type of activity for which HOME funds are used.
- If the housing is newly constructed, it must meet energy-efficiency standards.
- The housing must be available to Section 8 voucher holders.

Matching Requirement

Two stated goals of the HOME program are to leverage federal affordable housing funds by encouraging state, local, and private investment in affordable housing activities, and to increase the capacity of states and localities to meet their affordable housing needs.[34]

Accordingly, the HOME statute requires participating jurisdictions to match the HOME funds that they use in a fiscal year with their own 25% permanent contribution to affordable housing activities.

A PJ's matching funds can come from a wide variety of non-federal sources, including state or local governments, charitable organizations, and the private sector. The matching funds must be devoted to affordable housing activities that are eligible under the HOME guidelines, but they do not necessarily have to support projects that use HOME funds. The match can also take many forms, including in-kind contributions such as labor, construction materials, and land for HOME- eligible projects. Other contributions, such as foregone taxes, other foregone fees, and infrastructure improvements, may also count toward the matching requirement if they are used specifically for projects funded by HOME dollars. The matching requirement may not be met using federal funds.[35]

The matching requirement must be met in the same fiscal year that HOME funds are used, but if a jurisdiction provides more matching funds than are required in a given year, it can carry those funds forward to meet the matching requirement in subsequent years. The statute directs the Secretary to reduce or eliminate a participating jurisdiction's match requirement if the PJ certifies that it is under a condition of fiscal distress. The Secretary can choose to reduce or eliminate the match requirement if the President declares the jurisdiction to be a major disaster area.[36]

Although nearly all HOME funds are subject to the matching requirement, certain uses of funds are not required to be matched by the PJ. Funds that do not have to be matched include forgiven loans to Community Housing Development Organizations (CHDOs), funds used for administrative purposes (up to an allowable limit), and funds used to fill the threshold gap between a locality's formula allocation and its required $750,000 contribution to affordable housing activities, unless the locality obtains the latter from state HOME funds.

Set-Aside for Community Housing Development Organizations

As noted earlier, another stated purpose of the HOME authorizing legislation is to expand the capacity of non-profit agencies to provide affordable housing for low and very-low income households. HOME requires each participating jurisdiction to reserve at least 15% of its HOME funding for Community Housing Development Organizations (CHDOs). CHDOs are private nonprofit organizations that meet certain legal and organizational requirements and have the capacity and experience to carry out affordable housing projects. The funds reserved for CHDOs must be used to develop, manage, or sponsor affordable housing. CHDOs can engage in other activities using HOME funds, but any funding spent on projects in which the CHDO is not the developer, manager, or sponsor will not count toward the 15% set-aside requirement for CHDOs.[37]

HOME Subsidy Limits

When using HOME funds for owner-occupied housing rehabilitation, home buyer assistance, or rental housing activities, participating jurisdictions must follow restrictions on the minimum and maximum amounts of HOME funds that they can contribute to a given project. When participating jurisdictions use HOME funds for tenant-based rental assistance, they must establish both a maximum subsidy amount and a minimum tenant contribution to the tenant's rent.

Homeownership and Rental Housing. The minimum amount of HOME funds that can be used for new construction, rehabilitation, or acquisition of homeownership or rental housing is $1,000 multiplied by the number of HOME-assisted units in a project. The maximum per-unit subsidy for a project varies by participating jurisdiction and is based on the Federal Housing Administration's mortgage limits for moderate income multi-family housing.[38]

Tenant-Based Rental Assistance. The maximum HOME subsidy amount for tenant-based rental assistance is the difference between 30% of the household's adjusted monthly income and a jurisdiction-wide rent limit established by the participating jurisdiction. The rent limit must conform to certain parameters established by HUD.[39] Each participating jurisdiction is also required to set a minimum tenant contribution for tenant-based rental assistance. The minimum tenant contribution can either be a flat dollar amount or a percentage of tenant income.

Administration and Monitoring

A participating jurisdiction may use up to 10% of the funds it is allocated in a fiscal year for administrative purposes. Participating jurisdictions must also comply with record-keeping and monitoring requirements to ensure that they are using funds appropriately, making progress toward their housing goals, and generally funding activities in line with their Consolidated Plans.

RECENT FUNDING, DATA, AND TRENDS

Annual Appropriations

Each year, during the annual appropriations process, Congress appropriates funding to the HOME account within HUD's overall appropriation. The HOME account received an appropriation of $1.5 billion in FY1992, the first year in which it was funded.[40] Since FY2000, the annual appropriation to the HOME account has fluctuated between $1.6 billion and $2 billion. Appropriations increased between FY2000 and FY2004, from $1.6 billion to just over $2 billion, but then fell between FY2005 and FY2008. The FY2009 appropriation for the HOME program, over $1.8 billion, was slightly higher than the FY2008 appropriation.

While most of the funding appropriated to the HOME account is used for the formula grants to states and localities discussed earlier in this report, the HOME appropriation also includes funding that is set aside for certain related affordable housing activities. These set-asides are discussed in more detail below. Amounts appropriated for set-asides generally increased between FY2000 and FY2004 along with the increase in appropriations to the entire HOME account, rising from $47 million to $150 million over that time period, but decreased again in subsequent years. In FY2008, $79 million was appropriated for HOME account set-asides. The amount of funding appropriated for set-asides fell to $16 million in FY2009, largely because HUD's housing counseling program was funded under its own account rather than as a set-aside within HOME and because the American Dream Downpayment Initiative was not funded. **Table 1** shows annual appropriations levels for the HOME program from

FY1992 to FY2009, including the amounts appropriated for formula grants and for set-asides.[41]

Table 1. Appropriations for the HOME Account, FY1 992-FY2009 ($ in millions).

Fiscal Year	HOME Formula Grants	HOME Set-Asides	HOME Account Total[a]
1992	1,460	40	1,500
1993	988	12	1,000
1994	1,213	62	1,275
1995	1,336	64	1,400
1996	1,361	39	1,400
1997	1,332	68	1,400
1998	1,438	62	1,500
1999	1,550	50	1,600
2000	1,553	47	1,600
2001	1,734	62	1,796
2002	1,743	53	1,796[b]
2003	1,850	137	1,987
2004	1,855	150	2,006
2005	1,785	115	1,900
2006	1,677	81	1,757
2007	1,677	81	1,757
2008	1,625	79	1,704
2009	1,809[c]	16[d]	1,825[e]
Total	26,177	1,202	27,378

Source: Data taken from HUD's FY1994-FY2009 Budget Justifications and P.L. 111-8.

a. Totals may not add due to rounding. All appropriations figures are post-rescission and do not include any supplemental emergency or disaster funding.

b. The original HOME appropriation for FY2002 was $1,796 million, with $103 million of that amount accounting for HOME set-asides. This included $50 million for a "Downpayment Assistance Initiative," a precursor to the American Dream Downpayment Initiative (ADDI). However, the appropriation for the downpayment assistance program was subject to the program's being authorized by June 30, 2002. This authorization did not occur in time, and a supplemental FY2002 appropriations bill (P.L. 107-206) rescinded the $50 million appropriation for downpayment assistance.

c. Estimated by CRS based on the total HOME account appropriation and amount of funding for set-asides.

d. The FY2009 appropriation for HOME did not include set-asides for either the American Dream Downpayment Initiative or housing counseling (housing counseling was funded under its own account). Both programs are discussed in further detail below.

e. This total does not include additional funding for the HOME account appropriated in the American Recovery and Reinvestment Act of 2009 (ARRA, P.L. 111-5), which provided emergency supplemental appropriations for a number of programs. ARRA appropriated an additional $2.25 billion to the HOME program to be distributed to states based on FY2008 HOME allocations; however, rather than being used for traditional HOME activities, this funding was to be used to provide gap financing for stalled Low-Income Housing Tax Credit projects.

Formula Grants

In FY2008, every state received a HOME formula grant. The median state grant amount was about $9.9 million, and the mean grant was over $24.5 million.[42] The mean is pulled upward by a few states that received especially large formula grant allocations: for example, California received the largest state allocation at over $54 million. Five states received the minimum grant amount of $3 million, and a sixth state, Wyoming, received the minimum grant amount plus the additional $500,000 awarded to states that have no localities receiving their own HOME formula grants.

In FY2008, 591 localities or consortia also received their own HOME formula grant allocations.[43] The median grant to localities was about $840,500, and the mean grant was around $1.6 million.[44] Again, the mean grant amount is significantly higher than the median because a few localities received especially large grants. In particular, New York City received a grant of almost $112 million, close to three times the size of the next largest formula grant to a locality and over twice the next highest formula grant amount awarded (the grant to the state of California). The smallest formula grant amount to a locality was just above $248,000 and was awarded to Bay City, Michigan.[45]

The **Appendix** at the end of this report shows the number of participating jurisdictions (localities and consortia) in each state in FY2008. It also shows the total combined formula grant funding that each state and its participating jurisdictions received that year, and the percentage of total HOME funding for formula grants that each state's allocation represents.

HOME Account Set-Asides

In addition to providing funding for formula grants to states and localities, the appropriation to the HOME account includes funds that are set aside for related housing programs. Two major HOME account set-asides are discussed in this section.[46]

American Dream Downpayment Initiative

From FY2003 through FY2008, funding for the American Dream Downpayment Initiative (ADDI) was provided in the HOME account.[47] Congress chose not to fund ADDI in FY2009.

ADDI was created by the American Dream Downpayment Act (P.L. 108-186), signed into law on December 16, 2003.[48] The program aims to increase homeownership, especially among low- income and minority populations, by providing formula funding to all fifty states[49] and qualified local jurisdictions for downpayment and closing cost assistance for first-time home buyers. States and localities can use ADDI funds to provide closing cost and downpayment assistance up to $10,000 or 6% of a home's purchase price, whichever is greater. Additionally, up to 20% of ADDI funds can be used to assist homeowners with rehabilitation costs, as long as the rehabilitation is completed within a year of the home's purchase.

The formula used to award ADDI funds to states is based on the number of low-income households residing in rental housing in the state relative to the nation as a whole. For localities, the grant amount is based on the number of low-income households residing in rental housing in the jurisdiction relative to the entire state. In order for a local jurisdiction to receive its own allocation of ADDI funds, it must have a population of at least 150,000 or be eligible for a minimum grant of $50,000 under the ADDI formula.

While supporters of ADDI say that the program plays an important role in increasing homeownership, critics argue that it is duplicative because states and localities can already choose to use their HOME funds for downpayment assistance. ADDI was originally authorized to receive $200 million annually through FY2007, but the program has never received more than $86 million in appropriations. The Consolidated Appropriations Act, 2008 (P.L. 110-161) appropriated $10 million to ADDI and extended the program through the end of FY2008. President Bush's budget requested $50 million for ADDI in FY2009; however, the Omnibus Appropriations Act, 2009 (P.L. 111-8) did not include funding for ADDI.

Housing Counseling

From FY1997 through FY2008, funding for housing counseling was appropriated as a set-aside in the HOME account. Through the housing counseling program, authorized under section 106 of the Housing and Urban Development Act of 1968 (P.L. 90-448),[50] HUD competitively awards funding to HUD-approved agencies that provide counseling on a range of housing issues.

In each of the last several years, President Bush requested that housing counseling be funded through its own account, but until FY2009 Congress continued to fund housing counseling as a set-aside in the HOME account. In FY2009, Congress appropriated $65 million for housing counseling in its own account rather than as a set-aside within HOME. This amount is $15 million more than the appropriation for housing counseling in FY2008.

Leveraging

Leveraging refers to a program's ability to use its own program dollars to attract additional funding from other sources. Leveraging goals and potential funding sources vary by program, but leveraging can be an important concept for affordable housing because attracting multiple funding sources makes projects more feasible. Attracting other types of funding for affordable housing can also help to build the capacity of organizations that might not be able to undertake projects without the assistance of HOME funds. While HOME does not have a specific leveraging requirement, either in statute or in regulation, one of the stated goals of the HOME program is to attract state, local, and private funding for affordable housing activities for low- income households.[51]

HUD reports leveraging statistics for several of its programs, including HOME. According to HUD, every dollar of HOME funds used for housing units that were completed between FY1992 (the first year in which the program was first funded) and November 30, 2008 attracted $3.70 in non-HOME funds.[52] The Government Accountability Office (GAO) has analyzed the leveraging statistics that HUD and the Department of the Treasury report for various programs, and has calculated alternatives to the way that HUD reports its leveraging statistics in order to look at the different types of non-HOME funding that HOME-assisted projects attract.[53]

GAO found that projects that use HOME dollars do attract private funds and state and local funds. However, HUD's reported leverage ratio of non-program dollars to program dollars may overstate HOME's ability to attract non-federal funding for affordable housing because HOME projects also make use of other federal funding. Using data on HOME projects completed in FY2006 only, HUD's reported leverage ratio for the program in that year is $4 of other funding for every dollar of HOME funding. Using the same data, GAO found that much of the non- HOME program funding included in HUD's reported leveraging measure for the program comes from other federal sources.[54] Specifically, as **Figure 1** illustrates, HOME-assisted units that were completed in FY2006 used $2.36 billion in HOME funding, $4.52 billion in private funding, $3.14 billion in other federal funding, and $1.79 billion in state or local funding. This works out to $1.92 of private spending, $1.33 of other federal spending, and $0.76 of state or local spending for every dollar of HOME funding. A leverage ratio that only took into account other non-federal sources of funding for HOME-assisted projects completed in 2006 would be $2.68 for every dollar of HOME funding ($1.92 of private funding and $0.76 of state and local funding). This is $1.32 less than the reported leverage ratio that includes all non-program funds. One reason for the relatively large amount of other federal spending on HOME projects is that in GAO's analysis, equity from Low Income Housing Tax Credits (LIHTCs) was counted as other federal funding. Many affordable housing projects use both HOME funding and funds raised by LIHTCs.

Calculating alternative leverage measures for the HOME program, such as those presented by GAO, may provide a more complete picture of how well HOME is meeting its stated purpose of leveraging federal funding to attract other types of funding for affordable housing, including contributions from states, localities, and private entities.

Subsidy Layering

HOME funds may be combined with other federal resources to support affordable housing projects. Using a combination of federal funds from different sources for a single project is known as subsidy layering. The HOME statute and regulations require a participating jurisdiction that plans to use both HOME funds and other federal funds for a project to submit a subsidy layering certification with its consolidated plan. The certification must provide a strategy for evaluating funding commitments for affordable housing projects, and must ensure that the aggregate amount of federal funds, including HOME funds, that is invested in a housing project is no more than is necessary to provide affordable housing.[55]

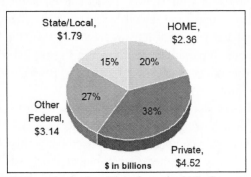

Source: Figure prepared by CRS on the basis of data from the U.S. Government Accountability Office, GAO- 08-136, *More Information on Leverage Measures' Accuracy and Linkage to Program Goals is Needed in Assessing Performance.*

Figure 1. Funding Sources for HOME-Assisted Units Completed in FY2006.

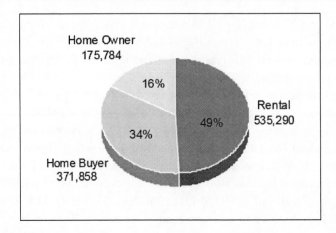

Source: Figure prepared by CRS on the basis of data from HUD's *HOME Program National Production Report as of 11/30/08*, available at http://www.hud.gov/offices/cpd/affordablehousing/ reports/production/113008.pdf. Numbers may not add due to rounding.

Figure 2. Percentage of Completed HOME Units by Unit Type (Through November 30, 2008).

How Participating Jurisdictions Use HOME Funds

HUD reports a number of HOME program performance statistics. These include statistics on the types of completed units that have used HOME funding, the eligible activities funded with HOME dollars, and the income level of households that benefit from HOME funds.

Breakdown of Unit Types

Between the beginning of the HOME program and November 30, 2008, nearly 882,000 physical units of affordable housing have been constructed, rehabilitated, or acquired using HOME funding, and an additional 201,000 families have been assisted through tenant-based rental assistance (TBRA). Together, this amounts to over 1 million physical units and TBRA-assisted households that have benefitted from HOME funds since the program's inception. As explained earlier, units assisted with HOME funds can be homeowner units, home buyer units, or rental units. Rental units and tenant-based rental assistance together represent the largest share of all completed units that have received HOME funding since the program's inception, followed by home buyer units. As shown in **Figure 2**, 49% of all completed units to date are rental units (including households receiving TBRA), 34% are home buyer units, and 16% are homeowner units.

In addition to statistics on completed units, HUD also reports how much HOME funding was used for each unit type. Since the program began, over $16.5 billion of HOME funding has been spent on units that were completed as of November 30, 2008. As shown in **Figure 3**, 53% of HOME funding that contributed to completed units was used for rental units or TBRA, while 28% was used for home buyer units and 19% for homeowner units.

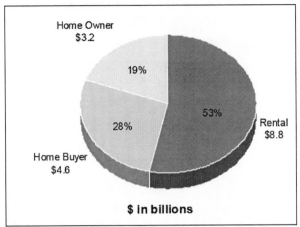

Source: Figure prepared by CRS on the basis of data from HUD's *HOME Program National Production Report as of 11/30/08*, available at http://www.hud.gov/offices/cpd/affordable housing/reports/production/113008.pdf. Numbers may not add due to rounding.

Figure 3. Percentage of HOME Funding by Unit Type (Through November 30, 2008).

Breakdown of Eligible Activities

As described earlier in this report, eligible uses of HOME funds generally fall into four categories: owner-occupied housing rehabilitation activities, assistance to home buyers, rental housing activities, and tenant-based rental assistance (TBRA). The HOME statute specifies that rehabilitation of both rental and homeowner units should be given priority over other types of eligible uses of HOME funds, such as acquiring or constructing affordable housing. As shown in **Figure 4**, of the over 1 million physical units and TBRA households that have been assisted using HOME funding, over 34% were rehabilitated units, 28% were acquired units, and 19% were newly constructed units. Nineteen percent of "units" were households that received TBRA rather than physical housing units.

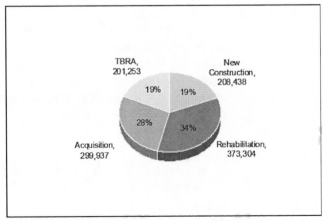

Source: Figure prepared by CRS on the basis of data from HUD's *HOME Program National Production Report as of 11/30/08*, available at http://www.hud.gov/offices/cpd/affordablehousing/ reports/production/113008.pdf. Numbersmay not add due to rounding.

Figure 4. Percentage of Completed HOME Units by Activity Type (Through November 30, 2008).

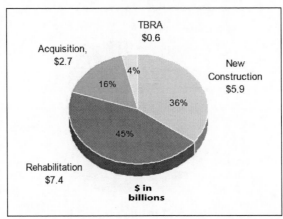

Source: Figure prepared by CRS on the basis of data from HUD's *HOME Program National Production Report as of 11 /30/08*,available at http://www.hud.gov/offices/cpd/affordablehousing/ reports/production/113008.pdf. Numbers may not add due to rounding.

Figure 5. Percentage of HOME Funding by Activity Type (Through November 30, 2008).

The breakdown of total HOME funding used for each eligible activity looks somewhat different than the number of units completed for each eligible activity. This is because some activities are more expensive than others. As **Figure 5** illustrates, nearly 45% of HOME funds actually spent since the program's inception were used for rehabilitation, 36% of funds were used for new construction, 16% were used for acquisition, and 3.5% were used for tenant-based rental assistance.

The difference between the percentage of funding going toward each activity and the percentage of completed units of each activity type reflects the difference in average costs for each activity: on average, an acquired unit costs $8,985 in HOME funds, while a rehabilitated unit costs $19,822 and a newly constructed unit costs $28,238. The average amount of tenant-based rental assistance received by a household is $2,855.[56]

Beneficiaries of HOME Funds

As required by statute, all HOME funds benefit families with incomes at or below 80% of area median income. Not surprisingly, HOME funds that are used for rental activities (including tenant-based rental assistance and the construction, acquisition, and rehabilitation of rental housing) benefit a lower-income population than funds that are used for homeowner and home buyer units. As explained earlier in this report, HOME funds that are used for rental activities must target a lower-income population than funds used for homeowner or home buyer activities.[57] Households at the lowest end of the income spectrum are also more likely to rent than to own their homes.

Figure 6 shows the percentage of funding for each HOME-assisted activity that has benefitted households at different income levels. As of November 30, 2008, HUD reported that more than three-quarters of funds disbursed for tenant-based rental assistance benefitted families with incomes at or below 30% of area median income, as did 43% of funds used for completed rental units. In contrast, less than one-third of funds used for completed occupied homeowner units benefitted households with incomes at or below 30% of area median income, and only 6% of funds used for completed home buyer units benefitted households with incomes in this range.

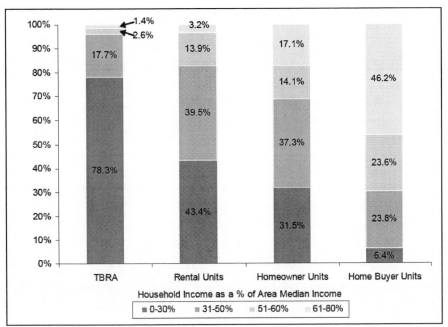

Source: Figure prepared by CRS on the basis of data from HUD's *HOME Program National Production Report as of 11/30/08*, available at http://www.hud.gov/offices/cpd/affordablehousing/ reports/production/113008.pdf. Numbers may not add due to rounding.

Figure 6. Percentage of HOME Funds Used to Benefit Different Income Groups, by Eligible Activity (Through November 30, 2008).

APPENDIX. DISTRIBUTION AND FUNDING TABLE

Table A-1. Distribution of Participating Jurisdictions and Formula Funding by State for FY2008 ($ in millions).

State	Number of PJs	Formula Grant Funding ($)[a]	% of Total Formula Grant Funding
Alabama	7	23.12	1.42
Alaska	1	3.97	0.24
Arizona	3	23.42	1.44
Arkansas	4	14.79	0.91
California	97	236.39	14.50
Colorado	11	19.82	1.22
Connecticut	6	18.94	1.16
Delaware	2	4.78	0.29
Dist. of Columbia	0	8.41	0.52
Florida	36	73.35	4.50
Georgia	12	39.09	2.40
Hawaii	1	7.15	0.44
Idaho	1	6.33	0.39

Table A-1. (Continued).

State	Number of PJs	Formula Grant Funding ($)[a]	% of Total Formula Grant Funding
Illinois	17	68.64	4.21
Indiana	13	27.55	1.69
Iowa	6	13.73	0.84
Kansas	5	12.39	0.76
Kentucky	4	22.87	1.40
Louisiana	9	28.52	1.75
Maine	2	7.73	0.47
Maryland	7	22.98	1.41
Massachusetts	19	43.22	2.65
Michigan	22	46.35	2.84
Minnesota	6	20.60	1.26
Mississippi	3	15.81	0.97
Missouri	8	28.02	1.72
Montana	3	5.65	0.35
Nebraska	2	8.24	0.51
Nevada	5	11.01	0.68
New Hampshire	2	5.98	0.37
New Jersey	27	44.23	2.71
New Mexico	2	10.04	0.62
New York	28	183.33	11.25
North Carolina	19	37.77	2.32
North Dakota	1	3.51	0.22
Ohio	23	60.48	3.71
Oklahoma	5	18.62	1.14
Oregon	6	19.80	1.21
Pennsylvania	31	68.89	4.23
Puerto Rico	11	30.88	1.89
Rhode Island	3	8.64	0.53
South Carolina	13	18.38	1.13
South Dakota	1	3.91	0.24
Tennessee	9	28.26	1.73
Texas	43	107.53	6.60
Utah	4	8.43	0.52
Vermont	1	3.91	0.24
Washington	14	31.18	1.91
West Virginia	5	11.97	0.73
Wisconsin	11	25.78	1.58
Wyoming	0	3.50	0.21
State Totals	591	1,629.94	100.00

Source: U.S. Department of Housing and Urban Development, Community Planning and Development Program Formula Allocations for FY2008, spreadsheet available at http://www.hud.gov/ offices/cpd/about/budget/budget08/ index.cfm.

a. Formula funding totals include both the state grant and grants to PJs within the state.

Table A-2. Distribution of Participating Jurisdictions and Formula Funding, Insular Areas for FY2008 ($ in millions).

Insular Area[a]	Number of PJs	Formula Grant Funding ($)[b]	% of Total Formula Grant Funding
American Samoa	—	0.31	9.33
Guam	—	1.27	38.52
Northern Marianas	—	0.58	17.74
Virgin Islands	—	1.13	34.41
Insular Areas Total	—	3.29	100.00

Source: U.S. Department of Housing and Urban Development, Community Planning and Development Program Formula Allocations for FY2008, spreadsheet available at http://www.hud.gov/offices/cpd/about/budget/budget08/index.cfm.

a. The HOME appropriation for formula grants only includes funding for states and localities; insular areas are funded by a set-aside equal to 0.2% of the appropriation for HOME formula grants. The percentages of formula grant funding for insular areas reflect the percentage of the set-aside funding that each insular area received.

b. Formula funding totals include both the state grant and grants to PJs within the state.

End Notes

[1] For more information on how HUD has distributed funds to states, and on how much funding has been obligated and expended to date, see HUD's Tax Credit Assistance Program website at http://www.hud.gov/recovery/tax-credit.cfm.

[2] U.S. Congress, Senate Committee on Banking, Housing, and Urban Affairs and House Committee on Banking, Finance, and Urban Affairs, *A New National Housing Policy: Recommendations of Organizations and Individuals Concerned about Affordable Housing in America*, joint committee print, 100th Cong., 1st sess., October 1987, S. Prt. 100-5 8 (Washington: GPO, 1987), p. V.

[3] The National Housing Task Force, *A Decent Place to Live*, March 1988.

[4] U.S. Congress, Senate Committee on Banking, Housing, and Urban Affairs, Subcommittee on Housing and Urban Affairs, hearing on the report of the National Housing Task Force, 100th Cong., 2nd sess., April 12 and 14, 1988, S. Hrg. 100-689 (Washington: GPO, 1988), pp. 1-10. "Affordable housing" can be defined differently in different contexts, but is generally understood to mean housing that costs 30% or less of a household's income. Households that pay more than 30% of their income for housing are considered cost-burdened, and households that pay more than 50% of their income for housing are considered severely cost-burdened.

[5] Ibid., p. 8.

[6] CDBG was established by the Housing and Community Development Act of 1974 (P.L. 93-3 83).

[7] Eligible activities that can be undertaken with CDBG funds are codified at 42 U.S.C. 5305. For more information on CDBG and federal housing assistance programs in general, see CRS Report RL34591, *Overview of Federal Housing Assistance Programs and Policy*, by Maggie McCarty et al..

[8] S. Hrg. 100-689, hearing before the Subcommittee on Banking, Housing, and Urban Affairs on the report of the National Housing Task Force, p. 21.

[9] U.S. Congress, Senate Committee on Banking, Housing, and Urban Affairs, *National Affordable Housing Act*, report to accompany S.566, 101st Cong., 2nd sess., S.Rept. 101-316 (Washington: GPO, 1990), pp.1-5.

[10] 42 U.S.C. § 12721.

[11] Other programs authorized by NAHA include the Homeownership and Opportunity for People Everywhere (HOPE) program, which is no longer funded, and the Housing Opportunities for Persons with AIDS (HOPWA) program. For more information on HOPWA, see CRS Report RL343 18, *Housing for Persons Living with HIV/AIDS*, by Libby Perl.

[12] The HOME statute is codified at 42 U.S.C. § 12722 et. seq. Regulations can be found at 24 CFR Part 92.

[13] U.S. Department of Housing and Urban Development web page, *HOME Investment Partnerships Program*, available at http://www.hud.gov/offices/cpd/affordablehousing/programs/home/. Low-income households are generally defined as households with incomes at or below 80% of area median income (AMI), and very-low income households are defined as those households with incomes at or below 50% of AMI.

[14] 42 U.S.C. § 12722.

[15] A metropolitan city is defined to be the central city of a metropolitan statistical area (MSA), as defined by the Office of Management and Budget (OMB), or any other city within a metropolitan area with a population of at least 50,000 people. An urban county is defined to be a county in a metropolitan area that is authorized by state law to undertake essential community development and housing assistance activities in its unincorporated areas and either (1) has a population of at least 200,000 people, excluding metropolitan cities within the county, with at least 100,000 of that population residing in unincorporated areas or included units of general local government, or (2) has a population of at least 100,000 people, a population density of at least 5,000 people per square mile, and includes no incorporated places (as defined by the U.S. Census Bureau) within its borders. These definitions can be found at 42 U.S.C. § 5302(a)(4) and 42 U.S.C. § 5302(a)(6).

[16] The minimum direct allocation threshold is reduced to $335,000 in years when Congressional appropriations for HOME are less than $1.5 billion.

[17] The minimum contribution to affordable housing activities is reduced to $500,000 in years when Congressional appropriations for HOME are less than $1.5 billion.

[18] The Secretary can choose to revoke a locality's designation as a participating jurisdiction if its contribution to affordable housing activities falls below $750,000 for three consecutive years, below $625,000 for two consecutive years, or if the jurisdiction does not receive a formula allocation of at least $500,000 in any single year (24 CFR § 92.107).

[19] 24 CFR § 92.50.

[20] A jurisdiction's net per capita income is computed by subtracting the per capita income of a family of three at the poverty threshold from the jurisdiction's per capita income. An index is constructed by dividing the national net per capita income by a jurisdiction's net per capita income (24 CFR § 92.50).

[21] Community Housing Development Organizations are private, non-profit organizations that meet certain legal and organizational requirements, as well as requirements concerning their capacity and experience related to affordable housing activities.

[22] The other programs are Community Development Block Grants (CDBGs), Emergency Shelter Grants (ESGs), and Housing Opportunities for Persons with AIDS (HOPWA). For more information on these programs, see CRS Report RL34591, *Overview of Federal Housing Assistance Programs and Policy*, by Maggie McCarty et al.. For more information specifically on ESG, see CRS Report RL33764, *The HUD Homeless Assistance Grants: Distribution of Funds*, by Libby Perl, and for more information specifically on HOPWA, see CRS Report RL343 18, *Housing for Persons Living with HIV/AIDS*, by Libby Perl.

[23] 24 CFR Part 91.1(b)(1).

[24] S. Hrg. 100-689, hearing before the Subcommittee on Banking, Housing, and Urban Affairs on the report of the National Housing Task Force, p. 21.

[25] U.S. Department of Housing and Urban Development webpage, *HOME Investment Partnerships Program*, available at http://www.hud.gov/offices/cpd/affordablehousing/=programs/home/.

[26] Activities that are prohibited uses of HOME funds are described at 42 U.S.C. § 12742(d) and 24 CFR § 92.214.

[27] 42 U.S.C. § 12722.

[28] Participating jurisdictions can base their calculation of 95% of the median purchase price of homes in the area on either the single family mortgage limits established for the Federal Housing Administration's single-family mortgage insurance program, found at 12 U.S.C. § 1709(b)(B)(i), or on a detailed market analysis that conforms to requirements set out by HUD, which can be found at 24 CFR § 92.254.

[29] HUD defines single-family housing to be "a one- to four-family residence, condominium unit, cooperative unit, combination of manufactured housing and lot, or manufactured housing lot." 24 CFR § 92.2.

[30] The methods by which participating jurisdictions can calculate 95% of the median purchase price of homes in the area are described in footnote 28.

[31] Fair market rents (FMRs) are calculated annually by HUD and are meant to reflect the cost of modest housing in a community. FMRs can be found on HUD's webpage at http://www.huduser.org/datasets/fmr.html.

[32] Participating jurisdictions must determine tenants' annual income according to the guidelines at 24 CFR § 92.203. HUD's maximum HOME rents will also take into account the number of bedrooms in a unit and average occupancy per unit.

[33] If rental units temporarily fail to meet either of the requirements governing the incomes of occupants of HOME-assisted units because of an increase in the current tenants' income, the unit is still meeting the requirements of this section as long as vacancies are filled according to these requirements.

[34] 42 U.S.C. § 12722.

[35] For the purposes of the matching requirement, equity derived from Low-Income Housing Tax Credits (LIHTCs) is considered federal funding. See U.S. Department of Housing and Urban Development CPD Notice 97-03, March 27, 1997, p. 14, available at http://www.hud.gov/offices/cpd/lawsregs/notices/1997/97-3.pdf. There is some disagreement over whether tax credits such as the LIHTC should be considered federal spending. Some argue that since tax credits represent foregone revenues, rather than government outlays, they should not be counted as federal spending; others argue that since tax credits represent money that otherwise would have accrued to the federal government, they should be counted as federal spending. For more information on the

LIHTC, see CRS Report RS22389, *An Introduction to the Design of the Low-Income Housing Tax Credit*, by Mark P. Keightley.

[36] The Secretary is required to reduce a jurisdiction's match requirement by 50% if the jurisdiction certifies that it is in a condition of fiscal distress and by 100% if the jurisdiction certifies that it is in a condition of severe fiscal distress. A jurisdiction other than a state is considered to be fiscally distressed if it (1) has an average poverty rate in the preceding calendar year that is equal to or greater than 125% of the average national poverty rate, or (2) has an average per capita income in the preceding calendar year that is less than 75% of the average national per capita income. A jurisdiction is considered severely fiscally distressed if it meets both of these conditions. The Secretary may choose to reduce a jurisdiction's match requirement by up to 100% if the jurisdiction is in an area in which a declaration of a disaster under the Stafford Act is in effect for any part of the fiscal year.

[37] U.S. Department of Housing and Urban Development, *Building HOME: A HOME Program Primer*, February 2006, page 3-1, available at http://www.hud.gov/offices/cpd/affordablehousing/training/materials/building/.

[38] These limits are published annually and are available from HUD Field Offices.

[39] For requirements governing rent limits, see 24 C.F.R. § 92.209.

[40] U.S. Department of Housing and Urban Development, *Detailed HOME Program Appropriation History for FY 1992-2005*, available at http://www.hud.gov/offices/cpd/affordablehousing/budget/index.cfm#home-allocs.

[41] HOME account set-asides are discussed later in this report and vary from year to year, but some programs commonly funded through HOME set-asides include the American Dream Downpayment Initiative, which provides funding for downpayment assistance; housing counseling; and technical assistance. Formula grant funding for insular areas is also included as a set-aside in the HOME account, and in some of the earlier years of the program, there was also a set-aside for formula grants for Indian tribes.

[42] The median state grant amount was $9,914,732 and the mean state grant amount was $24,562,219. Average and median state grant amounts include the fifty states, the District of Columbia, and Puerto Rico, but exclude grants to insular areas.

[43] Forty-nine states and Puerto Rico had at least one locality that was a participating jurisdiction and received its own HOME funding. Wyoming had no localities that qualified to receive their own allocations of HOME funds.

[44] Specifically, the median grant amount for localities was $840,508, and the mean grant amount for localities was $1,656,584 .

[45] Over 100 localities received formula grants under the $500,000 minimum in FY2008. These localities met the minimum funding threshold in the first year in which they became participating jurisdictions.

[46] Activities other than those described in this section sometimes receive funding through HOME set-asides, or have received such funding in the past. These activities include technical assistance and support for HUD's information systems, among others. Also, as noted earlier, formula grants for insular areas are also considered a HOME set-aside.

[47] Although funding was appropriated for downpayment assistance in FY2003, ADDI was not signed into law until December 2003. The FY2003 downpayment assistance funding was distributed according to a different formula and a different set of requirements than the ADDI funding in subsequent years.

[48] ADDI is codified at 42 U.S.C. § 12821, and the regulations governing the program can be found beginning at 24 CFR § 92.600.

[49] The definition of "state" is different under ADDI than under HOME. Specifically, ADDI does not include Puerto Rico as a state after FY2003. Insular areas are not eligible to receive ADDI funds. See 42 U.S.C. § 12821(a)(4) or the U.S. Department of Housing and Urban Development, *American Dream Downpayment Initiative Q&A*, revised May 5, 2005, available at http://www.hud.gov/offices/cpd/affordablehousing/programs/home/addi/qa.pdf.

[50] The housing counseling program is codified at 12 U.S.C. § 1701x(c), and the regulations governing the program are found at 24 CFR Part 214.

[51] 42 U.S.C. § 12722.

[52] U.S. Department of Housing and Urban Development, *HOME Program National Production Report as of 11/30/08*, December 4, 2008, available at http://www.hud.gov/offices/cpd/affordablehousing/reports/production/113008.pdf.

[53] U.S. Government Accountability Office, GAO-08-136, *More Information on Leverage Measures' Accuracy and Linkage to Program Goals is Needed in Assessing Performance*, January 2008, p. 50-53, available at http://www.gao.gov/new.items/d08136.pdf.

[54] Ibid.

[55] See 42 U.S.C. § 12742(f) and 24 CFR § 92.250(b).

[56] Average activity costs are for completed units as of November 30, 2008, and can be found in HUD's *HOME Program National Production Report as of 11/30/0*8, available at http://www.hud.gov/offices/cpd/affordablehousing/ reports/production/1 13008.pdf.

[57] 90% of funds used for tenant-based rental assistance or rental housing activities are required to benefit households with incomes at or below 60% of area median income, while the remaining 10% must benefit

households with incomes at or below 80% of area median income. HOME funds used for homeowner and home buyer housing are only required to benefit households with incomes at or below 80% of area median income.

In: An Overview of Federal Housing Assistance Programs   ISBN: 978-1-61122-419-1
Editor: Brandon C. Sherman   © 2011 Nova Science Publishers, Inc.

Chapter 4

THE HUD HOMELESS ASSISTANCE GRANTS: DISTRIBUTION OF FUNDS

Libby Perl

SUMMARY

Currently, the U.S. Department of Housing and Urban Development (HUD) distributes four Homeless Assistance Grants, each of which provides funds to local communities to finance a range of housing and supportive services options for homeless persons. These four grants—the Emergency Shelter Grants (ESG) program, the Supportive Housing Program (SHP), the Shelter Plus Care (S+C) program, and the Section 8 Moderate Rehabilitation for Single Room Occupancy Dwellings (SRO) program—were enacted as part of the McKinney-Vento Homeless Assistance Act (P.L. 100-77, as amended). Congress appropriates one lump sum for all four grants, and HUD then determines how the funds are allocated among the four programs.

The way in which the Homeless Assistance Grants are distributed will change in 2010 as the result of recently passed legislation. The Homeless Assistance Grants were reauthorized on May 20, 2009, as part of the Helping Families Save Their Homes Act (P.L. 111-22). The changes in P.L. 111-22 will have repercussions for the makeup of the Homeless Assistance Grants, the way in which funds are distributed to grantees, the purposes for which grantees may use funds, and the determination of who may be served under the law. The changes will take effect at the earlier of 18 months from the date of the law's enactment—on or about November 20, 2010—or three months from the date on which HUD publishes final regulations. Because the changes in P.L. 111-22 will not take place immediately, this report describes the way in which HUD currently distributes the Homeless Assistance Grants. For a discussion of changes, see the section of this report entitled "Reauthorization of the McKinney-Vento Homeless Assistance Grants."

HUD distributes the four Homeless Assistance Grants annually to eligible applicants, which include states, metropolitan areas, counties, nonprofit organizations, and public housing authorities. Funds for the ESG program are used primarily for the short-term needs of homeless persons, such as emergency shelter, while the SHP, S+C, and SRO programs address longer-term transitional and permanent housing needs. HUD uses one method to distribute funds for the ESG program and another method to distribute funds for the SHP, S+C, and SRO programs.

The ESG program distributes funds to states, counties, and metropolitan areas using the Community Development Block Grant (CDBG) program formula. In general, states and communities receive the same proportion of ESG funds that they received in CDBG funds the previous fiscal year. After they receive funds, states and communities then distribute them to homeless service providers, including nonprofit organizations and local government entities.

The SHP, S+C, and SRO grants are distributed through a competitive process called the Continuum of Care (CoC) application system (these three grants are sometimes referred to as the "competitive grants"). Through the CoC process, representatives from local community organizations work collaboratively to develop a plan for addressing homelessness in their area. They then determine which homeless services providers in the community should receive funding and submit a unified application to HUD. HUD then uses a multi-step process to determine which homeless services providers should receive funding. This involves both a formula aspect, through which HUD determines community need using the CDBG formula, and a competitive aspect, through which HUD assigns points for various elements included in the CoC application. President Obama's FY2010 budget proposes to modernize the CDBG formula. This would have implications for how the Homeless Assistance Grants are distributed in their current form as well as under P.L. 111-22.

INTRODUCTION

Homelessness in America has always existed, but it did not come to the public's attention as a national issue until the 1970s and 1980s, when the characteristics of the homeless population and their living arrangements began to change. Throughout the early and middle part of the 20th century, homelessness was typified by "skid rows"—areas with hotels and single-room occupancy dwellings where transient single men lived.[1] Skid rows were usually removed from the more populated areas of cities, and it was uncommon for individuals to actually live on the streets.[2] Beginning in the 1970s, however, the homeless population began to grow and become more visible to the general public. According to studies from the time, homeless persons were no longer almost exclusively single men, but included women with children; their median age was younger; they were more racially diverse (in previous decades the observed homeless population was largely white); they were less likely to be employed (and therefore had lower incomes); they were mentally ill in higher proportions than previously; and individuals who were abusing or had abused drugs began to become more prevalent in the population.[3]

A number of reasons have been offered for the growth in the number of homeless persons and their increasing visibility. Many cities demolished skid rows to make way for urban development, leaving some residents without affordable housing options.[4] Other possible factors contributing to homelessness include the decreased availability of affordable housing generally, the reduced need for seasonal unskilled labor, the reduced likelihood that relatives will accommodate homeless family members, the decreased value of public benefits, and changed admissions standards at mental hospitals.[5] The increased visibility of homeless people was due, in part, to the decriminalization of actions such as public drunkenness, loitering, and vagrancy.[6]

In the 1980s, Congress first responded to the growing prevalence of homelessness with several separate grant programs designed to address the food and shelter needs of homeless individuals.[7] Then, in 1987, Congress enacted the Stewart B. McKinney Homeless Assistance Act (McKinney Act), which created a number of new programs to comprehensively address the needs of homeless people, including food, shelter, health care, and education (P.L. 100-77). The act was later renamed the McKinney-Vento Homeless Assistance Act (McKinney-Vento) in P.L. 106-400 after its other prominent sponsor, Bruce F. Vento.[8]

Among the programs authorized in the McKinney Act were four grants to provide housing and related assistance to homeless persons: the Emergency Shelter Grants (ESG) program, the Supportive Housing Demonstration program, the Supplemental Assistance for Facilities to Assist the Homeless (SAFAH) program, and the Section 8 Moderate Rehabilitation Assistance for Single Room Occupancy Dwellings (SRO) program. These four programs, administered by the U.S. Department of Housing and Urban Development (HUD), were created to provide temporary and permanent housing to homeless persons, along with supportive services. Over the years, Congress has changed the makeup of the Homeless Assistance Grants, but there are still four currently-funded programs, three of which were part of the original McKinney Act. The four existing grants are the ESG program, the Supportive Housing Program (SHP), the Shelter Plus Care (S+C) program, and the SRO program.

On May 20, 2009, for the first time since 1992, the Homeless Assistance Grants were reauthorized as part of the Helping Families Save Their Homes Act (P.L. 111-22). The new law will change the makeup of the four existing grants—the SHP, S+C, and SRO programs will be combined into one grant called the "Continuum of Care Program;" the ESG program will be renamed the "Emergency Solutions Grants;" and rural communities will have the option of competing for funds under a new Rural Housing Stability Assistance Program. The way in which the funds are distributed, the purposes for which grantees may use funds, and the people who may be served will also change. Because the changes in P.L. 111-22 will not take effect until the earlier of 18 months from the date of its enactment—on or about November 20, 2010—or three months from the date on which HUD publishes final regulations, this report continues to describe how HUD currently distributes the four existing Homeless Assistance Grants. For more information about the changes in P.L. 111-22, see the section of this report entitled "Reauthorization of the McKinney-Vento Homeless Assistance Grants."

THE ROLE OF CONGRESS AND HUD IN THE FUNDING PROCESS

Since creating the four Homeless Assistance Grants in 1987, Congress has played a decreasing role in how funds are allocated among them. Initially, from FY1987 to FY1994, Congress appropriated funds separately for each of the four programs. However, beginning in FY1995 and continuing to the present, Congress has appropriated one lump sum for all four programs, and HUD has then determined how those funds are distributed among the ESG,

SHP, S+C, and SRO programs. (For a distribution of the grants from FY1987 through FY2009, see **Table 1**.)[9]

After Congress makes its annual appropriation for the Homeless Assistance Grants (this amount was approximately $1.677 billion in FY2009—P.L. 111-8), HUD first allocates a portion of the total appropriation to the ESG program. This amount is generally between 10% and 15% of the total appropriation. HUD bases this range of funding on the proportion of funds Congress devoted to the program in its FY1994 appropriation. After HUD has set aside the ESG funds from the appropriation, it sets aside funds to renew S+C permanent housing contracts in a separate account.[10] In every HUD appropriations act since FY2001, Congress has required HUD to provide funds to renew existing S+C contracts on an annual basis, as long as HUD determines that the S+C projects are needed and meet program requirements. The amount remaining after the ESG funds and S+C renewal funds are deducted from the total appropriation is then available for the SHP and SRO programs, and for new S+C projects. These remaining funds are not specifically dedicated to any of the three programs.

After determining which funds are available for the ESG program, S+C renewals, and the SHP, S+C, and SRO programs, HUD uses two methods to distribute the funds to grantees— one for the ESG program and another for the three remaining programs. HUD awards the funds allocated to the ESG program through a formula allocation, and the SHP, S+C, and SRO program funds through a competitive application system. For this reason, the SHP, S+C, and SRO programs are sometimes called the competitive Homeless Assistance Grants.

THE EMERGENCY SHELTER GRANTS PROGRAM

The ESG program, the oldest of the four existing Homeless Assistance Grants, was established one year prior to enactment of McKinney-Vento as part of the Continuing Appropriations Act for FY1987 (P.L. 99-591).[11] The funds distributed through the ESG program provide for the emergency shelter and service needs of homeless persons. The program uses the Community Development Block Grant (CDBG) program dual formula to distribute funds to both local communities (called "entitlement areas" and defined as metropolitan cities and urban counties[12]) and states (called "non-entitlement areas") for distribution in communities that do not receive funds directly. Puerto Rico is considered a state under the CDBG formula and the District of Columbia is an entitlement community. The territories (Guam, the Northern Mariana Islands, the Virgin Islands, and American Samoa) receive 0.2% of the ESG allocation which is then distributed based on population.[13] Tribes do not receive funds through ESG; instead, funds for homeless assistance are distributed through the Indian Community Development Block Grant.[14]

Table 1. Funding for Homeless Assistance Grants, FY1987- FY2009 ($ in thousands).

Fiscal Year	Emergency Shelter Grants (ESG) (a)	Single Room Occupancy (SRO) (b)	Shelter Plus Care[a] (S+C) (c)	Supportive Housing Program[b] (SHP) (d)	Total Funds for HUD Homeless Programs (see note) (e)
1987	60,000	35,000	—	59,000	195,000[c]
1988	8,000	—	—	65,000	72,000
1989	46,500	45,000	—	80,000	171,500
1990	73,164	73,185	—	126,825	284,004[d]
1991	73,164	104,999	—	149,988	339,414[e]
1992	73,164	105,000	110,533	150,000	449,960[f]
1993	49,496	105,000	266,550	150,443	571,489
1994	113,840	150,000	123,747	334,000[g]	822,747[h]
1995	155,218	136,000	164,000	630,000	1,120,000[i]
1996	113,841	48,000	89,000	606,000	823,000
1997	113,727	24,000	61,000	663,000	823,000
1998	164,993	10,000	117,000	596,000	823,000
1999	150,000	17,000	151,000	556,000	975,000
2000	150,000	20,000	95,000	784,000	1,020,000
2001	149,670	14,000	174,000	760,000	1,122,525
2002	150,000	10,400	178,700	788,200	1,122,525
2003	149,025	11,200	237,000	865,400	1,217,037
2004	159,056	12,900	322,800	906,900	1,259,525
2005	158,720	14,000	304,400	860,900	1,229,214
2006	158,400	988	322,900	881,700	1,326,600
2007	160,000	1,600	383,000	942,200	1,441,600
2008	160,000	2,371	406,164	1,007,891	1,585,990
2009	160,000	⌐	⌐	⌐	1,677,000

Sources: The FY2009 Omnibus Appropriations Act (P.L. 111-8), HUD Congressional Budget Justifications FY1 988-FY2009 (all grants through FY1994, competitive grants from FY2002 to FY2005, and total funds for HUD homeless programs), HUD Community Planning and Development grantee list FY1993-FY2009 (ESG from FY1 993 through FY2009), HUD's Office of Special Needs (competitive grants for FY1987 and from FY1995 through FY2001), and CRS analysis of HUD's award announcement for FY2006, FY2007, and FY2008 competitive grants, http://www.hud.gov/offices/cpd/homeless/budget/index.cfm.

Note: Until FY1 995, Congress separately appropriated funds for each of the four Homeless Assistance Grants. Since then, however, Congress has appropriated one amount for all four grants and HUD has divided the funds. Therefore, amounts in columns (a) through (d) in the years FY1987 through FY1994 represent appropriations, and those from FY 1995 forward represent funds distributed to grantees. The amounts for each of the four separate grant programs may add up to more or less than the amount in column (e) "Total for HUD Homeless Programs," which is the amount appropriated for HUD homeless program activities in a given fiscal year. In some years, this could be due to the use of carryover funds, and in others, the sum of the four separate grants may add up to less than the total due to allocations to other funds like technical assistance, data collection, or the Interagency Council on Homelessness.

a. The S+C program was authorized in 1990 by P.L. 10 1-645 and first received funding in FY1992.

b. From FY1987 to FY1993, SHP was a demonstration program. In FY1987, it was called the Transitional Housing Demonstration Program (P.L. 99-591). SHP as it currently exists was authorized in P.L. 102-550.

c. The total includes $15 million for the Supplemental Assistance for Facilities to Assist the Homeless (SAFAH) program. In 1992, P.L. 102-550 incorporated elements of SAFAH and the Supportive Housing Demonstration Program into the new Supportive Housing Program.

d. The total includes $10,830,000 for the SAFAH program.

e. The total includes $11,263,000 for the SAFAH program.

f. The total includes $11,263,000 for the SAFAH program.

g. In P.L. 103-124, Congress provided that of the amount appropriated for SHP, an amount not to exceed $50 million could be used for the Safe Havens Demonstration Initiative and $20 million for the Rural Housing Demonstration Program.

h. The total includes $100 million for the Innovative Homeless Initiatives Demonstration Program.

i. The total includes $25 million for the Innovative Homeless Initiatives Demonstration Program.
j. As of the date of this report, FY2009 competitive grants had not been awarded.

The CDBG program formula is meant to distribute funds based on a community's need for development; the ESG program has used the CDBG formula to target funds for homeless assistance since its inception.[15] The formula awards funds to metropolitan cities and urban counties (70% of funds) and to the states for use in areas that do not receive funds directly (30% of funds).[16] The CDBG formula uses a combination of five factors to award funds to recipient communities. (The CDBG formula uses four separate methods to award funds; this paper does not discuss the details of these methods.) The five factors are population, the number of persons in poverty, housing overcrowding (homes in which there is more than 1.01 persons per room), the age of housing (the number of housing structures built prior to 1940), and the extent of growth lag in a given community (the lack of population growth in a community compared to the growth rate it would have had if it had grown at the rate of other communities).[17] The factors are measured as ratios between the recipient community and all grant recipients. The CDBG formula was last changed in 1977 (P.L. 95-128).

After the CDBG formula determines the amount of ESG funds each state and community receives, they, in turn, allocate the funds to local government entities and nonprofit organizations that provide services for homeless persons. These recipient organizations may use funds for four main purposes: the renovation, major rehabilitation or conversion of buildings into emergency shelters; services such as employment counseling, health care, and education; homelessness prevention activities such as assistance with rent or utility payments; and operational and administrative expenses.[18] States and communities must ensure that not more than 30% of the total ESG funds they receive is used for services, not more than 30% is used for homeless prevention activities, not more than 10% is used for staff costs, and not more than 5% is used for administrative costs.[19]

Distribution of ESG Funds

As a condition for receiving ESG funds, states and communities must present HUD with a consolidated plan explaining how they will address community development needs within their jurisdictions. The consolidated plan is required in order for communities to participate in four different HUD grant programs, including ESG.[20] The plan is a community's description of how it hopes to integrate decent housing, community needs, and economic needs of low- and moderate- income residents over a three- to five-year time span.[21] Consolidated plans are intended to be collaborative efforts of local government officials, representatives of for-profit and non-profit organizations, and community members. HUD may disapprove a community's consolidated plan with respect to one or more programs, although communities have 45 days to change their plans to satisfy HUD's requirements.[22] If HUD disapproves the ESG portion of the plan, the applicant community will not receive ESG funds.

If HUD approves a community's consolidated plan, the community will receive ESG funds based on its share of CDBG funds from the previous fiscal year. However, the community must have received at least 0.05% of the total CDBG allocation in order to qualify to receive ESG funds.[23] In cases where a community would receive less than .05% of the total ESG allocation, its share of funds goes to the state to be used in areas that do not receive their own ESG funds.[24] For example, if a community received 0.08% of the total CDBG allocation to the states in FY2000, it would receive that same percentage of ESG funds in FY2001. In FY2008, 361 states, cities, counties, and territories received ESG funds.[25] The $160 million that HUD allocated for ESG represented approximately 10% of the total Homeless Assistance Grants distributed. For an overview of how funds are distributed, see **Figure 1**.

After the recipient states and entitlement communities receive their ESG funds, they distribute them to local government entities or nonprofit organizations that provide services to homeless persons. These recipient organizations have been previously determined by the state or local government through an application process in which organizations submit proposals—HUD is not involved in this process. Each recipient organization must match the federal ESG funds dollar for dollar.[26] The match may be met through the value of donated buildings, the lease value of buildings, salary paid to staff, and volunteer time counted at $5 an hour.[27]

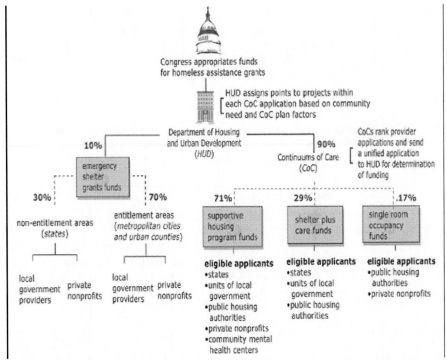

Source: Chart prepared by CRS on the basis of 42 U.S.C. § 11373, "HUD FY2008 Notice of Funding Availability," *Federal Register*, vol. 73, no. 133, July 10, 2008. Percentages are based on the FY2008 distribution of the Homeless Assistance Grants.

Figure 1. Distribution of the HUD Homeless Assistance Grants.

THE THREE COMPETITIVE HOMELESS ASSISTANCE GRANTS AND THE CONTINUUM OF CARE

The bulk of the funding for the Homeless Assistance Grants is awarded to the three competitive grant programs: the SHP, S+C, and SRO programs. In FY2008, almost 90% of the total amount of funds distributed to the four grant programs went to the competitive grants. The composition of the homeless programs that are part of the competitive grant process has remained relatively stable since the passage of McKinney-Vento in 1987. The three existing programs have together comprised the competitive grants since FY1992. Both the SHP and the SRO program were part of the original McKinney Act in 1987, and the S+C program was added in 1990 (P.L. 10 1-645). Congress later made two other programs, the Safe Havens for Homeless Individuals Demonstration Program and the Rural Homeless Housing Assistance Program (both enacted in P.L. 102-550), part of McKinney-Vento, and gave HUD authority to allocate funds to them from the SHP appropriation. However, HUD never allocated funds.

Table 2. Characteristics of the SHP, S+C, and SRO Programs.

Program Characteristics	Supportive Housing Program (SHP)	Shelter Plus Care (S+C)	Single Room Occupancy (SRO)
Eligible Uses of Funds	• Transitional Housing • Permanent Housing • Supportive Services • Operating Expenses	• Permanent Housing	• Permanent Housing
Eligible Applicants	• States • Local Government Entities • PHAs • Private Nonprofits • Community Mental Health Centers	• States • Local Government Entities • PHAs	• PHAs • Private Nonprofits
Eligible Populations	• Families and individuals (transitional housing and services only) • Individuals with disabilities	• Individuals with disabilities and their families	• Individuals
Match Requirements	• Dollar for Dollar (acquisition, rehabilitation, or construction) • 20% (services) • 25% (operating expenses)	• Equal amount of funds for services	• No match requirement
FY2008 Percentage of Competitive Funds	71.16%	28.68%	0.17%

Source: The McKinney-Vento Homeless Assistance Act, Title IV, Subtitles C, E, and F, 42 U.S.C. §§ 11381- 11389, 11401, and 11403-1 1407b. CRS analysis of HUD FY2008 Continuum of Care Awards, http://www.hud.gov/offices/cpd/homeless/budget/2008/index.cfm.

An Overview of the Three Competitive Grants

The three competitive Homeless Assistance Grants each perform somewhat different functions, but all three have a unified focus in that they concentrate on the longer-term needs of homeless individuals and families rather than their emergency requirements. These longer-term needs include transitional housing (up to 24 months), permanent housing, and supportive services. Supportive services are designed to help homeless individuals with a variety of issues that might prevent them from being able to find and maintain permanent housing (for example, employment counseling, health care, and child care). Differences among the programs occur in the eligible uses of funds, the way in which housing to homeless persons is provided, match requirements by grant recipients, and the eligible populations served. (For a breakdown of some of these distinctions, see **Table 2**.)

The Supportive Housing Program

The SHP provides funds for transitional housing for homeless individuals and families for up to 24 months, permanent housing for homeless individuals with disabilities, and supportive services.[28] In FY2008, slightly more than 71% of total HUD competitive grant funds went to recipients as SHP grants.[29] Eligible applicants for SHP grants include states, local government entities, public housing authorities (PHAs), private nonprofit organizations, and community mental health centers.[30] Grant recipients can provide housing together with services, or can choose to provide services only (without a housing program component). Specifically, funds may be used to acquire and/or rehabilitate buildings that will be used either to provide supportive housing or buildings that will be used to provide supportive services only. Funds may also be used to *construct* buildings that will be used for supportive housing (but not supportive services only).[31]

In addition to financing physical structures, grantees may use funds to provide services like case management, health care, child care, housing assistance, nutritional counseling, and employment assistance. Grant recipients may provide these services themselves, or through contracts with outside providers. In addition, grant recipients may use funds to pay for up to 75% of their annual operating expenses and to help implement a Homeless Management Information System (HMIS)[32] to keep records regarding the homeless individuals served within their community.

Recipients of SHP grants are required to meet match requirements. All of the matching funds must be provided by cash sources,[33] but the level of non-federal funds required varies with the type of activity undertaken. Funds that are to be used for acquisition, rehabilitation, or new construction must be matched with an equal amount of the grant recipient's own funds.[34] Those SHP grantees that receive funds for supportive services must provide at least a 20% match with funds from other sources, while grantees that receive funds for operating expenses must provide at least a 25% match of these funds on their own.[35]

The Shelter Plus Care Program

The S+C program provides permanent supportive housing through rent subsidies for homeless individuals with disabilities and their families. In FY2008, approximately 29% of total competitive grant funds went to S+C grantees.[36] The S+C rent subsidies may be tenant-based vouchers, project-based rental assistance, or sponsor-based rental assistance.[37] Eligible applicants for the S+C grants are states, local government entities, and PHAs.[38] The S+C program requires grant recipients to match the amount of grant funds they receive for rental assistance with an equal amount of funds that they will use to provide supportive services.[39] The services under S+C are similar to those provided in the SHP, and include activities like physical and mental health care, substance abuse counseling, child care services, case management, and educational and job training.[40] Grant recipients can fulfill their match requirement with cash, the value of a lease, salary expenses for employees, or the time of volunteers.

The Single Room Occupancy Program

The Single Room Occupancy (SRO) program provides permanent housing to homeless individuals in efficiency units similar to dormitories, with single bedrooms, community bathrooms, and kitchen facilities. In FY2008, 0.17% of total competitive funds awarded went to SROs.[41] The SRO program does not require homeless residents to have a disability and does not fund supportive services. Eligible applicants for SRO grants are PHAs and private nonprofit organizations.[42] SRO units are funded as part of HUD's Section 8 Moderate Rehabilitation program, which requires grant recipients to spend at least $3,000 per unit to rehabilitate property to be used for SRO housing in order to bring the property into compliance with HUD's housing quality standards.[43] Grant recipients are reimbursed for the costs of rehabilitating SRO units through Section 8 rental assistance payments that they receive over a ten-year contract period. The costs of rehabilitation are amortized and added to a base rental amount. The maximum amount that a building owner can spend per unit and still be reimbursed is $21,500 as of FY2008 (this amount is updated annually).[44] After the ten-year rental contracts expire, they are not renewed through the Homeless Assistance Grant competition, but through a separate HUD account on an annual basis.[45]

RESIDENT CONTRIBUTIONS TO HOUSING COSTS

In the SHP, S+C, and SRO programs, residents are asked to pay a portion of their income toward rent, if they are able. In all three programs, rent may not exceed the greater of 30% of adjusted income, 10% of gross income, or if a family receives welfare benefits, the portion of the benefit designated for housing costs.

Distribution of the Competitive Grants

The three competitive grants are distributed to eligible applicant organizations through a complex, multi-step process that involves both formula and competitive elements. HUD first uses the CDBG formula to determine the need levels of local communities (generally, a combination of cities and counties); the need level is effectively the maximum amount of funding that a given community can receive. HUD then determines through a competition whether applicant organizations that provide services to homeless persons qualify for funds. In the early years that the Homeless Assistance Grants existed, individual homeless services providers applied to HUD directly for funds. However, since FY1996 HUD has required applicants to participate in a collaborative community process called the Continuum of Care (CoC) application system if they want to receive SHP, S+C, or SRO funds. For an overview of how funds are distributed, see **Figure 1**, at the end of this section.

The Continuum of Care

HUD developed the CoC as both a way for communities to plan services that will address the needs of homeless persons, and the method through which service providers apply for HUD funds.[46] Under the CoC strategy, local communities establish CoC advisory boards made up of representatives from local government agencies, service providers, and community members who meet to establish local priorities and strategies to address homelessness in their communities. The CoC plan that results from this process is meant to contain elements that address the continuum of needs of homeless persons: prevention of homelessness, emergency shelter, transitional housing, permanent housing, and supportive services provided at all stages of housing.[47] The CoC system was created in 1993 as the Innovative Homeless Initiatives Demonstration Program, a grant program that provided funding to communities so that they could become more cohesive in their approach to serving homeless people.[48] Since then, nearly every community in the country has become part of a CoC, with approximately 468 CoCs in existence as of 2008, including those in the territories.[49]

Since the FY1996 grant application process for the competitive Homeless Assistance Grants, the CoC system has also been the vehicle through which local service providers apply for HUD competitive grants.[50] The process of applying for the competitive Homeless Assistance Grants begins at the local level when individual applicant organizations apply to their CoC advisory boards to be included in a unified CoC application to HUD for funding. Continuums have flexibility in how they set up their application processes, called the "review and ranking" process, and may have written guidelines available for applicants. HUD requires that the process be fair, and CoCs must explain in their grant applications to HUD the methods they use to ensure fairness, together with a list of any complaints they received from applicant organizations.[51] Applicant organizations may also address fairness and other concerns directly to HUD.

Each CoC selects the homeless assistance projects that it thinks should be funded and prioritizes them in a list that is included in an overall CoC application to HUD. The CoC application packet accompanying the list has multiple parts. It includes an overall CoC application with information about the CoC structure and assessment of community needs, and individual applications for each listed project that the CoC recommends for funding. Continuums send the entire application packet to HUD, which in turn determines the projects that will be funded, and how much funding each will receive. Note that HUD determines funding at the individual *project* level, not the CoC level, although HUD considers factors involving the CoC in making its decisions.

HUD Determination of CoC Pro Rata Need

Before the CoC applications even arrive at HUD, the agency goes through a process where it calculates each community's "pro rata need." Pro rata need is meant to represent the dollar amount that each community (cities and counties) needs in order to address homelessness. HUD determines a pro rata need amount for each community and then adds together the individual need amounts of the communities within a CoC to arrive at a pro rata need amount for the entire Continuum. This CoC pro rata need amount is essentially the maximum amount of HUD Homeless Assistance Grant funds for which a CoC can qualify. Pro rata need does not include amounts needed to renew S+C contracts or amounts for new

Samaritan Bonus or Rapid Re- Housing projects (these two latter projects are described in the next section of this report, "Special Activities"). CoCs qualify for either a "preliminary pro rata need" (PPRN) level or a "hold harmless need" (HHN) level.

Preliminary Pro Rata Need

To calculate preliminary pro rata need, HUD takes the proportion of funds each community is entitled to under the ESG program (which uses the CDBG formula), and multiplies this proportion by the total amount of competitive funds available to grantees (after subtracting the amount needed for S+C renewals) to arrive at a dollar amount of preliminary pro rata need. For example, if a city is eligible for 0.08% of total ESG funds, and $1.1 billion is available for the competitive Homeless Assistance Grants in a given year, the dollar amount of preliminary pro rata need assigned to that community is $960,000. The preliminary pro rata need amount for each city and county within a CoC is then added together to arrive at a total preliminary pro rata need amount for the CoC.

Hold Harmless Pro Rata Need

HUD applies a hold harmless level of need in cases where the total cost of a CoC's one-year renewal of SHP contracts exceeds the preliminary pro rata need amount. In these cases, an amount equal to the difference between preliminary pro rata need and the cost of SHP renewals is added to preliminary pro rata need to bring the CoC up to a hold harmless level (effectively this means that the cost of SHP one-year renewals is the hold harmless level). For example, a Continuum's total cost of renewing SHP contracts is $4 million, but the preliminary pro rata need is only calculated to be $2.3 million. The difference between these two amounts ($1.7 million) is added to preliminary pro rata need ($2.3 million) to arrive at the hold harmless need level of $4 million. Beginning with the FY2005 grant competition, CoCs may choose to reallocate their hold harmless need from existing SHP projects to new projects under any of the three competitive grants. In the FY2008 competition, CoCs could also choose to reallocate SHP renewal funds to an HMIS project.

Final Pro Rata Need

Final pro rata need (FPRN) is the higher of PPRN or HHN. Whether the CoC is in PPRN status or HHN status, in order to receive sufficient funding for existing projects that must be renewed, the CoC must prioritize those renewal projects within the final pro rata need level, or they will not receive sufficient funding.

Threshold Review

When CoC applications arrive at HUD, the agency first goes through a threshold review of the individual project applications within each CoC application. In this process, HUD looks at various eligibility factors to ensure that every participant in the proposed projects (from applicant organizations to clients who will be served) are eligible for the Homeless Assistance Grants for which they are applying. The following list is illustrative of the factors that HUD considers, and does not include every element that HUD reviews.[52]

- HUD confirms that applicants are eligible by law to operate the program for which they are seeking funds. For example, only PHAs and private nonprofit organizations may operate an SRO project.

- Individual applicants must show an ability to provide matching funds for their projects.
- The applications must demonstrate that the proposed projects are eligible for funding, for example that the population to be served is eligible for assistance, that the projects will be accessible to persons with disabilities, that they are cost effective, and that the applicant organizations are participating (or will participate) in any local Homeless Management Information System.
- HUD assesses the potential quality of proposed projects by ensuring that the type of housing and its location fit the needs of participants, and that participants will be assisted with a variety of services.
- In order to receive funding, projects must comply with civil rights and fair housing requirements, employ, to the extent feasible, low- and very low-income persons, meet environmental requirements, and request funding in accordance with each grant's guidelines.

Scoring the Applications

In the final step, HUD reviews each individual project application and assigns points to each project that the Continuums have recommended for funding. Until the FY2008 competition, HUD awarded a total of 100 points in two categories: points for need (40 points) and for CoC factors (60 points). Need was based on each individual project's ranking within a CoC's application, while CoC factors were based on various characteristics and performance outcomes of CoCs. However, in the FY2008 competition, HUD eliminated points for need; instead, need is accounted for in the pro rata need determination process. The entire 100 points are now awarded on the basis of CoC factors. Note that even though points are based on CoC applications, points are awarded to individual projects within the CoC application. This means that each project receives the same score.

The points that are awarded to projects on the basis of CoC factors are used to determine which projects will be funded. Projects that score above a certain point threshold will receive full funding up to their final pro rata need. In cases of ties, HUD has established a tie-breaking system.[53] The threshold number of points varies from year to year. For example, in the FY2006 competition, 86 points were needed.[54] However, in FY2007, only projects that scored 90.25 points or more received full funding.[55] In FY2008, the threshold was 78.25.[56] Certain projects—SHP projects that CoCs propose for renewal, projects that CoCs propose to fund with reallocated SHP funds, and new HMIS projects—may still be funded even if they do not receive enough points to meet the threshold funding level, as long as the projects fall within their CoC's final pro rata need level. The SHP contract extensions may be made for up to one year in these cases.[57]

Points for Continuum of Care Factors

The CoC factors that HUD scores may vary from year to year. In the most recent Notice of Funding Availability for FY2008, there are five categories in which projects are scored.[58]

- CoC Housing, Services, and Structure: HUD awards points for the existence of an inclusive and outcome-oriented community process to develop a CoC strategy, and a fair and impartial project review and selection process. The strategy should be comprehensive, addressing the continuum of services, and designed to serve all homeless subpopulations. In addition, the CoC should have created, maintained, and built upon housing and services available to meet the needs of homeless persons. A total of 14 points may be awarded in this category.

- Homeless Needs and Data Collection: This category awards points on the basis of a CoCs understanding of the number of homeless individuals in the CoC's area and their needs, as well as a CoC's progress in implementing an HMIS to track and provide an unduplicated count of homeless persons. A total of 24 points may be awarded in this category.

- CoC Strategic Planning: HUD awards points in this category to Continuums with 10-year plans to end chronic homelessness, and those with discharge policies for persons leaving institutional care (for example, correctional facilities, hospitals, or foster care). The category also considers whether CoCs propose projects that address unmet needs in the community, are able to estimate the cost to renew SHP and S+C projects for the next five years, and are able to leverage funds from other sources. A total of 16 points may be awarded in this category.

- CoC Performance: The factors considered in this category include steps that CoCs have taken to meet their goals, whether CoCs have increased the number of permanent housing beds for chronically homeless individuals, whether there has been a decrease in chronic homelessness, the success that homeless individuals have in remaining in permanent housing, the success of homeless individuals in gaining employment and access to available government programs and funds, the record of CoC projects in hiring low- and very low-income employees, the implementation of energy-efficiency measures in housing and community facilities, and the existence of a local plan to remove regulatory barriers to affordable housing. A total of 28 points may be awarded in this category.

- Emphasis on Housing Activities: Within this category, HUD awards points to Continuums based on the percentage of funds to be used to provide housing (versus services). CoCs need not use all funds for housing in order to receive the maximum number of available points. A total of 18 points may be awarded in this category.

Allocation of the Grants

Despite the fact that Continuums of Care serve as intermediaries between HUD and individual homeless service providers during the application process, funds go directly to service providers, not to the CoC. Projects receive funding for between one and ten years depending on the type of project and whether it is a new contract or a renewal. New SHP projects are funded for two or three years, while renewals are funded for one to three years.[59] Initial S+C contracts run for five years, renewals are made for one year at a time, and SRO projects are funded for ten years (renewals take place outside the Homeless Assistance Grant application process).[60] Grant recipients enter into a grant agreement with HUD, and, if the grant involves construction, work must begin within 18 months of HUD's grant award letter and be completed within 36 months.[61] Activities that are not contingent on construction must begin within 12 months of receipt of the grant award letter.

SPECIAL ACTIVITIES

In recent years, HUD has distributed funds to serve homeless individuals through programs that are not directly part of the four Homeless Assistance Grants discussed in this report. Each of the three programs—the Samaritan Housing Initiative, the Rapid Re-Housing Demonstration Program, and the Homelessness Prevention and Rapid Re-Housing Program—reflects different policy priorities when it comes to serving homeless individuals. The oldest of the three initiatives, the Samaritan Housing Initiative (sometimes referred to as the Samaritan Bonus), funds permanent supportive housing for a group of individuals considered chronically homeless, single adults (typically men) often with mental illnesses and substance abuse issues. A second initiative, the Rapid Re-Housing Demonstration, for which Congress appropriated funds in FY2008, focuses on finding housing for homeless families with children, a group sometimes thought to be neglected in favor of serving chronically homeless individuals. Finally, the most recent of the three initiatives, the Homelessness Prevention and Rapid Re-Housing Program (HPRP), emphasizes the prevention of homelessness, something for which only a small portion of HUD funds have been used in the past.

Samaritan Housing Initiative

Although the Samaritan Bonus has been part of the CoC competition since FY2005, until the FY2008 competition funds for the bonus had been computed as part of the pro rata need process. FY2008 was the first year in which funds for the Samaritan Bonus were awarded separately. HUD's Samaritan Bonus must be used by CoCs specifically to create new permanent supportive housing for chronically homeless individuals. A chronically homeless person is defined as an individual with a disabling condition who has been continuously homeless for one year or has had four episodes of homelessness in the last three years.[62] In the past, CoCs could not create more than one project with Samaritan Bonus funds, but in FY2008, CoCs could propose and receive funding for one or more projects. A CoC may qualify for additional funds under the Samaritan Bonus up to a maximum of 15% of its preliminary pro rata need or $6 million, whichever is lower. For example, if a Continuum has a preliminary pro rata need of $2 million with a hold- harmless level that brings its need level up to $3 million, it may receive a Samaritan Bonus of $300,000 (15% of $2 million). In the FY2007 competition, 199 CoCs received the Samaritan Bonus, totaling $94 million.[63] HUD has not announced the number of CoCs that received the Samaritan Bonus in FY2008.

Rapid Re-Housing Demonstration Program

Rapid re-housing is a process targeted to assist homeless families with dependent children that have one or more moderate barriers to achieving and maintaining permanent housing. Through supportive services to address these barriers, together with short-term housing assistance, the hope is that families will be able to maintain permanent housing. In the FY2008 Consolidated Appropriations Act (P.L. 110-161), Congress appropriated $25 million for a Rapid Re-Housing Demonstration Program. HUD awarded the funds through a competitive process to 23 projects proposed by Continuums of Care for funding. The announcement of grant award recipients was made on February 19, 2009.[64]

Rapid Re-Housing grantees are to provide supportive services and transitional housing assistance to help families move to permanent housing as quickly as possible. Under the Rapid Re-Housing grant, service providers may fund transitional housing for one of two time periods, to be determined by the service provider at the time it assesses the needs of a given family. These two time periods are either 3-6 months or 12-15 months. Grantees may not use more than 30% of funds for supportive services.[65] Among the moderate barriers to achieving permanent housing that families must face in order to be eligible for Rapid Re-Housing services are (1) temporary financial strain, (2) inadequate employment or loss of employment, (3) inadequate childcare resources, (4) an ability to overcome a low level of education or command of the English language, (5) legal problems that can be addressed by a service provider, (6) minimal mental health issues or prior substance use, and (7) poor rental and credit history.[66]

Rapid Re-Housing grants were awarded through a separate, 100-point competition in which each CoC could apply for only one grant. HUD conducted a threshold review, much like the one HUD uses to determine eligibility of projects in the competition for the three competitive grants. Then, eligible applicants were scored on five factors: (1) experience in operating rapid re-housing projects, (2) the ability to assess the needs of families, (3) the applicant's relationship with other service providers in the community, (4) the ability to maintain affordable housing stock, (5) the existence of centralized intake, and (6) a threshold level of shelter beds that are reported in a homeless management information system within the CoC.[67] A CoC's score on the application for Rapid Re-Housing funds was added to its CoC score in the competitive grant process to determine which projects were funded.

The New Homelessness Prevention and Rapid Re-Housing Program

Congress appropriated $1.5 billion for a new Homelessness Prevention and Rapid Re-Housing Program (HPRP) as part of the American Recovery and Reinvestment Act (P.L. 111-5), which was signed by the President on February 17, 2009. The funds are being distributed to states and local communities using the ESG program formula to determine allotments. On February 25, 2009, HUD announced how the funds would be distributed.[68] Although funds will be distributed via the ESG formula, unlike the ESG program, where only 30% of funds may be used for homelessness prevention activities, all funds are to be used for activities to prevent homelessness or to quickly find housing for those who have become homeless. In addition, because the amount of HPRP funds available greatly exceeds typical ESG appropriations, more cities and counties qualify for the minimum HPRP grant of $500,000; under HPRP, 337 cities qualify for their own grant (compared to 203 that received FY2009 ESG allocations) and 148 urban counties qualify for their own HPRP grant (compared to 102 that received funds under the FY2009 ESG grants). As with ESG, grantee state and local governments may allocate funds to subgrantees that are agencies within government or private nonprofit organizations. Unlike ESG, there are no match requirements for HPRP funds. Grantees must expend at least 60% of funds within two years of the date that the funds are made available by HUD, and 100% of funds within three years.

On March 19, 2009, HUD released a notice in which it detailed requirements for grantees and subgrantees.[69] Recipients may use funds to assist individuals and families who find themselves in two different sets of circumstances—those who, but for HPRP assistance, would become homeless and those who currently meet HUD's definition of homelessness.[70] In both cases, those assisted should only require temporary assistance in order to find and retain housing, and must have incomes at or below 50% of area median income (considered very low income).[71] Funds may be used for short-term rental assistance (up to 3 months) or medium-term rental assistance (4-18 months), for security or utility deposits, utility payments, help with moving expenses, and hotel vouchers. Recipients may also use funds for activities to help families find and maintain housing such as help with housing searches, outreach to landlords, credit repair, and legal services. The notice explicitly states that funds may not be used for mortgage costs.[72] In order to qualify for funds, communities were required to amend their consolidated plans to describe how they would use the funds and submit the amended plan to HUD by May 18, 2009. HUD was to approve consolidated plan amendments by July 2, 2009,[73] and expects to enter into grant agreements by September 1, 2009.[74]

REAUTHORIZATION OF THE MCKINNEY-VENTO HOMELESS ASSISTANCE GRANTS

On April 2, 2009, identical versions of bills to reauthorize the McKinney-Vento Homeless Assistance Grants were introduced in both the House and Senate. The two bills, H.R. 1877 and S. 808, were both entitled the Homeless Emergency Assistance and Rapid Transition to Housing (HEARTH) Act. On May 6, 2009, Senator Reed, the sponsor of S. 808, proposed adding the bill as an amendment to S. 896, the Helping Families Save Their Homes Act, which was being considered by the full Senate.[75] Senator Reed's amendment was approved, and later that same day the Senate approved S. 896. The House approved S. 896 on May 19, 2009, and, due to small differences between the House- and Senate-passed versions, the Senate approved the House-passed measure that same day. On May 20, 2009, the President signed the bill into law as P.L. 111-22. Prior to this, the Homeless Assistance Grants had not been reauthorized since 1992 (P.L. 102-550). The changes in the HEARTH Act will take effect at the earlier of 18 months from the date of its enactment—on or about November 20, 2010—or three months from the date on which HUD publishes final regulations.

The changes in P.L. 111-22 will have repercussions for the makeup of the Homeless Assistance Grants (the three competitive grants will be consolidated into one grant), the way in which funds are distributed to grantees, the purposes for which grantees may use funds, and the determination of who may be served under the law. This section describes the major changes that the HEARTH Act makes to the Homeless Assistance Grants.

Consolidation of the Competitive Homeless Assistance Grants

The HEARTH Act removes the distinctions among the three competitive Homeless Assistance Grants and replaces them with one consolidated grant program called the "Continuum of Care Program." Applicants will no longer apply for one of the three existing grants—S+C, SHP, or SRO—based on the type of housing and services they want to provide. Instead, the new consolidated grant will provide funds for permanent housing, transitional housing, supportive services, and re-housing activities.

In consolidating the competitive grants, the HEARTH Act will maintain some aspects of the current Continuum of Care application system and will codify the system in law (currently much of the application system has been established through the grant funding process). Under P.L. 111-22, HUD will review applications from Collaborative Applicants—local entities that will determine funding priorities and jointly submit a single application to HUD on behalf of all local applicant organizations (much like the existing Continuum of Care). Currently, although CoCs submit one application to HUD, the Department must still review the individual project applications from organizations seeking funding. This change from separate project applications to a single Collaborative Applicant application will mean the difference between HUD reviewing hundreds rather than thousands of applications.[76] Collaborative Applicants may also choose to apply to HUD to be "Unified Funding Agencies;" the Unified Funding Agencies will have authority to receive grant awards directly from HUD and distribute them to individual awardee organizations. Otherwise, HUD will continue using its current practice of distributing funds directly to individual project applicants.

P.L. 111-22 will also require certain set-asides within the Continuum of Care Program to provide housing for homeless populations.

- At least 30% of funds (not including those for permanent housing renewals) must be used to provide permanent supportive housing to individuals with disabilities or families with an adult head of household (or youth in the absence of an adult) who has a disability. This requirement will be reduced proportionately as communities increase permanent housing units for those individuals and families, and will end when HUD determined that a total of 150,000 permanent housing units had been provided for homeless persons with disabilities since 2001.
- At least 10% of funds must be used to provide permanent housing for families with children.

Collaborative Applicants that are successful in reducing or eliminating homelessness through permanent housing will receive bonuses that they can use for any eligible activity under the Continuum of Care Program as well as homelessness prevention activities.

P.L. 111-22 also institutes a new program to allow certain high-performing communities to have greater flexibility in the way that they use their funds. To be designated high-performing, a Collaborative Applicant will have to meet requirements regarding the average length of homelessness in their communities, repeat instances of homelessness, community involvement and outreach activities, effectiveness in reducing homelessness, and success in achieving independent living among homeless families with children and youth.

Collaborative Applicants designated "high performing" will be able to use their grant awards for any eligible activity under the Continuum of Care Program, as well as for homelessness prevention activities.

Regarding the pro rata need process currently used to determine how funds are distributed to communities (which uses the CDBG formula, in part, to determine need), the HEARTH Act requires HUD to create a new formula for determining need within two years of the bill's enactment using "factors that are appropriate to allocate funds to meet the goals and objectives of" the Continuum of Care program. P.L. 111-22 will give the HUD Secretary the authority to adjust the formula to ensure that Collaborative Applicants have sufficient funds to renew existing contracts for one year.

The HEARTH Act authorizes the Continuum of Care Program, together with the Emergency Solutions Grants Program (described below) at $2.2 billion in FY2010 and such sums as necessary for FY2011. P.L. 111-22 provides that renewals of permanent housing contracts may be funded through either the Homeless Assistance Grants account or the project-based Section 8 account.

Definition of "Homeless Individual" and "Chronically Homeless Person"

The HEARTH Act expands the definition of "homeless individual" that was codified in the McKinney-Vento Homeless Assistance Act when the law was originally enacted.[77] Under the original law, a homeless individual is defined as an individual who lacks a fixed, regular, and adequate nighttime residence and who resides in a temporary shelter (including welfare hotels, congregate shelter, and transitional housing for those with mental illnesses), resides in an institution as a temporary residence, or a in place not designed for human habitation.

The HEARTH Act amends the current definition of homeless individual to include all those persons living in transitional housing, not just those residing in transitional housing for the mentally ill as in current law. P.L. 111-22 also includes in the definition persons living in hotels or motels paid for by a government entity. In addition, the new law adds to the current definition those individuals and families who meet all of the following criteria:

- Will "imminently lose their housing," whether it be their own housing, housing they are sharing with others, or a hotel or motel not paid for by a government entity. Imminent loss of housing will be evidenced by:
  - an eviction requiring an individual or family to leave their housing within 14 days;
  - a lack of resources that would allow an individual or family to remain in a hotel or motel for more than 14 days; or
  - credible evidence that an individual or family would not be able to stay with another homeowner or renter for more than 14 days.
- Have no subsequent residence identified.
- Lack the resources needed to obtain other permanent housing.

HUD practice prior to passage of the HEARTH Act was to consider those individuals and families who would imminently lose housing within seven days to be homeless.

Another change to the definition of homeless individual is that the HEARTH Act considers homeless anyone who is fleeing a situation of domestic violence or other life-threatening condition. In addition, P.L. 111-22 adds to the definition of homeless individual unaccompanied youth and homeless families with children who are defined as homeless under other federal statutes[78] and who (1) have experienced a long-term period without living independently in permanent housing; (2) have experienced instability as evidenced by frequent moves; and (3) can be expected to continue in unstable housing due to factors such as chronic disabilities, chronic physical health or mental health conditions, substance addiction, histories of domestic violence or childhood abuse, the presence of a child or youth with a disability, or multiple barriers to employment. In general, however, Collaborative Applicants will not be able to use more than 10% of grant funds to serve those individuals and families defined as homeless under other federal statutes.

P.L. 111-22 also expands the current definition of "chronically homeless person," which is defined in regulation.[79] Under the regulation, the term is defined as an *unaccompanied individual* who has been homeless continuously for one year or on four or more occasions in the last three years, and who has a disability. The HEARTH Act adds to the definition those homeless *families* with an adult head of household (or youth where no adult is present) who has a disability. The definition of disability specifically includes post traumatic stress disorder and traumatic brain injury. Note, however, that to be considered chronically homeless, an individual or family has to be living in a place not meant for human habitation, a safe haven, or an emergency shelter; the HEARTH Act's proposed changes to the definition of "homeless individual" do not apply to chronic homelessness. In addition, a person released from an institution will be considered chronically homeless as long as, prior to entering the institution, they otherwise met the definition of chronically homeless person, and had been institutionalized for fewer than 90 days.

Homelessness Prevention

The HEARTH Act also expands the opportunities for grantees to engage in homelessness prevention activities. Currently, only ESG funds may be used for homelessness prevention activities such as payment of rent or utility bills, limited to 30% of a state's or a community's allocation. P.L. 111-22 expands the eligible activities and funding level of the Emergency Shelter Grants Program and renames it the "Emergency Solutions Grants Program." The new law allocates 20% of funds made available by Congress for the Homeless Assistance Grants to the newly named program (currently somewhere between 10% and 15% of funds are reserved for the ESG program). P.L. 111-22 expands the list of supportive services that can be provided with ESG program funds from those concerned with "employment, health, drug abuse, or education," to include family support services for homeless youth, victim services, and mental health services.

The new ESG program also allows funds to be used for short- or medium-term rental assistance and housing relocation and stabilization services for individuals and families at risk of homelessness. The bill defines the term "at risk of homelessness" to include an individual or family with income at or below 30% of area median income, who has insufficient income to attain housing stability, who has moved frequently for economic reasons, and who lives in unstable housing (examples of unstable housing are enumerated in the law). The term also includes all individuals and families defined as homeless under other federal statutes as "at risk." Under the updated ESG program in the HEARTH Act, the amount of funds that grant recipients can use for emergency shelter and related supportive services are limited, thereby requiring that a portion of funds be used for rental assistance and services for those at risk of homelessness. Specifically, recipients cannot use more than the greater of 60% of their ESG allocation, or the amount they had used prior to enactment of the HEARTH Act, for emergency shelter and related services.

Rural Homelessness

In the area of rural homelessness, the HEARTH Act retains portions of McKinney-Vento's rural homelessness grant program (Title IV, Subtitle G of McKinney-Vento), a program that has not been funded, as the Rural Housing Stability Assistance Program. The program reserves not less than 5% of Continuum of Care Program funds for rural communities to apply separately for funds that would otherwise be awarded as part of the Continuum of Care Program. Unlike the Continuum of Care program, rural communities will be able to serve persons who do not necessarily meet HUD's definition of "homeless individual." P.L. 111-22 provides that HUD may award grants to rural communities to be used for (1) re-housing or improving the housing situation of those who are homeless or are in the worst housing situations in their geographic area, (2) stabilizing the housing situation of those in imminent danger of losing housing, and (3) improving the ability of the lowest-income residents in the community to afford stable housing. The HEARTH Act adds to the list of eligible activities under the rural grants the construction or rehabilitation of transitional or permanent housing as well as the leasing of property or payment of rental assistance for these purposes.

OTHER ISSUES REGARDING THE HOMELESS ASSISTANCE GRANTS

Despite the enactment of McKinney-Vento reauthorization legislation, there are other factors involved in the distribution of the Homeless Assistance Grants that may continue to be issues of concern to those interested in how funds are allocated. An ongoing concern has been the amount of funds required to renew existing housing and services contracts, leaving a relatively small share of funding to support new projects. Another issue is the way in which the CDBG formula affects the distribution of the Homeless Assistance Grants. While enactment of the HEARTH Act may mean that the CDBG formula will not be used in the distribution of competitive funds in the future, the CDBG formula will continue to be used to distribute ESG funds.

Renewals of the Competitive Homeless Assistance Grants

In recent years Congress has shown some concern about the cost of renewing existing permanent supportive housing contracts through the S+C and SHP programs, while also funding new permanent housing units.[80] Currently a large percentage of competitive Homeless Assistance Grant funds are used to renew existing SHP and S+C contracts. For example, in FY2008 approximately 86% of competitive grant funds were used to renew existing contracts. (For the percentage allocation of the FY2008 competitive grants see **Figure 2.**) In its FY2010 budget, HUD estimates that of the nearly $1.8 billion requested by the President, approximately 84% would be used to renew existing projects.[81] Since FY2001, Congress has required funds to be set aside funds for S+C renewals in order to protect the existing permanent housing contracts, but SHP renewals are not similarly protected. They are simply part of the competition for all remaining funds.

Congress has also shown concern over sufficient funds for both new and renewal projects due to the need for additional housing facilities to meet the needs of chronically homeless individuals.[82] A chronically homeless person is defined as an individual with a disabling condition who has been homeless continuously for a year or more, or has had at least four episodes of homelessness in three years.[83] In 2002, President Bush established an initiative to end chronic homelessness within ten years, and as a result, many states and communities are making efforts to provide housing for chronically homeless individuals. At the beginning of the chronic homelessness initiative, it was estimated that 150,000 to 200,000 new housing units were needed in this effort. In FY2008, around 19% of competitive grants— approximately $274 million—funded projects for chronically homeless individuals.[84] This was down from FY2007 when 25% of competitive grants ($330 million) funded projects for chronically homeless individuals. In FY2007, HUD estimated that 20,000 chronically homeless individuals moved into permanent supportive housing.[85]

HUD has changed the way it calculates pro rata need in order to help CoCs to free up funds for new permanent housing projects. With the FY2005 competition for available funds, HUD enabled CoCs to eliminate funding for existing SHP projects from their priority lists while still qualifying for the hold harmless level of pro rata need funds that would have been required to renew those SHP projects. This enables the funds that otherwise would have been directed toward renewals to be used to create new permanent housing projects.[86] Although this allows CoCs to defund projects that they do not think should receive grants, it does not address what CoCs can do about renewing projects they think are worth funding while also funding projects that would create new housing.

The Role of the Community Development Block Grant Formula

The Community Development Block Grant (CDBG) formula has determined how ESG funds are distributed since the inception of the program in 1986, and has been used in the distribution of the competitive grants since at least FY1995. The effectiveness of using the CDBG formula to target funds to services for homeless persons has been questioned at various times. Two General Accounting Office (now Government Accountability Office) reports from the late 1980s noted that the CDBG formula might not be the best way to target funds to areas that most need homeless assistance funds.[87] Congress, too, has questioned the relationship between the formula and homelessness. In FY2001, the Senate Appropriations Committee noted that "the CDBG formula has no real nexus to homeless needs," and urged HUD to hasten its development of a method for counting homeless individuals.[88] HUD responded with a report that proposed alternative methods for determining community need for homeless assistance.[89]

The newly enacted HEARTH Act (P.L. 111-22) responded to these concerns, in part by directing HUD to develop a formula for determining need for the competitive Continuum of Care Program within two years of the law's enactment. As discussed earlier in this report, the competitive Homeless Assistance Grants currently use the CDBG formula to determine a community's need for funds. However, the competitive grants will continue to use the CDBG formula until HUD implements a new formula, and the HEARTH Act does not change the use of the CDBG formula to distribute ESG funds.

The CDBG formula has also been questioned as the best way of targeting funds for its intended purpose—community development—and changing the formula has been the subject of discussion for a number of years. If Congress were to change the CDBG formula, the way in which the Homeless Assistance Grants are distributed would also change. The current formula factors used to distribute funds are: population, the number of persons in poverty, housing overcrowding (homes in which there are more than 1.01 persons per room), the age of housing (the number of housing structures built prior to 1940), and the extent of growth lag in a given community (the lack of population growth in a community compared to the growth rate it would have had if it had grown at the rate of other communities).[90] In 2005, HUD released a report in which it examined the effectiveness of the CDBG formula in targeting communities that are in need of development. Among the report's criticisms of the formula was that the use of the population variable means that some fast-growing communities with low development needs may still receive increasing CDBG grants.[91] Another criticism was that the poverty variable may provide college towns with a disproportionate share of funds by counting college students as living in poverty.[92] A third potential problem with the formula the report noted was that the age of housing and growth lag factors do not necessarily reflect communities' needs for development. In some communities, housing built prior to 1940 has been rehabilitated and gentrified, while in others it has been torn down or subject to neglect.[93] As a result, some communities with refurbished pre-1940s housing may qualify for more CDBG funds than deteriorating communities that have demolished their older housing.

The 2005 HUD report also proposed alternative factors for the CDBG formula.[94] Among these was a formula that would not require a split of funds between entitlement communities (which currently receive 70% of funds) and non-entitlement communities (which receive 30% of funds) and would use the following factors:

- the number of people in poverty, excluding college students;
- housing that is 50 years old or older and occupied by a household in poverty;
- female-headed households with children under the age of 18; and
- overcrowding.

The President's FY2010 budget proposes to change the CDBG formula, and replace it with this HUD-proposed formula.[95] The budget proposes that the CDBG formula be modernized to "better target funds to communities with the greatest economic need," and noted that any new formula would include hold-harmless provisions to allow transition time for communities that might receive a lower share of total funds to adjust to the revised allocations.

End Notes

[1] Peter H. Rossi, *Down and Out in America: The Origins of Homelessness* (Chicago: The University of Chicago Press, 1989), pp. 20-2 1, 27-28.

[2] Ibid., p. 34.

[3] Ibid., pp. 39-44.

[4] Ibid., p. 33.

[5] Ibid., pp. 181-194, 41. See, also, Martha Burt, *Over the Edge: The Growth of Homelessness in the 1980s* (New York: Russell Sage Foundation, 1992), pp. 31-126.

[6] *Down and Out in America*, p. 34; *Over the Edge*, p. 123.

[7] These programs included the Emergency Food and Shelter Program (P.L. 98-8), the Emergency Shelter Grants Program (P.L. 99-59 1), and the Transitional Housing Demonstration Program (P.L. 99-59 1). In 1987, all three were incorporated into the Stewart B. McKinney Homeless Assistance Act (P.L. 100-77), although the Transitional Housing Demonstration Program was renamed the Supportive Housing Demonstration Program.

[8] For information about other programs created by the McKinney Act, see CRS Report RL3 0442, *Homelessness: Targeted Federal Programs and Recent Legislation*, coordinated by Libby Perl.

[9] In addition to funds for the four grant programs, the congressional appropriation has also at times contained funds for items like training and technical assistance, data collection, and the Interagency Council on Homelessness. These amounts make up a small percentage of the total appropriation.

[10] Department of Housing and Urban Development, "Notice of Funding Availability, Continuum of Care Homeless Assistance," *Federal Register*, vol. 73, no. 133, July 10, 2008, p. 39849 (hereinafter FY2008 NOFA).

[11] The ESG program was initially part of H.R. 5313, which was incorporated into H.Rept. 99-1005, the Conference Report to accompany H.J.Res. 738, which became P.L. 99-591.

[12] See 42 U.S.C. 11373(a), which refers to the statute governing the Community Development Block Grant at 42 U.S.C. §§ 5302(a)(4)-(6). A metropolitan city is the central city within a metropolitan statistical area, or a city of 50,000 or more within a metropolitan statistical area, and an urban county is a county within a metropolitan area that has a population of 200,000 or more, or 100,000 or more if the county contains no incorporated areas.

[13] 24 C.F.R. § 576.5(a).

[14] U.S. Department of Housing and Urban Development, *Emergency Shelter Grants Program FY2008 Operating Instructions*, October 2008, p. 2, http://www.hudhre.info/documents/ESG_OperatingInstructions_2008.pdf.

[15] For a description of the factors used in the CDBG formula, see the section of this report entitled, "The Role of the Community Development Block Grant Formula."

[16] 42 U.S.C. §§ 5306(a) - (d).

[17] 42 U.S.C. § 5306.

[18] 42 U.S.C. § 11374(a).

[19] Ibid.

[20] The other programs are the Community Development Block Grant program, the HOME program, and the Housing Opportunities for Persons with AIDS (HOPWA) program. For more information about HOME, see CRS Report R401 18, *An Overview of the HOME Investment Partnerships Program*, by Katie Jones, and for more information about HOPWA, see CRS Report RL343 18, *Housing for Persons Living with HIV/AIDS*, by Libby Perl.

[21] 24 C.F.R. § 91.1(a).

[22] 24 C.F.R. § 91.500.

[23] 42 U.S.C. § 11373.

[24] 42 U.S.C. § 11373(b).

[25] HUD Office of Community Development, http://www.hud.gov/offices/cpd/about/budget/budget08/index.cfm.

[26] 42 U.S.C. § 11375(a).

[27] Ibid.

[28] At least 10% of total SHP funds must be used for supportive services, at least 25% must be used for projects that serve families with children, and at least 25% must be used for projects that serve homeless persons with disabilities. 42 U.S.C. § 11389(b).

[29] Based on CRS analysis of HUD FY2008 Continuum of Care Awards, http://www.hud.gov/offices/cpd/homeless/budget/2008/index.cfm.

[30] 42 U.S.C. § 11382(1).

[31] 42 U.S.C. § 11383.

[32] HMIS is a data collection, organization, and storage initiative to keep records of homeless persons receiving services. For more information see CRS Report RL33956, *Counting Homeless Persons: Homeless Management Information Systems*, by Libby Perl.

[33] 24 C.F.R. § 583. 145.

[34] 42 U.S.C. § 11386(e).

[35] FY2008 NOFA, pp. 39842-39843.

[36] Based on CRS analysis of HUD FY2008 Continuum of Care Awards, http://www.hud.gov/offices/cpd/homeless/budget/2008/index.cfm.

[37] 42 U.S.C. §§ 11404-1 1406b. In sponsor-based housing, recipient states, local governments, or PHAs contract with private nonprofit organizations or community mental health agencies to operate the housing. 24 C.F.R. § 582.100(c).

[38] 42 U.S.C. § 11403g(2).

[39] 42 U.S.C. § 1 1403b(a).

[40] 24 C.F.R. § 582.5.

[41] Based on CRS analysis of HUD FY2008 Continuum of Care Awards, http://www.hud.gov/offices/cpd/homeless/budget/2008/index.cfm.

[42] 42 U.S.C. § 11401(j).

[43] 24 C.F.R. § 882.802.

[44] HUD publishes the maximum amount of expenditures annually, taking account of changes in construction costs. See FY2008 NOFA, p. 39849.

[45] Ibid.

[46] The development of the Continuum of Care system is described in *Priority: Home! The Federal Plan to Break the Cycle of Homelessness*, The U.S. Department of Housing and Urban Development, 1994, pp. 73-75.

[47] Barnard-Columbia Center for Urban Policy, *The Continuum of Care: A Report on the New Federal Policy to Address Homelessness*, U.S. Department of Housing and Urban Development, December 1996, p. 9.

[48] See U.S. Department of Housing and Urban Development, "Funding Availability for Fiscal Year 1994 for Innovative Project Funding Under the Innovative Homeless Initiatives Demonstration Program," *Federal Register* vol. 58, no. 243, December 21, 1993, pp. 67616-67618.

[49] "HUD-Defined CoC Names and Numbers Listed by State," Revised April 2008, http://www.hud.gov/offices/adm/ grants/nofa08/coclisting.pdf.

[50] U.S. Department of Housing and Urban Development, "Continuum of Care Homeless Assistance; Funding Availability," *Federal Register* vol. 61, no. 52, March 15, 1996, pp. 10865-10877.

[51] Exhibit I of Continuum of Care application, http://www.hud.gov/offices/adm/hudclips/forms/files/40090-1.doc. This document is from the 2007 application. For FY2008 funds, HUD implemented an online application system, and application materials are not available.

[52] For all of the eligibility factors, see FY2008 NOFA, pp. 39846-39849.

[53] Ibid., p. 39853.

[54] Statement of Mark Johnston, Deputy Assistant Secretary for Special Needs, HUD Office of Community Planning and Development, FY2007 Continuum of Care NOFA Webcast, March 27, 2007, http://www.hud.gov/offices/cpd/ homeless/index.cfm.

[55] HUD SuperNOFA Broadcast slides, February 21, 2008, p. 8, http://www.hudhre.info/documents/2007_debrief_broadcast.ppt.

[56] HUD Debriefing Broadcast slides, April 22, 2009, p. 11, http://www.hudhre.info/documents/CoCDebrief BroadcastSlides_2008.pdf.

[57] FY2008 NOFA, p. 39852.

[58] Ibid., pp. 39850-39852.

[59] Ibid., p. 39848.

[60] Ibid., p. 39845.

[61] Ibid., p. 39854.

[62] 24 C.F.R. § 91.5.

[63] HUD SuperNOFA Broadcast slides, February 21, 2008, p. 15, http://www.hudhre.info/documents/2007_debrief_broadcast.ppt.

[64] For a list of the grant recipients, see HUD's news release, http://www.hud.gov/news/release.cfm?content=pr09-010. cfm.

[65] FY2008 NOFA, p. 39843.

[66] Ibid., p. 39846.

[67] Ibid., p. 39852.

[68] The list of HPRP recipients is available at http://www.hud.gov/recovery/homeless-prevention.cfm.

[69] U.S. Department of Housing and Urban Development, Notice of Allocations, Application Procedures, and Requirements for Homelessness Prevention and Rapid Re-Housing Program Grantees under the American Recovery and Reinvestment Act of 2009, March 19, 2009, http://www.hud.gov/recovery/hrp-notice.pdf.

[70] Ibid., pp. 5-6.

[71] Ibid. p. 23.

[72] Ibid., p. 20.

[73] Ibid., p. 31.

[74] Ibid., p. 2.

[75] See S.Amdt. 1040.

[76] The HEARTH Act also allows individual organizations to apply directly to HUD for funds if they are not reasonably permitted to participate as part of the collaborative application process.

[77] 42 U.S.C. § 11302.

[78] For more information about the definition of homelessness under other federal programs, see the section entitled "Defining Homelessness" in CRS Report RL30442, *Homelessness: Targeted Federal Programs and Recent Legislation*, coordinated by Libby Perl.

[79] 24 C.F.R. § 91.5.

[80] In order to better anticipate the need for renewal funds, beginning in FY2002, Congress asked HUD to estimate five- year projections for renewing SHP and S+C contracts. Conference Report to accompany H.R. 2620, *Department of Veterans' Affairs, Housing and Urban Development, and Independent Agencies Appropriation Act*, 107th Cong., 1st sess., November 6, 2001, H.Rept. 107-272. HUD has provided these estimates in its FY2003, FY2006, and FY2007 Congressional Budget Justifications.

[81] U.S. Department of Housing and Urban Development, *FY2010 Congressional Budget Justifications*, p. W-4, http://www.hud.gov/offices/cfo/reports/2010/cjs/cpd2010.pdf (hereinafter *FY2010 HUD Budget Justifications*).

[82] See, for example, Senate Committee on Banking, Housing and Urban Affairs, Subcommittee on Housing and Urban Development, *HUD's Fiscal Year 2003 Budget and Legislative Proposals*, 107th Cong., 2nd sess., February 13, 2002, S. Hrg. 107-839, pp. 14-16, http://banking.senate.gov/_files/107839.pdf.

[83] 24 C.F.R. § 91.5.

[84] HUD news release, February 19, 2009, http://www.hud.gov/news/release.cfm?content=pr09-010.cfm.

[85] HUD SuperNOFA Broadcast slides, February 21, 2008, p. 16, http://www.hudhre.info/documents/ 2007 _debrief _broadcast.ppt.

[86] U.S. Department of Housing and Urban Development, "Notice of Funding Availability, Continuum of Care Homeless Assistance," *Federal Register*, vol. 70, no. 53, March 21, 2005, pp. 14283-14284.

[87] U.S. General Accounting Office, *Homelessness: Implementation of Food and Shelter Programs Under the McKinney Act*. GAO/RCED-88-63. December 1987, p. 33, http://archive.gao.gov/d29t5/134578.pdf, and *Homelessness: HUD's and FEMA 's Progress in Implementing the McKinney Act*. GAO/RCED-89-50. May 1989, pp. 46-48, http://archive.gao.gov/d25t7/138597.pdf.

[88] S.Rept. 106-410. The statement was made regarding the competitive Homeless Assistance Grants.

[89] U.S. Department of Housing and Urban Development. Office of Community Planning and Development. *Report to Congress: Measuring "Need" for HUD's McKinney-Vento Homeless Competitive Grants*, 2001.

[90] 42 U.S.C. § 5306.

[91] Todd Richardson, *CDBG Formula Targeting to Community Development Need*, U.S. Department of Housing and Urban Development, February 2005, p. 46, http://www.huduser.org/Publications/pdf/CDBGAssess.pdf.

[92] Ibid., p. 47.

[93] Ibid., pp. 48-50.

[94] Ibid., pp. 61-84.

[95] *FY2010 HUD Budget Justifications*, p. Q-10.

In: An Overview of Federal Housing Assistance Programs ISBN: 978-1-61122-419-1
Editor: Brandon C. Sherman © 2011 Nova Science Publishers, Inc.

Chapter 5

AN OVERVIEW OF THE SECTION 8 HOUSING PROGRAMS

Maggie McCarty

SUMMARY

The Section 8 low-income housing program is really two programs: the voucher program and the project-based Section 8 program. Vouchers are portable subsidies that low-income families can use to lower their rents in the private market. Vouchers are administered at the local level by quasi-governmental public housing authorities (PHAs). Project-based Section 8 is a form of rental subsidy that is attached to a unit of privately owned housing. Low-income families who move into the housing pay a reduced rent, on the basis of their incomes.

The Section 8 program began in 1974, primarily as a project-based rental assistance program. However, by the mid-1980s, project-based assistance came under criticism for seeming too costly and concentrating poor families in high- poverty areas. Congress stopped providing new project-based Section 8 contracts in 1983. In their place, Congress created vouchers as a new form of assistance. Today, vouchers — numbering more than 2 million — are the primary form of assistance provided under Section 8, although over 1 million units still receive project-based assistance under their original contracts or renewals of those contracts.

Congressional interest in the Section 8 program has increased in recent years, particularly as the program costs have rapidly grown, led by cost increases in the voucher program. In order to understand why costs are rising so quickly, it is important to first understand how the program works and its history. This report presents a brief overview of that history and introduces the reader to the program. For more information, see CRS Report RL33929, *Recent Changes to the Section 8 Voucher Renewal Funding Formula*; CRS Report RL34002, *Section 8 Housing Choice Voucher Program: Issues and Reform Proposals in the 110th Congress*; and CRS Congressional Distribution Memorandum, *Factors Behind Cost Increases in the Section 8 Housing Choice Voucher Program, FY2000-FY2004*, all by Maggie McCarty.

This report will be updated as warranted.

INTRODUCTION

The rental assistance programs authorized under Section 8 of the United States Housing Act of 1937 (42 U.S.C. § 1437f) — Section 8 project-based rental assistance and tenant-based vouchers — have become the largest component of the Department of Housing and Urban Development's (HUD) budget, with appropriations of more than $22 billion in FY2008. The rising cost of providing rental assistance is due, in varying degrees, to expansions in the program, the cost of renewing expiring longterm contracts, and rising costs in housing markets across the country. The most rapid cost increases have been seen in the voucher program.

Partly out of concern about cost increases, and partly in response to the administrative complexity of the current program, the Administration has called for reform of the voucher program and its funding each year since 2002. In response, Congress has enacted changes to the way that it funds the voucher program and the way that PHAs receive their funding. Congress has not enacted the program reforms advocated by the Administration, although it has considered its own reform proposals.

In order to understand why the program has become so expensive and why reforms are being considered, it is first important to understand the mechanics of the program and its history. This paper will provide an overview of the Section 8 program and its history. For more information, see CRS Report RL33929, *Recent Changes to the Section 8 Voucher Renewal Funding Formula*; CRS Report RL34002, *Section 8 Housing Choice Voucher Program: Issues and Reform Proposals in the 110th Congress*; and CRS Congressional Distribution Memorandum, *Factors Behind Cost Increases in the Section 8 Housing Choice Voucher Program, FY2000-FY2004*, all by Maggie McCarty.

Background Information

From 1937 until 1965, public housing and the subsidized mortgage insurance programs of the Federal Housing Administration (FHA) were the country's main forms of federal housing assistance. As problems with the public housing and other bricks and mortar federal housing construction programs (such as Section 235 and Section 236 of the National Housing Act) arose — particularly their high cost — interest grew in alternative forms of housing assistance. In 1965, a new approach was adopted (P.L. 89-117). The Section 23 program assisted low-income families residing in leased housing by permitting a public housing authority (PHA)[1] to lease existing housing units in the private market and sublease them to low-income and very low-income families[2] at below-market rents. However, the Section 23 program did not ameliorate the growing problems with HUD's housing construction programs and interest remained in developing and testing new approaches. The Experimental Housing Allowance Program is one example of such an alternative approach.

Table 1. The Experimental Housing Allowance Program.

The Experimental Housing Allowance Program (EHAP) began with a mandate to HUD from Congress in 1970 to test the impacts and feasibility of providing low-income families with allowances to assist them in obtaining existing, decent rental housing of their choice (P.L. 91-152). Congress was interested specifically in finding the answers to several key questions:

- How many families would make use of allowance payments?
- What kind of housing would they choose and in what neighborhoods?
- How would housing markets respond to the increased demand for housing?
- At what cost could a housing allowance program be administered?

In order to answer these questions, HUD contracted for the conduct of three experiments: the *Demand Experiment* to test how families would respond to a housing allowance, the *Supply Experiment*, to test how markets would respond to subsidies and the *Administrative Agency Experiment*, to test the administrative capacity and funds required to administer a housing allowance program. The first reports came out in 1973, and a final report was issued in 1980. The EHAP's key findings are listed below:

- In order to ensure housing quality, subsidies have to be tied to housing standards; however, stricter housing standards limit participation. Participation is also linked to subsidy amount; as the subsidy increases, so does participation.
- Mobility and location of residence are mainly governed by ties to relatives, neighbors, and friends and are not affected by housing allowance payments.
- A housing allowance program has virtually no effect on the price of housing and does not stimulate new construction or major rehabilitation. However, it does help preserve the existing housing stock by stimulating repairs.
- A housing allowance program can be effectively administered at the local level.

The early findings of EHAP helped to set the tone for the debate that created the Section 8 program.

(Raymond Struyk, "Policy Questions and Experimental Responses," in *Housing Vouchers for the Poor: Lessons from a National Experiment*, edited by Raymond Struyk and Marc Bendick Jr. [Washington: Urban Institute Press, 1981].)

Due to criticisms about cost, profiteering, and slumlord practices in federal housing programs, President Nixon declared a moratorium on all existing federal housing programs, including Section 23, in 1973. During the moratorium, HUD revised the Section 23 program and sought to make it the main assisted housing program of the federal government. However, at the same time, Congress was considering several options for restructuring subsidized housing programs. After all the debates and discussions that typically precede the passage of authorizing legislation were completed, Congress voted in favor of a new leased housing approach, and the Section 8 program was created.

EARLY SECTION 8

The Section 8 program is named for Section 8 of the United States Housing Act of 1937. The original program, established by the Housing and Community Development Act of 1974 (P.L. 93-383), consisted of three parts: new construction, substantial rehabilitation, and existing housing certificates. The 1974 Act and the creation of Section 8 effectively ended the Nixon moratorium. In 1978, the moderate rehabilitation component of the program was added, but it has not been funded since 1989. In 1983, the new construction and substantial rehabilitation portions of the program were repealed, and a new component — Section 8 vouchers — was added. In 1998, existing housing certificates were merged with and converted to vouchers.

New Construction and Substantial Rehabilitation

Under the new construction and substantial rehabilitation components of the early Section 8 program, HUD entered into long-term (20- or 40-year) contracts with private for-profit, non-profit, or public organizations that were willing to construct new units or rehabilitate older ones to house low- and very low-income tenants. Under those contracts, HUD agreed to make assistance payments toward each unit for the duration of the contract. Those assistance payments were subsidies that allowed tenants residing in the units to pay 25% (later raised to 30%) of their adjusted income as rent. The program was responsible for the construction and rehabilitation of a large number of units. Over 1.2 million units of housing with Section 8 contracts that originated under the new construction and substantial rehabilitation program still receive payments today.

By the early 1980s, because of the rising costs of rent and construction, the amount of budget authority needed for the Section 8 rental assistance program had been steadily increasing while the number of units produced in a year had been decreasing. At the same time, studies emerged showing that providing subsidies for use in newly constructed or substantially rehabilitated housing was more expensive than the cost of providing subsidies in existing units of housing. Also, because contracts were written for such long terms, appropriators had to provide large amounts of budget authority each time they funded a new contract (see below for an illustration of the implication of long-term contracts). As the budget deficit grew, Members of Congress became concerned with the high costs associated with Section 8 new construction and substantial rehabilitation, and these segments of the Section 8 program were repealed in the Housing and Urban-Rural Recovery Act of 1983 (P.L. 98-181).

Moderate Rehabilitation

The Housing and Community Development Amendments of 1978 (P.L. 95-557) added the moderate rehabilitation component to the Section 8 program, which expanded Section 8 rental assistance to projects that were in need of repairs costing at least $1,000 per unit to make the housing decent, safe, and sanitary. Over the next 10 years, however, this component of the program was fraught with allegations of abuse; the process of awarding contracts was considered unfair and politicized. Calls for reform of the moderate rehabilitation program led to its suspension. It has not been funded since 1989.

Existing Housing Certificates

The existing housing certificate component of the Section 8 program was created in the beginning of the Section 8 program and continued until 1998. Under the existing housing certificate program, PHAs and HUD would enter into an Annual Contributions Contract (ACC) for the number of units that would be available to receive assistance. Contracts were originally written for five years and were renewable, at HUD's discretion, for up to 15 years. In the contract, HUD agreed to pay the difference between the tenant's rental payment and the contract rent of a unit. The contract rent was generally limited to the HUD-set Fair Market Rent (FMR) for the area.

Table 2. What Do Long Term Contracts Mean for Congress?

The following example illustrates how Congress appropriates funds for long-term contracts, compared to one-year contracts.

In 2003, a housing subsidy cost an average of $6,000 per year. If Congress wanted to fund 10 new Section 8 subsidies in 2003, the cost of doing so would depend on the length of the contract Congress decided to fund:

If the contract was a **40-year** contract, as was the case in the beginning of the Section 8 program, then Congress must appropriate:

$$10 \text{ vouchers} \times \$6,000 \times 40 \text{ years} = \textbf{\$2.4 million.}*$$

If the contract was a **one-year** contract, as is the case with Section 8 contracts today, then Congress must appropriate:

$$10 \text{ vouchers} \times \$6,000 \times 1 \text{ year} = \textbf{\$60,000.}$$

Thus, it would have cost Congress less in 2003 to provide one year contracts than it would have to provide multiyear contracts. The trade-off is the cost in subsequent years. For example, assume that Congress intends to maintain those 10 subsidies in 2004. If Congress funded those subsidies under 40-year contracts in 2003, then the subsidies would not require new funding again until 2043, meaning Congress would not have to provide appropriations in 2004; however, if Congress funded those subsidies under one-year contracts in 2003, then the subsidies would require another year's worth of funds in 2004.

* Note, this example does not include an estimate for inflation. When funding multi-year contracts, Congress generally includes an estimate of inflation and adds it to the total cost.

Table 3. What is Fair Market Rent (FMR)?

FMRs are gross rent estimates that include both shelter rent paid by the tenant to the landlord and the cost of tenant-paid utilities, except telephones. Each year, HUD sets FMRs either at the 40th percentile rent or at the 50th percentile rent for each metropolitan or non-metropolitan statistical area in the nation, as well as for each state. For most areas, the FMR is set at the 40th percentile rent paid by recent movers, which means that 40% of all standard quality rental housing units rented within the past 18 months have rents at or below the FMR. For some high cost areas, the FMR is set at the 50th percentile rent or the median rent, so that 50% of standard units fall at or below the FMR. In some low-cost communities, the FMR is raised to the statewide FMR, if it is higher.

After entering into a contract with HUD, PHAs would advertise the availability of certificates for low-income tenants. The existing housing certificate program was primarily tenant-based, meaning that the assistance was attached to the tenant. Families selected to receive assistance were given certificates as proof of eligibility for the program; with their certificates, families could look for suitable housing in the private market. Housing was considered suitable if it rented for the FMR or less and met Housing Quality Standards (HQS).[3] Once the household found a unit, they signed a lease and agreed to pay 30% of their adjusted income for rent. The remainder of the rent was paid by HUD to the landlord on behalf of the tenant. If a family vacated a unit in violation of the lease, HUD had to make rental payments to the landlord for the remainder of the month in which the family vacated, and pay 80% of the contract rent for an additional month. If the family left the unit at the end of their lease, they could take their certificate with them and use it for their next home. HUD also paid the PHA an administrative fee for managing the program. The amount of this administrative fee was set by Congress in appropriations legislation each year.

PHAs were permitted to use up to 15% of their Section 8 certificates for project-based housing. In project-based Section 8 existing housing, the subsidy was attached to the unit, which was selected by the PHA, and not to the tenant. This meant that when a tenant vacated a unit, another eligible tenant would be able to occupy it, and HUD would subsidize the rent as long as a contract was in effect between the PHA and the owner.

In 1998, the Quality Housing and Work Opportunity Reconciliation Act (QHWRA) (P.L. 105-276) merged the Section 8 existing housing certificate program with the voucher program (see below) and converted all certificates to vouchers, effectively ending the Section 8 existing housing certificate program.

The Voucher Program

The largest component of today's Section 8 program, the voucher program, was first authorized by the Housing and Urban-Rural Recovery Act of 1983 (P.L. 98-181). It was originally a demonstration program, but was made permanent in 1988. Like the Section 8 existing housing certificate program, the voucher program is administered by PHAs and is tenant-based, with a project-based component. However, under the voucher program, families can pay more of their incomes toward rent and lease apartments with rents higher than FMR.

TODAY'S SECTION 8 PROGRAM

Today's Section 8 program is really two programs, which, combined, serve almost 3.5 million households.

Section 8 Project-Based Rental Assistance

The first program under Section 8 can be characterized as Section 8 project- based rental assistance. This program includes units created under the new construction, substantial rehabilitation, and moderate rehabilitation components of the earlier Section 8 program that are still under contract with HUD. Although no new construction, substantial rehabilitation, or moderate rehabilitation contracts have been created for a number of years, about 1.3 million of these units are still funded under multiyear contracts that have not yet expired and do not require any new appropriations, or multiyear contracts that had expired and are renewed annually, requiring new appropriations.

Families that live in Section 8 project-based units pay 30% of their incomes toward rent. In order to be eligible, families must be low-income; however, at least 40% of all units must be available for very low-income families. If a family leaves the unit, the owner will continue to receive payments as long as he or she can move another eligible family into the unit.

Owners of properties with project-based Section 8 rental assistance receive a subsidy from HUD, called a Housing Assistance Payment (HAP). HAP payments are equal to the difference between the tenant's payments (30% of income) and a contract rent, which is agreed to between HUD and the landlord. Contract rents are meant to be comparable to rents in the local market, and are typically adjusted annually by an inflation factor established by HUD or on the basis of the project's operating costs. Project-based Section 8 contracts are managed by contract administrators. While some HUD regional offices still serve as contract administrators, the Department's goal is to contract the function out entirely to outside entities, including state housing finance agencies, PHAs, or private entities.

When project-based HAP contracts expire, the landlord can choose to either renew the contract with HUD for up to five years at a time (subject to annual appropriations) or convert the units to market rate. In some cases, landlords can choose to "opt-out" of Section 8 contracts early. When an owners terminates an HAP contract with HUD, either through opt-out or expiration — the tenants in the building are provided with enhanced vouchers designed to allow them to stay in their unit (see discussion of enhanced vouchers below). In 2008, about 4,000 Section 8 project- based rental assistance contracts were expected to expire; it is unclear how many will choose to renew.

In 2000, about 60% of the households that lived in project-based Section 8 units were elderly households, about 15% were disabled households, and about 21% were non-elderly, non-disabled households with children. Of the non-elderly, non-disabled households (including the approximately 5% who did not have children), about half received income solely from work, about 16% received income solely from welfare, about 10% combined work and welfare, and about 20% reported no income or income from other sources (such as child support). The average earnings of the non- elderly, non-disabled households were a little more than $11,000 per year.[4]

Section 8 Tenant-Based Housing Choice Vouchers

When QHWRA merged the voucher and certificate programs in 1998, it renamed the voucher component of the Section 8 program the Housing Choice Voucher program. The voucher program is funded in HUD's budget through the tenant-based rental assistance account. The federal government currently funds more than 2 million Section 8 Housing Choice Vouchers. PHAs administer the program and receive an annual budget from HUD. Each has a fixed number of vouchers that they are permitted to administered and they are paid administrative fees.

Table 4. Income Thresholds for a Three-Person Family in Selected Areas in 2007.

	HUD Very Low-Income Limits	Hud Extremely Low-Income Limits	HHS Poverty Guidelines
Jefferson County, MS	$17,450	$10,500	$17,170
Missoula, MT	24,550	14,700	17,170
New York, NY	31,900	19,150	17,170
San Francisco, CA	50,900	30,550	17,170

Source: Department of Housing and Urban Development 2007 Income Limits and Department of Health and Human Services 2007 Poverty Guidelines.

Vouchers are tenant-based in nature, meaning that the subsidy is tied to the family, rather than to a unit of housing. In order to be eligible, a family must be very low-income (50% or below area median income (AMI)),[5] although 75% of all vouchers must be given to extremely low-income families (30% or below AMI). To illustrate the regional variation in these definitions of low-income and their relationship to federal definitions of poverty, **Table 1** compares HUD's income definitions to the Department of Health and Human Service's (HHS) poverty guidelines for several geographic areas. Note that HHS poverty guidelines are uniform in all parts of the country (except for Alaska and Hawaii, not shown in the following table).

Families who receive vouchers use them to subsidize their rents in private market apartments. Once an eligible family receives an available voucher, the family must find an eligible unit. In order to be eligible, a unit must meet minimum housing quality standards (HQS) and cost less than 40% of the family's income[6] plus the HAP paid by the PHA. The HAP paid by the PHA for tenant-based vouchers, like the HAP paid for Section 8 project-based rental assistance, is capped; however, with tenant-based vouchers, PHAs have the flexibility to set their caps anywhere between 90% and 110% of FMR (up to 120% FMR with prior HUD approval). The cap set by the PHA is called the payment standard. Once a family finds an eligible unit, the family signs a contract with HUD, and both HUD and the family sign contracts with the landlord. The PHA will pay the HAP (the payment standard minus 30% of the family's income), and the family will pay the difference between the HAP and the rent (which must total between 30% and 40% of the family's income). After the first year, a family can choose to pay more than 40% of their income towards rent. PHAs may also choose to adopt minimum rents, which cannot exceed $50. (See box below for an example.)

Once a family is using a voucher, the family can retain the voucher as long as the PHA has adequate funding for it and the family complies with PHA and program requirements. If a family wants to move, the tenant-based voucher can move with the family. Once the family moves to a new area, the two PHAs (the PHA that originally issued the voucher and the PHA that administers vouchers in the new area) negotiate regarding who will continue to administer the voucher.[7]

The voucher program does not contain any mandatory time limits. Families exit the program in one of three ways: their own choice, non-compliance with program rules (including non-payment of rent), or if they no longer qualify for a subsidy. Families no longer qualify for a subsidy when their incomes, which must be recertified annually, have risen to the point that 30% of that income is equal to rent. At that point the HAP payment will be zero and the family will no longer receive any subsidy.

Table 5. How is a Voucher Subsidy Calculated?

First, a PHA sets a payment standard. A payment standard is a maximum subsidy level that is equal to anywhere between 90% and 110% of Fair Market Rent (FMR). Then, a PHA calculates a maximum Housing Assistance Payment (HAP). A HAP is the amount that the PHA will pay the landlord and it is equal to the greater of the rent for an apartment or the payment standard, minus 30% of a family's income. The family can then go out to the rental market and find an apartment. In order to be approved that apartment cannot rent for more than the maximum HAP plus 40% of a family's income. If the rent for the unit is less than the HAP plus 30% of a household's income, the household must still pay 30% of their income toward rent, but the HAP will be reduced.

For example, consider a family who earns $900 per month and lives in a community with an FMR of $800 per month for the appropriate size apartment. If their PHA has a payment standard of 110% of FMR, then the maximum HAP a family can receive is $610 per month [($800 * 110%) - ($900 * 3 0%)]. The family can therefore shop for an apartment with a rent of up to $970 per month [$610 + ($900 * 40%)].

If the family finds an apartment for $970 per month, the PHA will pay the maximum HAP ($610) and the family will pay 40% of their income per month ($360).

If the family finds an apartment for less than the payment standard, say $750 per month, the family will pay 30% of their income toward rent, and the PHA will pay the difference between the rent and 30% of the family's income. In this case, the family will pay $270 [$900 * 30%] and the PHA will pay $480 [$750 - (900 * 30%)].

In 2000, about 17% of households with vouchers were elderly households, about 22% were disabled households, and about 53% were non-elderly, non-disabled households with children. Of the non-elderly, non-disabled households (including the approximately 8% that did not have children), about half received their income solely from work, about 20% received their income solely from welfare, about 6% combined work and welfare, and about 22% reported no income or income from other sources (such as child support). The average earnings of the non-elderly, non- disabled households were a little more than $12,000 per year.[8]

Project-Based Vouchers

Vouchers, like Section 8 existing housing certificates, can be project-based. In order to project-base vouchers, a landlord must sign a contract with a PHA agreeing to set-aside up to 25% of the units in a development for low-income families. Each of those set-aside units will receive voucher assistance as long as a family that is eligible for a voucher lives there. Families that live in a project-based voucher unit pay 30% of their adjusted household income toward rent, and HUD pays the difference between 30% of household income and a reasonable rent agreed to by both the landlord and HUD. PHAs can choose to project-base up to 20% of their vouchers. Project-based vouchers a portable; after one year, a family with a project-based voucher can convert to a tenant-based voucher and then move, as long as a tenant-based voucher is available.

Tenant Protection or Enhanced Vouchers

Another type of voucher, called a tenant protection voucher, is given to families that were already receiving assistance through another HUD housing program, before being displaced. Examples of instances when families receive tenant-protection vouchers include when public housing is demolished or when a landlord has terminated a Section 8 project-based rental assistance contract. Families that risk being displaced from project-based Section 8 units are eligible to receive a special form of tenant-protection voucher, called an enhanced voucher. The "enhanced" feature of the voucher allows the maximum value of the voucher to grow to be equal to the new rent charged in the property, as long as it is reasonable in the market, even if it is higher than the PHA's payment standard. They are designed to allow families to stay in their homes. If the family chooses to move, then the enhanced feature is lost and the voucher becomes subject to the PHA's normal payment standard.

Special Purpose Vouchers

The voucher program also has several special programs or uses. These include family unification vouchers and vouchers used for homeownership. Family unification vouchers are given to families for whom the lack of adequate housing is a primary factor in the separation, or threat of imminent separation, of children from their families or in preventing the reunification of the children with their families. According to the Child Welfare League of America, HUD has awarded 33,497 family unification vouchers to PHAs since the inception of the program.[9]

While there are no specifically authorized "homeownership vouchers," since 2000 certain families have been eligible to use their vouchers to help pay for the monthly costs associated with homeownership. Eligible families must work full-time or be elderly or disabled, be first-time homebuyers, and agree to complete first-time homebuyer counseling. PHAs can decide whether to run a homeownership program and an increasing number of PHAs are choosing to do so. According to HUD's website, more than 5,700 families have closed on homes using vouchers.[10]

Family Self-Sufficiency Coordinators

The Family Self Sufficiency (FSS) program was established by Congress as a part of the National Affordable Housing Act of 1990 (P.L. 101-625). The purpose of the program is to promote coordination between the voucher program and other private and public resources to enable families on public assistance to achieve economic self-sufficiency. Families who participate in the program sign five-year contracts in which they agree to work toward leaving public assistance. While in the program, families can increase their incomes without increasing the amount they contribute toward rent. The difference between what the family paid in rent before joining the program and what they would owe as their income increases is deposited into an escrow account that the family can access upon completion of the contract. For example:

> If a family with a welfare benefit of $450 per month begins working, earning $800 per month, the family's contribution towards rent increases from $135 per month to $240 per month. Of that $240 the family is now paying towards rent, $105 is deposited into an escrow account. After five years, the family will have $6,300 plus interest in an escrow account to use for whatever purpose the family sees fit.

PHAs receive funding for FSS coordinators, who help families with vouchers connect with services, including job training, child care, transportation and education.

Demonstrations

Two large-scale demonstrations are currently under way in the Section 8 voucher program. The Moving to Opportunity Fair Housing Demonstration (MTO) was authorized in 1992 (P.L. 102-550, P.L. 102-139). MTO combines housing counseling and services with tenant-based vouchers to help very low-income families with children move to areas with low concentrations of poverty. The experimental demonstration was designed to test the premise that changes in an individual's neighborhood environment can change his or her life chances. Since participating families were selected between 1994 and 1998, the full results of the 10-year demonstration are not yet available. However, HUD has published several interim evaluations of the short- and mid-term impacts of MTO. They have found some improvements in housing quality, neighborhood conditions, safety and child and adult health for families that moved to lower-poverty areas. Mixed effects were found on youth delinquency and risky behavior. Small positive impacts were found on child education, but no impacts have yet been seen on employment, earnings, or receipt of public assistance.[11]

The Moving to Work Demonstration, authorized in 1996 (P.L. 104-134), was created to give HUD and PHAs the flexibility to design and test various approaches for providing and administering housing assistance. The demonstration directed HUD to select up to 30 PHAs to participate. The goals were to reduce federal costs, provide work incentives to families, and expand housing choice. MTW allows participating PHAs greater flexibility in determining how to use federal Section 8 voucher and Public Housing funds by allowing them to blend funding sources and experiment with rent rules, with the constraint that they had to continue to serve approximately the same number of households. It also permits them to seek exemption from most Public Housing and Housing Choice Voucher program rules. An evaluation for MTW published in January 2004 reported:

> The local flexibility and independence permitted under MTW appears to allow strong, creative [P]HAs to experiment with innovative solutions to local challenges, and to be more responsive to local conditions and priorities than is often possible where federal program requirements limit the opportunity for variation. But allowing local variation poses risks as well as provides potential benefits. Under MTW, some [P]HAs, for instance, made mistakes that reduced the resources available to address low-income housing needs, and some implemented changes that disadvantaged particular groups of needy households currently served under federal program rules. Moreover, some may object to the likelihood that allowing significant variation across [P]HAs inevitably results in some loss of consistency across communities.[12]

CONCLUSION

The combined Section 8 programs are the largest direct housing assistance program for low-income families. With a combined FY2008 budget of more than $22 billion, they reflect a major commitment of federal resources. That commitment has led to some successes. More than 3 million families are able to obtain safe and decent housing through the program, at a cost to the family that is considered affordable. However, these successes come at a high cost to the federal government. Given current budget deficit levels, Congress has begun to reevaluate whether the cost of the Section 8 programs, particularly the voucher program, are worth their benefits. Proposals to reform the program abound, and whether the current Section 8 programs are maintained largely in their current form, changed substantially, or eliminated altogether are questions currently facing Congress.

End Notes

[1] PHAs are state-chartered, quasi-governmental bodies that administer public housing and Section 8 vouchers.

[2] HUD uses a relative measure of income for determining benefits and eligibility for Section 8. "Low-income families" have adjusted gross incomes at or below 80% of the local area median income; "very low-income" families have adjusted gross incomes at or below 50% of the local area median income; and "extremely low-income" families have adjusted gross incomes at or below 30% of the local area median income

[3] Housing Quality Standards (HQS) are minimum standards set by HUD that set acceptable conditions for interior living space, building exterior, heating and plumbing systems, and general health and safety.

[4] CRS calculation of data in Jeffrey M. Lubell, Mark Shroder, Barry Steffen, "Work Participation and Length of Stay in HUD-Assisted Housing," *Cityscape*, vol. 6, no. 2 (2003).

[5] In some limited circumstances, families can earn up to 80% of AMI and still be eligible.

[6] This 40% cap on a tenant's contribution is in effect only for the first year. After the first year, if rent increases and the family wishes to continue to live in the unit, then the family can choose to contribute more than 40% of its income toward rent.

[7] The feature of a voucher that permits a family to move from one jurisdiction to another while retaining their assistance is referred to as portability. The administration of portability has proven to be complicated for PHAs. In some cases, the originating PHA is billed for the cost of the family's voucher by the receiving PHA; in other cases, the receiving PHA transitions the new family onto one if its vouchers and the original voucher reverts to the originating PHA. PHA advocacy groups have called for HUD to make regulatory reforms to ease the administration of portability.

[8] CRS calculation of data in Jeffrey M. Lubell, Mark Shroder, Barry Steffen, "Work Participation and Length of Stay in HUD-Assisted Housing," *Cityscape*, vol. 6, no. 2 (2003).

[9] HUD awarded 33,497 FUP vouchers from 1992 to 2001. Each award included five years of funding per voucher and the voucher's use was restricted to FUP-eligible families for those five years. At the end of those five years, PHAs were eligible to convert those FUP vouchers to regular vouchers. While the five-year use restrictions have expired for all FUP vouchers, according to surveys conducted by the Child Welfare League of America, the vast majority of PHAs have continued to use their original FUP vouchers for FUP-eligible families and some have even chosen to use some regular-purpose vouchers for FUP families. As a result of these two factors, it is unclear how many families are receiving FUP vouchers at this time.

[10] http://www.hud.gov/offices/pih/programs/hcv/homeownership/publiclist_vhosites.xls], accessed January 4, 2007.

[11] *Moving to Opportunity Fair Housing Demonstration Program Interim Impacts Evaluation, US Department of Housing and Urban Development*, Prepared by Larry Orr, et al., Abt Associates; and Lisa Sanbonmatsu, et al., National Bureau of Economic Research, September 2003.

[12] *Housing Agency Responses to Federal Deregulation: An Assessment of HUD's "Moving to Work" Demonstration*, U.S. Department of Housing and Urban Development, Prepared by Martin D. Abravanel et al., Urban Institute, January 2004.

In: An Overview of Federal Housing Assistance Programs   ISBN: 978-1-61122-419-1
Editor: Brandon C. Sherman   © 2011 Nova Science Publishers, Inc.

Chapter 6

RECENT CHANGES TO THE SECTION 8 VOUCHER RENEWAL FUNDING FORMULA

Maggie McCarty

SUMMARY

Changes enacted by Congress during the appropriations process in each of the past several years have significantly altered the way that public housing authorities (PHAs) receive funding to administer the Section 8 Housing Choice Voucher program. Prior to FY2003, PHAs received funding for each voucher they were authorized to administer, based on their average costs from the previous year, plus inflation, referred to as "unit-based" funding. Most PHAs were not using all of their vouchers, due in part to rental market conditions, and each year the Department of Housing and Urban Development (HUD) was able to recapture unspent funds. In FY2001 and FY2002, some Members of Congress began expressing concern about the underutilization of vouchers and the amount of recaptures.

Beginning in FY2003, and culminating in FY2006, Congress fundamentally changed the way PHAs received voucher funding. The changes were designed to limit the amount of unspent funds held by PHAs and limit the cost of vouchers, which had begun to grow rapidly in 2001 and 2002, due in part to market changes and in part to policy changes. In FY2006, PHAs were funded based on the amount of funding they had received in the previous year (regardless of changes in their costs and utilization), plus an inflation adjustment, prorated to fit within the amount appropriated. Under this formula, the funding needs of the program became more predictable, but some agencies received more funding than they were legally permitted to spend, while other agencies did not receive enough funding for all of the vouchers they were authorized to administer. The Bush Administration supported this conversion to a "budget-based" formula and requested that Congress enact permanent reforms to complement the new funding method. Low-income housing advocates and PHA industry groups generally opposed both the funding changes and the Bush Administration's proposed policy reforms.

In FY2007, after Democrats gained control of the Congress, Congress again changed the funding formula through the appropriations process. PHA funding was based on what they were spending in the previous year (rather than what they had been allocated in the previous year). As a result, PHAs that had not been spending all of their funding in FY2006 saw a reduction in funding in FY2007. Nonetheless, the funding provided was sufficient so that all PHAs received more than 100% of their 2006 costs and utilization. In FY2008 and FY2009, Congress adopted a cost and utilization-based formula similar to FY2007, but with a reduction in funding for PHAs with excess unspent funding in reserve. In FY2009, concerns were raised about how the implementation of the FY2009 formula may have left some PHAs without sufficient funding to continue serving all eligible families. Ultimately, Congress provided HUD with access to additional funding to help address shortfalls that could have resulted in families losing assistance. In FY2010, Congress again adopted a cost and utilization-based formula, a hybrid of the "unit- based" and "budget-based" models, but without a reduction for excess reserves.

During the period of "budget-based" funding formulas, utilization of both authorized vouchers and of available funding declined. Since the adoption of a cost and utilization-based funding model, utilization has begun to increase again. As utilization increases, the cost of the program to Congress increases. This presents a set of policy tradeoffs between the goal of cost containment and the goal of serving as many eligible families as possible. The Section 8 voucher renewal funding formula continues to be a source of debate in the annual appropriations cycle, as well as in Section 8 voucher reform bills, which have contained proposals for statutory formula changes. This report describes changes in the formula included in appropriations bills for FY2003 to the present. It will be updated to reflect further enacted legislation.

INTRODUCTION

Each year, Congress provides funding to the Department of Housing and Urban Development (HUD) to renew the more than 2.1 million Section 8 vouchers—also called Housing Choice Vouchers—authorized by Congress (see **Table 1** below). The Section 8 voucher program is federally funded and governed by federal rules, but is administered at the local level by quasi- governmental public housing authorities (PHAs). Section 8 vouchers are rental subsidies that low-income families use in the private market to help make up the difference between their rent and their expected contribution toward that rent (30% of adjusted income). The cost of a voucher to a PHA is the difference between the lesser of a tenant's actual rent or the maximum subsidy level set by the PHA—called a payment standard—and 30% of a tenant's income. That cost increases or decreases with changes in tenant incomes and changes in rents and payment standards. (For more information on Section 8 voucher reform proposals, see CRS Report RL34002, *Section 8 Housing Choice Voucher Program: Issues and Reform Proposals*, by Maggie McCarty.)

In recent years, Congress has enacted, and HUD has implemented, a series of changes in the way that voucher renewal funding is distributed to local PHAs. These changes have led to funding uncertainty for many PHAs, and has put pressure on Congress to adopt a permanent funding formula, possibly through enactment of Section 8 voucher reform legislation.

Table 1. Section 8 Voucher Renewal Funding,
FY2003-CY2010 (in billions of dollars).

	FY 2003[a]	FY 2004[a]	CY 2005[b]	CY 2006[b]	CY 2007[b]	CY 2008[b]	CY 2009[b]	CY 2010[b]
Renewal Funding	11.106	12.721	13.355	13.949	14.436	13.972[c]	14.284[d]	16.339

Source: Table prepared by CRS. Figures are derived from HUD budget documents. For more details, see CRS Appropriations Reports. Central Reserve funding, where applicable, is included. Amounts are not reduced for rescissions in prior year unobligated balances, but are reduced for rescissions from renewal funding.

a. HUD did not track separate budget authority for tenant-based and project-based rental assistance prior to FY2005. These figures come from a table provided on page 21 of H.Rept. 108-674.

b. Beginning in FY2005, the amount provided for renewals is allocated to PHAs on a calendar year basis, rather than a federal fiscal year basis.

c. The FY2008 appropriations act provided $ 14.695 billion for renewal funding in FY2008, but also rescinded $723 million in renewal funding available for FY2008. The amount shown here is reduced for the rescission. It is assumed that an amount equivalent to the amount rescinded was available from reserves for purposes of voucher renewals, meaning that a full $1 4.695 billion was available for renewals in CY2008.

d. The FY2009 appropriations act provided $ 15.034 billion for renewal funding in FY2009, but also rescinded $750 million in renewal funding available for FY2009. The amount shown here is reduced for the rescission. It is assumed that an amount equivalent to the amount rescinded was available from reserves for purposes of voucher renewals, meaning that a full $1 5.034 billion was available for renewals in CY2008.

This report discusses the renewal funding formula changes that Congress has enacted as a part of the annual appropriations process, starting in FY2003, and concludes with a discussion of their effects.

PRE-FY2003 FUNDING

Prior to FY2003,[1] PHAs administering the voucher program were funded based on their average annual per-voucher cost from the previous year, adjusted by an inflation factor and multiplied by the number of vouchers that the PHA was authorized to lease.[2] Each PHA was provided with a reserve equal to one month of voucher funding that could be used in the event that a PHA's voucher costs increased faster than the inflation factor established by HUD. Despite the fact that they received full funding, few PHAs were able to lease 100% of their authorized vouchers.[3] Low utilization rates were a major concern of Congress for several years.[4] While PHAs are expected to have utilization rates of at least 95%,[5] in FY2000 and FY2001, national voucher utilization rates were just over 91%.[6] Since PHAs were not utilizing all of their vouchers, they typically had low budget utilization as well, meaning that they had more money in their budgets than they needed, and they rarely had to dip into their one-month program reserves, even if their costs rose significantly. At the end of the year, HUD and each PHA would reconcile their budgets, and HUD was typically able to recapture excess funds from PHAs' reserves.[7]

HUD generally used this same formula—last year's actual costs, plus an inflation, times the number of authorized vouchers—each year to determine how much funding to request from Congress for the renewal of tenant-based Section 8 vouchers. HUD would also make available to Congress for rescission those unused funds that the agency had recaptured from PHAs. The end result of this system *for PHAs* was that their funding increased along with their costs. If their costs dropped, they were permitted to use some of their excess funds to create new vouchers, a process called maximized leasing. The end result of this system *for Congress* was that each year it provided more funds for voucher renewals than PHAs could reasonably be expected to use, and then recaptured those unused funds the following year to offset the cost of that year's appropriation.

FY2003-FY2006: THE EMERGENCE OF "BUDGET-BASED" FUNDING

FY2003 Funding Changes

In FY2003, Congress changed the way PHAs were funded in an attempt to limit recaptures of unspent funds and provide funding levels that better reflected actual use. Since actual use of vouchers was lower than authorized use, this change reduced the amount of appropriations needed for the program. HUD was directed in the annual appropriations bill to fund PHAs based on their average annual per-voucher cost from the previous year, increased by the inflation factor, and multiplied by the number of vouchers the PHA could *reasonably be expected to lease in that year* (rather than the larger number of *authorized* vouchers). Specifically, the law stated,

> The Secretary shall renew expiring section 8 tenant-based annual contributions contracts for each public housing agency ... based on the total number of unit months which were under lease as reported on the most recent end-of-year financial statement submitted by the public housing agency to the Department, adjusted by such additional information submitted by the public housing agency ... regarding the total number of unit months under lease at the time of renewal of the annual contributions contract, and by applying an inflation factor based on local or regional factors to the actual per-unit cost as reported on such statement. (P.L. 108-7, Title II, Section (1))

HUD implemented this provision so that PHAs' budgets were based on their utilization rates and costs as reported on their end-of-the-year statements, *or more recent data*, if available. As stated in guidance released by HUD:

> Renewal calculations under the [Federal Fiscal Year] 2003 Appropriation will be based on the total number of unit months under lease and actual cost data, as reported on the PHA's most recent year-end settlement or as subsequently submitted to HUD by the PHA. Actual costs will be adjusted by applying the [Annual Adjustment Factors]. Expiring voucher funding increments will generally be renewed for terms of three months. The use of the most recent leasing and cost data and the short renewal terms will enable HUD to calculate funding more accurately than previous procedures allowed. (HUD Notice PIH 2003-23, Issued September 22, 2003)

Congress also created a Central Reserve fund to be used by the Secretary to replenish PHA one- month reserves in the event that PHAs had to use their reserves to cover the costs of increased utilization or increased per-voucher costs. The language of the law stated, in regard to the Central Reserve fund:

> The Secretary may use amounts made available in such fund, as necessary, for contract amendments resulting from a significant increase in the per-unit cost of vouchers or an increase in the total number of unit months under lease as compared to the per-unit cost or the total number of unit months provided for by the annual contributions contract. (P.L. 108- 7, Title II, Section (2))

Finally, the bill instituted restrictions on maximized leasing, stating that none of the funds provided in the act could be used to support more vouchers than a PHA was authorized to lease in a year. This presented problems for PHAs that were over-leased.[8] Many had to refrain from reissuing vouchers once families left the program in order to get their leasing back to their authorized level.

FY2004 Funding Changes

The FY2004 appropriations law continued in the direction of the FY2003 law, instructing HUD to fund PHAs based on actual utilization of vouchers—rather than on the total number of vouchers they were authorized to lease—and restricting the use of funds for maximized leasing. Moreover, the conference report that accompanied the FY2004 appropriations law stated that the conferees were concerned about "spiraling" cost increases in the voucher program and that they expected the Secretary to control costs.[9] As stated in the conference report:

> The conferees are aware that the Secretary has the administrative authority to control the rapidly rising costs of renewing expiring annual contributions contracts (ACC), including the budget-based[10] practice of renewing expiring ACCs, and expect the Secretary to utilize these tools. (H.Rept. 108-235, Title II)

The FY2004 appropriations language was changed from FY2003 to state:

> The Secretary shall renew expiring section 8 tenant based annual contributions contracts for each public housing agency ... based on the total number of unit months which were under lease as reported on the most recent end-of-year financial statement submitted by the public housing agency to the Department, or as adjusted by such additional information submitted by the public housing agency to the Secretary as of August 1, 2003 (subject to verification), and by applying an inflation factor based on local or regional factors to the actual per-unit cost. (P.L. 108-199, Title II, Section (1))

The FY2004 language also varied from the FY2003 language in terms of how the Central Reserve fund could be used: In FY2003, the Central Reserve fund could be used to replenish PHA reserves that had been depleted due to either increased utilization rates or increased costs. In FY2004, the Secretary could use Central Reserve funds only to replenish reserves depleted because of increased utilization, *not* increased costs:

> Language proposed by the House and Senate is not included to allow the Central Fund to also be used for increased per-unit costs as such costs have been reflected in the amount provided for renewals. (H.Rept. 108-401, Division G, Title II)

HUD issued a notice on April 22, 2004 (PIH 2004-7) implementing the FY2004 appropriations law. According to the notice, PHAs' budgets would be based on their utilization rates from their end-of-the-year statements, or more recent data if available, and costs as reported on their end-ofthe-year statements as of August 1, 2003, adjusted by the annual adjustment factor (AAF), *but not adjusted by more recent data, even if available.* The notice stated that PHAs could appeal to the Secretary only if they could document that *rental* costs in their areas had risen higher than the inflation factor adopted by HUD. The notice proved controversial. Some housing advocates contended that Congress gave HUD the authority to use a broader measure of inflation than the AAF, taking into account not just rental costs but also other changes in PHAs' costs, such as utility costs and changes in their tenant populations. The notice was not modified, and on August 31, 2004, HUD granted the appeals requests of 380 agencies out of approximately 400 that applied, distributing a total of $160 million from the Central Reserve. However, HUD did not necessarily provide the full level requested in each appeal.

FY2005 Funding Changes

The final FY2005 Consolidated Appropriations Act (P.L. 108-447) moved the program further in the direction of budget-based funding. It directed the Secretary to fund PHAs based on their voucher costs and utilization rates as of May-July 2004 plus the HUD-published AAF, adjusted for new tenant protection vouchers.[11] If a PHA's May-July data were not available, HUD was directed to fund the agency based on February-April 2004 data, or if these data were not available, to fund the PHA based on its most recently submitted year-end financial statement, as of March 31, 2004. If the amount provided in the law was insufficient to fund all PHA budgets under this formula, then the Secretary was directed to prorate agency budgets. According to the conference report (H.Rept. 108-792), PHAs were expected to manage their voucher programs within their budgets for CY2005, regardless of their actual costs. The report also stated that "HUD shall provide agencies with flexibility to adjust payment standards and portability policies as necessary to manage within their 2005 budgets." Agency reserves were reduced from the one- month to the one-week level and no Central Reserve was provided to replenish depleted reserves. Finally, the act continued the prohibition on maximized leasing.

The FY2005 appropriations act made another important change to the way that PHAs received their voucher renewal funding. Rather than funding PHAs for the federal fiscal year (October 1, 2004-September 30, 2005), the act funded PHAs for the calendar year (January 1, 2005-December 3, 2005). The accounting change allowed for some one-time budget authority savings in the appropriations process. As a result, PHAs had to alter the way in which they budget for their voucher programs to a calendar-year cycle.

HUD published guidance implementing these provisions on December 8, 2004 (HUD Notice PIH 2005-1). Agencies received notification of their preliminary budget levels on December 17, 2004. At that time, PHAs were directed to inform HUD of any data errors within 10 days (although the deadline was later extended). The appeals were limited to data errors; agencies were told that they could not appeal the actual formula used for calculating their budgets. The final calculations, including a final proration factor, were published on January 21, 2005. Agencies were funded generally at 4.03% less than their May-July 2004 actual cost and utilization levels, plus the 2005 AAF. This proration factor of just less than 96% was implemented because the funding amount provided by Congress for voucher renewals was not sufficient to fund agencies at 100% of their formula eligibility.

According to CRS analysis of HUD funding data, the median change in PHA renewal budgets from FY2004 to FY2005 was an increase of 0.17%. This number hides a wide variance; the change at the fifth percentile was a decrease of 12% and the change at the 95th percentile was an increase of 14%. On February 25, 2005, HUD published Notice PIH 2005-9, entitled "[PHA] Flexibility to Manage the Housing Choice Voucher Program in 2005." It identified administrative options available to PHAs to lower their costs in 2005. Suggestions included lowering payment standards; reducing utility assistance to families; restricting portability;[12] reviewing rents to ensure they are reasonable in the market; suspending the reissuance of vouchers when families leave the program; restricting bedroom sizes; instituting minimum rents; monitoring income eligibility more strictly; and terminating assistance to families due to insufficient funds.

FY2006 Funding Formula

The FY2006 HUD Appropriations Act (P.L. 109-115) distributed renewal funding using roughly the same formula as FY2005. HUD allocated renewal funds to PHAs based on the amount they were eligible to receive in CY2005 (prior to proration), plus inflation (using the AAF), adjusted for additional tenant protection vouchers or vouchers that were reserved for project-based use,[13] and prorated to fit within the amount appropriated. The act provided the Secretary with $45 million to adjust the budgets of agencies in two categories: (1) those for whom the May-July period used as the basis for CY2005 funding represented unusually low leasing or costs and who applied to the Secretary for an adjustment; and (2) those whose costs had risen due to unforeseen circumstances or portability billings. The prohibition on maximized leasing was retained in FY2006. HUD issued projected funding letters to all PHAs on January 19, 2006; PHAs were directed to respond with concerns by February 3, 2006. Again, the amount provided by Congress was insufficient to fund PHAs at their full CY2006 formula eligibility, so PHAs were funded at about 94% of their eligibility.

Implications of Changes, FY2003-FY2006

The changes enacted up through FY2006, particularly those enacted in FY2005 and FY2006, gave incentives to PHAs to reduce their costs. Those changes, partnered with a cooled rental housing market,[14] worked together to reverse the "spiraling" cost growth trend seen in 2003.[15] According to CRS analysis of data provided by the Congressional Budget Office, average annual per voucher costs remained flat from calendar year 2004 to calendar year 2005 and declined by about 1.5% from calendar year 2005 through September 2006. Utilization also declined, from a peak of over 98% in 2004 to around 90% as of September 2006.[16] This drop in utilization translated into nearly 100,000 fewer households receiving assistance in 2006 compared to 2004.[17] Most PHAs were not spending all of their funding and therefore had accumulated reserve funds. CRS analysis of HUD data indicated that PHAs had accumulated, on average, unspent balances of 10% of their budget authority from January 2005 though September 2006. Nationally, budget utilization dropped from a high of over 98% in 2003 and 2004 to under 92% in 2006.[18]

FY2007-PRESENT: A COST AND UTILIZATION-BASED FUNDING MODEL

FY2007 Funding Formula

In FY2007, the debate continued between a strictly "budget-based" funding formula, in which PHAs are given a fixed pot of funding in which to administer their programs (such as in FY2006), and a "unit-based" formula, in which PHAs are funded based on what they need to maintain a certain voucher level (such as pre-FY2003).

For FY2007, then-President Bush requested that Congress continue to fund the voucher program using a budget-based formula similar to the one adopted in FY2005 and FY2006. The thenPresident's budget also requested that Congress lift the prohibition on maximized leasing, noting that, in a budget-based funding environment, some PHAs may be receiving more funding than they are permitted to use. According to CRS analysis of HUD data, as of the end of September 2006, 168 PHAs (or about 7% of all PHAs), were at their cap on authorized vouchers, so had excess funding they were not permitted to use to serve additional families from their waiting lists.

In the final FY2007 appropriations law (P.L. 110-5), Congress rejected President Bush's proposal. Instead, the law adopted a formula based on how much funding PHAs were using (similar to the formula enacted in FY2004), rather than a formula based on how much funding PHAs had received in the previous year. Specifically, in FY2007, PHAs received funding based on their leasing and cost data from their most recent 12 months of reported data, adjusted for the first-time renewal of tenant protection and HOPE VI vouchers and vouchers reserved for project-based contracts, inflated by the AAF, and prorated to fit within the amount appropriated. The law included a central reserve fund which the Secretary could use (1) for adjustments for PHAs that experienced a significant increase in renewal costs resulting from unforeseen circumstances or from voucher portability; and (2) for adjustments for public housing agencies experiencing a significant decrease in voucher funding, due to the formula shift, that could result in a loss of voucher units. The act continued the prohibition on over-leasing.

P.L. 110-28, an emergency supplemental funding bill, later amended the formula to provide exceptions for three categories of PHAs. First, certain Hurricane Katrina-affected agencies were funded on the basis of the higher of what they would have received under the

FY2007 formula or what they received in FY2006. Second, agencies that would have lost funding under the FY2007 formula and had been placed under receivership within the prior 24 months were funded on the basis of the higher amount they received in FY2006. Third, agencies that spent more in FY2006 than their FY2006 allocations plus their unspent voucher and administrative fee balances were funded on the basis of what they received in FY2006.

Under the FY2007 formula change, PHAs (except for those noted above) were funded based on the amount of funding they were *using* in FY2006, rather than the amount of funding they *received* in FY2006. Those PHAs with higher costs and utilization rates relative to their FY2006 budgets did better under the FY2007 enacted formula than they would have done under President Bush's proposed formula; those PHAs with lower costs and utilization relative to their FY2006 budgets did worse. However, the funding provided was sufficient to fund all PHAs at more than 105% of their eligibility.[19] And, given that the eligibility was set on current usage, the amount provided should have been sufficient for agencies to continue to serve at least the same number of families and, in some cases more (as long as they were within their caps).

The FY2007 formula contained elements of both a unit-based funding formula and a budget- based funding formula. The formula was unit-based, in that PHAs' funding allocations were based, in part, on the number of vouchers they were using, and they were subject to caps in the number of vouchers they could use. The formula was also budget-based, in that PHAs were given a fixed budget in which to administer their programs.

FY2008 Funding Formula

Then-President Bush's FY2008 budget request again included a proposal for a strictly "budget-based" voucher funding formula, similar to the one requested in FY2007 and in place for FY2005 and FY2006. Specifically, he requested that agencies be funded in FY2008 based on what they were eligible to receive in calendar year 2007, adjusted for the AAF, and for costs associated with Family Self Sufficiency (FSS) program deposits and tenant protection vouchers, and pro-rated to fit within the amount appropriated. The accompanying text indicated that the President would seek to re-benchmark the formula using more recent cost and utilization data in the future, possibly in FY2009, as a part of a larger reform proposal.

The FY2008 Consolidated Appropriations Act (P.L. 110-161) adopted a cost and utilization-based funding formula similar to the one adopted in FY2007. Specifically, it funded agencies based on their leasing and costs in the prior calendar year, adjusted for the AAF, and for costs associated with FSS deposits, tenant protection vouchers, and vouchers set-aside for project-based commitments. As in FY2007, it provided a central reserve fund to allow HUD to make adjustments to the budgets of certain agencies, and provided an alternative formula for several categories of agencies: Katrina-affected agencies, those under receivership, and those that spent beyond their allocations.

Unlike FY2007, the FY2008 Act included a rescission that affected agencies' total funding. Specifically, the act reduced each PHA's funding level by the amount by which their unusable reserves exceeded 7% of the total they received in FY2007. Unusable reserves are reserves—or Net Restricted Assets (NRA)—in excess of what agencies need to reach 100% leasing. They were called "unusable" because the prohibition on maximized leasing (or over-leasing) had been maintained, so PHAs were legally unable to use those reserves, or NRA, to lease additional vouchers and serve additional families. The FY2008 Act rescinded $723 million in FY2008 renewal funding, which is the amount that PHAs were estimated to have in unusable reserves above 7% of their funding. These provisions "freed-up" unusable NRA, allowing Congress to reduce the total amount of new appropriations it provided for voucher renewals in FY2008, without reducing the total amount of funding available to PHAs to use for renewals in FY2008.

FY2009 Funding Formula

Again in FY2009, then-President Bush asked Congress to adopt a strictly "budget-based" funding formula like the one adopted in FY2006, basing PHA renewal funding on the amount of funding they received in the previous year. Again, Congress rejected the President's request. The FY2009 omnibus funding bill directed HUD to fund PHAs using roughly the same hybrid, cost and utilization-based formula adopted in FY2008.

It directed HUD to fund PHAs based on the number of vouchers they had leased, and the cost of those vouchers in FY2008, adjusted for inflation and a few other factors. Then, each PHA's allocation was prorated, or reduced, by an amount that corresponded with HUD's estimate of a portion of their Net Restricted Assets (NRA), both usable and unusable. The aggregate NRA offset equaled the amount rescinded ($750 million). PHAs were expected to then supplement their allocations of new funding with their unused NRA. The act also included a $100 million renewal set-aside, to make adjustments for agencies under certain circumstances (i.e. PHAs that faced an increase in renewal costs due to portability or unforeseen circumstances, faced an increase in leasing between the end of the fiscal year and the start of the calendar year, or had unused project-based vouchers and special vouchers for veterans).

CY2009 Shortfall

As directed by Congress, HUD based the CY2009 allocations on the utilization and cost data submitted by PHAs for FY2008. HUD used this same data to estimate PHAs' NRA. In some cases, HUD's estimates of costs (plus inflation), utilization, and NRA did not accurately represent PHAs' CY2009 costs, utilization, and NRA balances. In some cases, the inaccurate estimates resulted from inaccurately reported data; in some cases, the difference resulted from significant changes in the cost and leasing conditions of agencies between the end of FY2008 and the start of CY2009 (a period not captured in the data).

Regardless of the reason, some PHAs found that their CY2009 funding was insufficient to cover the costs of all the vouchers they were using to serve families. HUD estimated that as many as 15% of PHAs administering the voucher program faced such shortfalls. The Department worked with agencies to determine which were facing shortfalls. Some were assisted with additional funding from the FY2009 $100 million renewal set-aside or $30 million in administrative fee funding that the Department had set aside for this purpose. HUD had also been advising agencies as to how they could cut costs to stay within their budgets.[20] Generally, if a PHA does not have sufficient funding to renew all of its vouchers, the PHA may have to stop issuing vouchers, and, in some cases, families may lose assistance. HUD asked that agencies that were facing shortfalls first contact the Department before terminating assistance to families.[21]

In response to concerns about families losing assistance, Congress enacted legislation permitting HUD to access some additional funding (up to $200 million) to shore-up the budgets of PHAs that were at risk of terminating assistance to families as a result of insufficient funding in CY2009.[22] This policy change effectively increased the amount of set-aside renewal funding provided to HUD in FY2009 to adjust agencies' budgets (originally, $100 million) and expanded its purposes to allow it to be used to prevent the termination of assistance.

FY2010 Funding Formula

FY2010 was the first budget request of the Obama Administration and it represented a different approach to voucher funding than that of the former Bush Administration. Specifically, the President's FY2010 budget requested a funding formula very similar to the model that had been in place since FY2007, based on PHAs' costs and utilization. The biggest difference in the request was that the Administration asked for the authority to offset agencies' budgets for excess reserves, at the Secretary's discretion, and then reallocate that offset funding to high-performing agencies or to agencies based on need. The budget also requested that the prohibition on over-leasing be lifted to allow PHAs to fully utilize their budgets.

The final FY2010 funding law (P.L. 111-117) adopted a funding formula similar to the one requested by the Administration and based on FY2009 cost and leasing data, adjusted for inflation and other factors. However, it did not provide the Secretary with the authority to offset agency budgets based on reserves, nor did it lift the prohibition on over-leasing. Unlike FY2008 and FY2009, the FY2010 allocation formula included no offset for unspent agency reserves.

Implications of Changes, FY2007-Present

As noted earlier, just prior to, and shortly after, the formula changes that began in FY2003, PHAs were serving as many, and in some cases more families, than they were authorized to serve, and they were spending nearly every federal dollar they received. Following the funding formula changes that were enacted between FY2003 and FY2006, PHAs were serving fewer families and spending a smaller share of the federal funding they received. Low utilization of both funding and vouchers was prevalent when the voucher funding formula was changed again in FY2007.

Since the change from a strictly "budget-based" funding formula to the recent hybrid cost and utilization-based model, the utilization patterns of PHAs have begun to change again. Funding utilization has begun increasing from a low of around 91% in 2006 to just under 94% by the beginning of 2009.[23] Further, by 2009, PHAs were serving over 100,000 more families than they were serving in 2006. This means that by 2009, PHAs were serving more families than they had in 2003, the previous high point in families served. While PHAs had accumulated large reserves during the budget-based formula days of 2005 and 2006, by the end of FY2009, much of those reserves had been spent down as a result of the rescissions enacted in FY2008 and FY2009. Per voucher costs, which remained relatively flat in CY2005 and CY2006, began rising again in CY2007, CY2008, and CY2009.[24]

LEGISLATIVE REFORM PROPOSALS

In recent years, some Members of Congress from both parties have introduced voucher reform legislation containing a statutory change to the voucher renewal funding formula. Most recently, in the 111th Congress, the Section 8 Voucher Reform Act of 2009 (H.R. 3045) would adopt a new funding formula similar to the formula in place in recent appropriations acts, but with several important differences. It would require HUD to use the most recent leasing and cost data for allocating funds to PHAs, eliminate the prohibition on maximized leasing, provide PHAs with reserves and replenish those reserves, provide HUD with a mechanism for reallocating unused funds, and permit PHAs to take advances against their next year's funding.[25]

However, it is important to note that even if a new funding formula were to be adopted through the authorizing process, the Appropriations Committees could override the formula by adopting a different allocation formula in the annual appropriations act, as it has each year since FY2003. It is unclear whether the Appropriations Committees would defer to the authorizing committees in this circumstance.

SUMMARY AND POLICY CONSIDERATIONS

Prior to FY2003, the Section 8 voucher program was funded much like an entitlement program; the amount provided by Congress was largely determined by a formula, limiting Congress's ability to constrain funding without facing the prospect of reducing the number of vouchers and providing little incentive for PHAs to restrain costs. In response to concern about inefficient funding allocations, as well as, later, rising costs, and in an attempt to obtain greater control over future cost growth, Congress enacted a series of funding changes, beginning with those enacted for FY2003. These changes resulted in a conversion of the program's funding structure into one more similar to other discretionary programs, in which grantees received an annual fixed sum of money, regardless of changes in their costs or the number of people served. While these changes gave Congress greater control over the program's budget, many PHAs argued the changes made the program more difficult to administer. PHAs have only limited control over their costs since the value of the subsidies provided to families are statutorily set (as roughly the difference between rent and 30% of income).

In areas where they did have control, such as in setting payment standards, selecting families from the waiting list, and issuing vouchers, many PHAs made changes. Some lowered their payment standards from 110% to 100% or less of local fair market rents. Since changes in payment standards only affect future families in the program, some PHAs undertook rent reasonableness reviews and reduced rents paid to landlords, some of whom accepted the cut, others of whom chose to no longer participate in the program. PHAs had the option of selecting higher-income families from their waiting lists (for whom subsidy costs are lower), although PHAs were still constrained by a requirement that 75% of all vouchers be targeted to the lowest- income families. Many PHAs intentionally reduced their utilization rates by not reissuing vouchers when families left the program. Agencies that intentionally lowered their utilization rates in order to save money in FY2004 likely encountered problems in FY2005, as their budgets were capped at their costs *and* utilization rates as of the third quarter of FY2004. It is likely that, at least for some PHAs whose costs had risen faster than their funding under the new formula, these changes resulted in fewer households receiving vouchers.

Data from HUD indicate that voucher costs leveled off and utilization rates declined from 2005 to 2006. According to CRS analysis of HUD data, average voucher costs declined by around 1.5% and average utilization declined by over 2% during that period. At the same time, some agencies were receiving more money than they were legally permitted to spend. Under the budget-based funding formulas in place in FY2005 and FY2006, PHAs' funding did not necessarily decrease if their costs decreased (for example, due to changes in the types of families served or changes in the rental market). Since maximized leasing was prohibited, some PHAs had funds that they were not permitted to spend, even if they had waiting lists for vouchers in their communities (7% of all PHAs had unusable funds, as of September 2006, according to CRS analysis).

The budget-based funding formula changes enacted through FY2006 were controversial with low-income housing advocates and PHA industry groups. Most low-income housing advocates called for a return to an actual-cost and unit-based formula. PHA advocacy groups were vocal about the difficult predicament they felt that the current formula put them in, given the statutory constraints under which they run their programs.

The FY2007 funding bill reversed recent trends by enacting a voucher renewal funding formula similar to the one that was in place when the changes first began. In FY2007, PHAs were funded based on the amount of funding *they were using* in the previous year, rather than the amount of money *they had received* in the previous year. As a result, PHAs that had large funding surpluses were eligible for less funding in FY2007, although funding for the program was sufficient to provide all PHAs with over 105% of their formula eligibility, meaning PHAs could continue to serve at least all of the families they had been serving. The FY2008 and FY2009 formulas followed the FY2007 formula closely, although they included reductions in the budgets of agencies that had more reserve funding than they were legally permitted to spend, paired with rescissions. These rescissions and offsets made unusable funding usable, and reduced the amount of appropriations needed to fund the program. The FY20 10 formula was very similar, but without a reduction to reserves, since reserves were greatly reduced as a result of the previous rescissions and increasing utilization.

Now that the strictly "budget-based" funding model has been replaced with a cost and utilization- based model, PHAs again have an incentive to increase their utilization and spend all of their funding. As a result, costs and utilization have begun rising again. Since costs and utilization are rising, so is the cost of the program to Congress. As in FY2003 and FY2004, these rising costs could put pressure on policy makers to find ways to again contain costs in the program. Past cost containment strategies have been effective at reducing costs, but have also led to a reduction in the number of families served, and accumulations of unspent and unusable funds. Policy makers wishing to pursue future cost containment strategies may want to tailor policies that attempt to maintain a level of service to families, while minimizing the accumulation of unspent funds. Section 8 voucher reform legislation has proposed formula changes designed to maximize the number of families served, but not necessarily to firmly cap future cost growth. Further, even if such legislation is enacted, it could be overridden by future appropriations legislation.

End Notes

[1] The formula in place prior to FY2003 was authorized by the Quality Housing and Work Opportunity Reconciliation Act of 1998 (P.L. 105-276, codified at 42 USC 1437f(dd)).

[2] PHAs "lease" vouchers when they sign contracts with tenants and landlords under which PHAs agree to provide payments to landlords on behalf of tenants. Each PHA has a fixed number of vouchers it is authorized to "lease."

[3] Low utilization during this period was attributed to a number of factors, including tight rental markets, low voucher limits (called payment standards), and, in some cases, poor management.

[4] Voucher utilization was the topic of Congressional hearings; an Appropriations subcommittee staff report on the topic was developed in the Senate (Empty Promises—Subcommittee Staff Report on HUD's Failing Grade on the Utilization of Section 8 Vouchers, September 12, 2000); and in the FY2001 appropriations law, Congress included language permitting PHAs to increase their payment standards to help increase utilization.

[5] According to HUD's Housing Choice Voucher Guidebook, 95% utilization is considered standard performance and 98% is considered high performance.

[6] Hearing before the House Subcommittee on VA, HUD and Independent Agencies, Hearing on the FY2003 HUD budget, 107th Congress, 2nd Session, March 19, 2002, document Part 6.

[7] HUD had the authority to permanently reallocate vouchers (and their accompanying funding) from PHAs that were not using all of their vouchers (and had surplus funding) to those PHAs that were using all of their vouchers and had excess demand. The Department published a notice in the Federal Register in November 2001 explaining the reallocation process, however, HUD never implemented the process or made any reallocations.

[8] Some PHAs were over-leasing on purpose, as a way to fully utilize their budgets. Other PHAs were over-leased because more families were able to use their vouchers than had been estimated by the PHAs.

[9] The Government Accountability Office (GAO) estimated that, between 1998 and 2004, per voucher costs grew 42% in nominal dollars (25% in real dollars). The highest rate of growth happened between 2002 and 2003 and between 2003 and 2004 at 11% per year. There were a number of factors driving this cost growth, ranging from changes in the way the program was administered to changing market conditions. For more information, see GAO report 06-405, *Policy Decisions and Market Factors Explain Changes in the Costs of the Section 8 Programs*. See also, CRS Congressional Distribution Memo, *Factors behind cost increases in the Section 8 Housing Choice Voucher Program, FY2000-FY2004*, by Maggie McCarty (available from the author).

[10] Budget-basing provides PHAs with a budget based on a fixed dollar amount, rather than a fixed number of vouchers.

[11] Tenant protection vouchers are given to families being displaced from other HUD assistance programs (such as public housing). PHAs' costs may increase from one year to the next because of an increase in the number of tenant protection vouchers they are administering.

[12] Vouchers are nationally portable, meaning that if a family moves from the jurisdiction of one PHA to another, the family retains its assistance. However, if the new jurisdiction does not wish to permanently accept the new voucher (a process called absorption), the new jurisdiction can bill the old jurisdiction. This can present budget problems for the old jurisdiction if rents are significantly higher in the new jurisdiction.

[13] Vouchers are project-based when they are set aside for use in a particular unit of housing. This adjustment is provided for PHAs who had artificially low utilization rates in May-July 2004 because they had reserved vouchers for new units that were under construction.

[14] Rental markets began softening in 2002 and 2003 and remained flat in 2004.

[15] For more information about factors influencing the rise in voucher costs during that period, see U.S. Government Accountability Office, *Rental Housing Assistance: Policy Decisions and Market Factors Explain Changes in the Costs of the Section 8 Programs*, GAO-06-405, April 28, 2006, http://www.gao.gov/products/GAO-06-405.

[16] Utilization rates for 2004 come from HUD's 2004 Performance and Accountability Report; utilization rates for 2006 come from CRS analysis of currently unpublished HUD data.

[17] Department of Housing and Urban Development, *Congressional Justifications, FY2010 Budget*, Figure C-1, pp. F-2.

[18] See footnote 17.
[19] Based on data from HUD's website, available at https://www.hud.gov/offices/pih/programs/hcv/forums/fund.ppt#261,8,HAPFundingHiglights.
[20] For more information, see the HUD presentation titled "Financial Management 2009," available at http://www.hud.gov/offices/pih/programs/hcv/webcasts/finman2009jun30.pdf; and "HUD Makes Funds Available to Housing Agencies with Section 8 Difficulties: HUD issues guidance to agencies to keep families housed," HUD News Release, HUD No. 09-143, July 31, 2009.
[21] Ibid.
[22] Specifically, P.L. 111-88 permitted HUD to allocate up to $200 million from the advance appropriation provided in FY2009 for use in FY2010 (which is available in the last quarter of CY2009) based on need, rather than based on the FY2009 funding formula.
[23] See footnote 17.
[24] Based on CRS analysis of HUD data.
[25] For more details, see CRS Report RL34022, *The Department of Housing and Urban Development: FY2008 Appropriations*, by Maggie McCarty et al.

In: An Overview of Federal Housing Assistance Programs ISBN: 978-1-61122-419-1
Editor: Brandon C. Sherman © 2011 Nova Science Publishers, Inc.

Chapter 7

USDA RURAL HOUSING PROGRAMS: AN OVERVIEW

Bruce E. Foote

SUMMARY

Title V of the Housing Act of 1949 authorized the Department of Agriculture (USDA) to make loans to farmers to enable them to construct, improve, repair, or replace dwellings and other farm buildings to provide decent, safe, and sanitary living conditions for themselves or their tenants, lessees, sharecroppers, and laborers. USDA was also authorized to make grants or combinations of loans and grants to those farmers who could not qualify to repay the full amount of a loan, but who needed the funds to make the dwellings sanitary or to remove health hazards to the occupants or the community.

While the act was initially targeted toward farmers, over time the act has been amended to enable USDA to make housing loans and grants to rural residents in general. Currently, the USDA housing programs are administered by the Rural Housing Service (RHS). The housing programs are generally referred to by the section number under which they are authorized in the Housing Act of 1949, as amended.

The rural housing programs include loans for the purchase, repair, or construction of single-family housing; loans and grants to remove health and safety hazards in owner-occupied homes; loans and grants for the construction and purchase of rental housing for farmworkers; loans for the purchase and construction of rental and cooperative housing for the elderly and for rural residents in general; rental assistance payments to make rental housing more affordable; interest subsidies to make homeownership loans more affordable and to enable production of rental housing that is affordable for the target population; and loans for developing building sites upon which rural housing is to be constructed.

This report will be updated as deemed necessary.

INTRODUCTION

Title V of the Housing Act of 1949 authorized the Department of Agriculture (USDA) to make loans to farmers to enable them to construct, improve, repair, or replace dwellings and other farm buildings to provide decent, safe, and sanitary living conditions for themselves or their tenants, lessees, sharecroppers, and laborers.[1] USDA was also authorized to make grants or combinations of loans and grants to those farmers who could not qualify to repay the full amount of a loan, but who needed the funds to make the dwellings sanitary or to remove health hazards to the occupants or the community.

While the act was initially targeted toward farmers, over time the act has been amended to enable USDA to make housing loans and grants to rural residents in general. Currently, the USDA housing programs are administered by the Rural Housing Service (RHS). The housing programs are generally referred to by the section number under which they are authorized in the Housing Act of 1949, as amended.

In the 1970s, there was concern that owners of some RHS-financed multifamily housing were prepaying their loans and converting the property to uses other than rental occupancy by low- and moderate-income families. Keeping federally assisted housing available for use by low- and moderate income occupants is referred to as housing preservation. In prior years, preservation related more to maintaining or improving the physical standards of the housing, but, since the late 1970s, preservation has related more to simply keeping the property available for use by the target population for whom it was initially constructed. Funding housing preservation, in both senses of the word, continues to be a concern for Congress.

Partly because housing projects for the elderly are more acceptable to communities than low-income projects in general, a relatively large number of projects funded through the Section 515 rural rental program are elderly projects. Occupants who were in their 60s upon initial occupancy may have aged 10, 20, or 30 years. Such occupants may have need for different services, and these have to be financed. Laws have changed regarding building accessibility requirements, and repairs must be made to meet those requirements. These also need to be financed.

When the majority of the Section 514 and 515 projects were originally financed, the owners were required to maintain a reserve of 10% of the project costs for future repairs and replacements. While 10% seemed adequate 30 years ago, many owners now find that these reserves are not adequate to finance needed repairs and replacements. This suggests a need for a change in law or regulation, but in the meantime, the projects may need additional loans to finance repairs.

In response to this need, P.L. 109-97 included $9 million for the cost of a demonstration program for the preservation and revitalization of Section 515 housing. The Administration's FY2007 budget proposal, however, would not fund this program in FY2007, and would transfer any balances to the multifamily housing rural voucher program. Language would provide that, subject to authorization, these funds could also be used for preservation and revitalization of Section 515 multifamily rental housing properties.

As in prior years, the FY2007 budget requests no funding for the Section 515 program. It may be argued that there would be a net loss of affordable rental housing in rural areas whenever owners prepay their loans and find other uses for the property instead of continuing its use as low-income rental property. This may be one of the reasons that Congress has continued to fund the program, though the funding has been at significantly lower levels than in the past. (See **Table 1b.**)

A bill, H.R. 5039, that was introduced in the 109th Congress would have amended the Housing Act of 1949 to direct USDA to carry out a revitalization program for Section 515 projects. Owners would have been given financial incentives to continue using their property as low- to moderate-income rental, but prepayment of the loans would also have been permitted if certain requirements are met.

Table 1a. Funding for Selected Rural Housing Programs, FY1980-FY2007 ($ in millions).

Fiscal Year	Section 502 Direct	Section 502 Guaranteed	Section 504 Loans	Section 504 Grants	Section 514	Section 516
1980	2,805.6	18.9	21.9	24.0	24.6	22.3
1981	2,577.9	5.8	17.9	22.7	18.5	10.5
1982	2,476.4	na	10.0	13.6	1.9	14.9
1983	2,137.1	na	7.1	12.5	4.0	7.5
1984	1,844.9	na	7.2	12.5	5.5	9.8
1985	1,789.9	na	7.9	12.5	17.6	11.2
1986	1,155.7	na	7.0	13.9	10.4	10.8
1987	1,144,2	na	5.9	12.5	10.7	7.1
1988	1,270.9	na	7.6	12.5	11.4	11.2
1989	1,266.8	na	11.3	12.5	11.4	9.4
1990	1,310.8	na	11.6	12.6	11.3	10.8
1991	1,2691.7	38.4	11.2	12.8	13.8	10.4
1992	1,253.8	214.4	11.3	12.8	15.9	13.5
1993	1,291.3	539.8	11.8	14.3	16.3	15.9
1994	1,656.8	725.9	25.2	27.5	15.7	40.6
1995	931.3	1,048.8	29.5	27.8	15.1	11.0
1996	1,016.4	1,700.0	35.1	25.7	15.0	10.0
1997	706.4	2,000.0	30.9	17.6	15.0	8.4
1998	1,007.8	2,822.5	30.3	25.7	14.6	10.0
1999	922.9	2,977.0	25.5	21.3	20.0	13.1
2000	1,140.9	2,150.5	27.4	30.4	28.8	19.3
2001	1,074.7	2,341.6	30.8	33.7	33.2	9.9
2002	1,080.6	2,418.7	32.0	31.2	47.3	14.5
2003	1,038.2	3,086.7	32.1	33.7	55.9	7.0
2004	1,351.5	3,233.4	33.6	32.4	24.1	6.8
2005	1,140.7	3,045.5	34.7	31.6	32.9	30.4
2006	1,129.3	2,895.0	32.9	30.7	19.9	25.9
2007*	1,165.5	3,908.7	31.2	27.7	9.6	26.1

Source: Prepared by the Congressional Research Service based on documents from the U.S. Department of Agriculture.

na = program was not authorized in the years shown.

* USDA estimate based on amount appropriated.

**Table 1b. Funding for Selected Rural Housing Programs,
FY1980-FY2007 ($ in millions).**

Fiscal Year	Section 515	Section 521	Section 523 Self Help Housing Grants	Section 524 Site Loans	Section 533	Section 538
1980	881.3	393.0	6.2	0.8	na	na
1981	864.8	423.0	13.1	0.5	na	na
1982	953.7	403.0	4.7	0	na	na
1983	802.0	398.0	10.2	0.3	na	na
1984	919.0	123.7	5.0	0.2	na	na
1985	903.0	111.0	9.4	0	na	na
1986	652.3	168.3	5.1	0	19.1	na
1987	554.9	275.3	7.6	0.2	19.1	na
1988	554.9	275.3	5.7	0	19.1	na
1989	554.9	275.4	8.3	0.4	19.1	na
1990	571.0	296.4	5.3	0.1	19.1	na
1991	576.3	311.1	12.0	0.6	23.0	na
1992	573.9	319.8	7.8	0.4	23.0	na
1993	573.9	404.0	16.9	0.6	23.0	na
1994	512.4	446.7	11.9	0.1	23.0	na
1995	183.3	523.0	12.9	0	22.0	na
1996	151.0	540.5	12.9	0.6	11.0	23.7
1997	152.5	520.2	26.2	0.1	7.6	51.8
1998	149.4	541.4	26.7	0.4	11.1	78.7
1999	114.4	583.4	26.2	3.1	7.2	74.8
2000	113.8	639.6	28.0	0.6	5.5	99.7
2001	114.1	685.7	17.6	3.7	7.4	101.8
2002	118.4	701.0	26.5	0.5	8.6	99.4
2003	115.0	723.7	40.0	1.2	10.3	102.0
2004	115.9	580.6	35.3	3.2	9.3	99.4
2005	99.2	592.0	42.1	0.4	8.8	97.2
2006	98.2	646.7	34.0	3.0	10.8	98.4
2007**	90.4	329.4	34.4	1.9	9.5	63.0

Source: Prepared by the Congressional Research Service based on documents from the U.S. Department of Agriculture = program was not authorized in the years shown.

* $12,000 was provided for sites in South Dakota.

** USDA estimate based on amount appropriated.

Descriptions of the rural housing programs are presented below in the order of the sections under which they are authorized in the Housing Act of 1949. Note that most of the programs involve direct loans from USDA, while others involve USDA-insured loans from private lenders. USDA is one of the few government agencies that makes direct loans to borrowers. The report concludes with a discussion of current legislative issues. Tables are presented that show funding for various rural housing programs since FY1980.

SINGLE-FAMILY HOUSING LOANS (SECTION 502)

Section 502 of the Housing Act of 1949 gave USDA authority to make housing loans to farm owners to construct or repair farm dwellings and other buildings, for themselves or their tenants, lessees, sharecroppers, and laborers. The act was amended in 1961 to make nonfarm rural residents eligible for the Section 502 loans.[2] Amendments by the Housing and Urban Development Act of 1965 authorized the purchase and repair of previously occupied dwellings, as well as the purchase of building sites.[3] Amendments in 1968 enabled borrowers to receive interest credits to reduce the interest rate to as low as 1%.[4] The Housing and Urban Development Act of 1970 enabled Section 502 loans to be made for homes on leased land, as long as the remaining term of the lease extends beyond the repayment period of the loan.[5]

In 1977, Section 502 was amended to authorize USDA to guarantee loans made by private lenders to above-moderate-income borrowers in rural areas.[6] Funding for guaranteed loans was discontinued in 1983. The Housing and Community Development Act of 1987 directed USDA to carry out a three-year demonstration program, under which moderate-income borrowers may obtain guaranteed loans under Section 502 for the purchase of single-family homes.[7] A permanent guaranteed loan program was authorized in 1990 by the Cranston-Gonzalez National Affordable Housing Act.[8]

Under the present Section 502 program, borrowers may obtain loans for the purchase or repair of new or existing single-family housing in rural areas. Borrowers may either obtain direct loans from USDA or obtain loans from private lenders that are guaranteed by USDA.

Borrowers with income of 80% or less of the area median may be eligible for the direct loans, and may receive interest credit to reduce the interest rate to as low as 1%. The loans are repayable over a 33-year period. In a given fiscal year, at least 40% of the units financed under this section must be made available only to very low-income families or individuals.[9] The loan term may be extended to 38 years for borrowers with incomes below 60% of the area median.

Borrowers with income of up to 115% of the area median may obtain USDA-guaranteed loans from private lenders. Guaranteed loans may have up to 30-year terms. Priority is given to first-time homebuyers, and USDA may require that borrowers complete a homeownership counseling program.

In recent years, Congress and the Administration have been increasing the funding for the guaranteed loans and decreasing funding for the direct loans.

About 98% of the Section 502 loans are used for home purchases. The homes to be financed must be "modest" in cost and design, and must be located in rural areas serviced by the Agriculture Department. To be eligible for a Section 502 loan, a borrower must have the means to repay the loan but be unable to secure reasonable credit terms elsewhere.

MODERNIZING RURAL HOMES (SECTION 504)

For farmers without sufficient income to qualify for a Section 502 loan, Section 504 of the Housing Act of 1949 authorized loans, grants, or combinations of loans and grants to make farm dwellings safe and sanitary or to remove health hazards.[10] Low-income nonfarm homeowners became eligible for the program in 1961.[11] Eligibility was extended to leasehold property in 1970.[12] The 1983 Housing Act made the program available to very low-income homeowners only.[13] The act also eliminated congressionally mandated loan and grant limits for individual homeowners and gave USDA the authority to set those limits.

Under current regulations, rural homeowners with incomes of 50% or less of the area median may qualify for USDA direct loans to repair their homes. Loans are limited to $20,000, and have a 20-year term at a 1% interest rate. Owners who are aged 62 or more may qualify for grants of up to $7,500 to pay for needed home repairs. To qualify for the grants, the elderly homeowners must lack the ability to repay the full cost of the repairs. Depending on the cost of the repairs and the income of the elderly homeowner, the owner may be eligible for a grant for the full cost of the repairs, or for some combination of a loan and a grant that covers the repair costs. The combination loan and grant may total no more than $20,000.

CONSTRUCTION DEFECTS/UNDERSERVED AREAS (SECTION 509)

Section 504 of the Housing and Community Development Act of 1977 added Section 509(c) to the Housing Act of 1949.[14] Under Section 509(c), USDA is authorized to receive and resolve complaints concerning construction of Section 502 housing by contractors. If a contractor refuses or is unable to honor a warranty, the borrower may be eligible for a grant for the cost of correcting the defects. The borrower must begin the process within 18 months of the completion of the home. Related costs, such as temporary living expenses, may be included in the grant.

The Cranston-Gonzalez National Affordable Housing Act amended Section 509 by adding subsection (f).[15] In each fiscal year, USDA is required to designate 100 counties and communities as "targeted underserved areas" that have severe unmet housing needs. The USDA must set aside 5% of each fiscal year's lending authority under Sections 502, 504, 515, and 524, and reserve it for assistance in targeted underserved areas. Colonias, however, are given priority for assistance with the reserved funds.[16] The USDA must also set aside sufficient Section 521 rental assistance that may be used with the Section 514 and Section 515 programs. (See Section 521, discussed below.)

Under the Housing Application Packaging Grant (HAPG) program, nonprofit organizations, community development organizations, state or local governments, or their agencies may receive grants from USDA to help interested parties prepare applications for USDA housing loans in targeted underserved areas and colonias.

HOUSING FOR FARM LABORERS (SECTIONS 514 AND 516)

The Housing Act of 1961 added Section 514 to the Housing Act of 1949.[17] Under Section 514, loans are made to farm owners, associations of farm owners, or nonprofit organizations to provide "modest" living quarters, basic household furnishings, and related facilities for domestic farm laborers. The loans are repayable in 33 years and bear an interest rate of 1%. To be eligible for Section 514 loans, applicants must be unable to obtain financing from other sources that would enable the housing to be affordable by the target population.

Individual farm owners, associations of farmers, local broad-based nonprofit organizations, federally recognized Indian tribes, and agencies or political subdivisions of local or state governments may be eligible for loans from USDA to provide housing and related facilities for domestic farm labor. Applicants who own farms or who represent farm owners must show that the farming operations have a demonstrated need for farm labor housing, and the applicants must agree to own and operate the property on a nonprofit basis. Except for state and local public agencies or political subdivisions, the applicants must be unable to provide the housing from their own resources and unable to obtain the credit from other sources on terms and conditions that they could reasonably be expected to fulfill. The applicants must be unable to obtain credit on terms that would enable them to provide housing to farm workers at rental rates that would be affordable to the workers. The USDA state director may make exceptions to the "credit elsewhere" test when (1) there is a need in the area for housing for *migrant* farm workers and the applicant will provide such housing, and (2) there is no state or local body or nonprofit organization that, within a reasonable period of time, is willing and able to provide the housing.

Applicants must have sufficient capital to pay the initial operating expenses. It must be demonstrated that, after the loan is made, income will be sufficient to pay operating expenses, make capital improvements, make payments on the loan, and accumulate reserves.

In 1964, the 1949 Housing Act was amended to add Section 516.[18] The Section 516 program permitted qualified nonprofit organizations, Indian tribes, and public bodies to obtain grants for up to two-thirds of the development cost of farm labor housing. Applicants must demonstrate that there is a need for such housing, and that there is reasonable doubt that the housing would be built without USDA assistance. Grants may be used simultaneously with Section 514 loans if the necessary housing cannot be provided by financial assistance from other sources. The section was amended in 1970 to permit grants of up to 90% of the development cost of the housing.[19] The 1983 Housing Act provides that in decisions on approving applications under these two sections, USDA shall consider only the needs of farm laborers and make the determination without regard to the extent or nature of other housing needs in the area.[20] The act also requires that, in a given fiscal year, up to 10% of the funds available under Section 516 shall be made available to assist eligible nonprofit agencies in providing housing for domestic and migrant farm workers.[21]

Nonprofit organizations, Indian tribes, and local or state agencies or subdivisions may qualify for Section 516 grants to provide low-rent housing for farm labor. The organizations must be unable to provide the housing from their own resources, and be unable to secure credit (including Section 514 loans) on terms and conditions that the applicant could reasonably be expected to fulfill. Applicants must contribute at least 10% of the total development costs from their own resources or from other sources, including Section 514 loans. The housing and related facilities must fulfill a "pressing need" in the area, and there must be reasonable doubt that the housing can be provided without the grant.

The Housing and Community Development Act of 1987 redefined "domestic farm labor" to include persons (and the family of such persons) who receive a substantial portion of their income from the production or handling of agricultural or aquacultural products.[22] They must be U.S. citizens or legally admitted for permanent residence in the U.S. The term includes retired or disabled persons who were domestic farm labor at the time of retiring or becoming disabled. In selecting occupants for vacant farm labor housing, USDA is directed to use the following order of priority: (1) active farm laborers, (2) retired or disabled farm laborers who were active at the time of retiring or becoming disabled, and (3) other retired or disabled farm laborers.

Farm labor housing loans and grants to qualified applicants may be used to buy, build, or improve housing and related facilities for farm workers, and to purchase and improve the land upon which the housing will be located. The funds may be used to install streets, water supply and waste disposal systems, parking areas, and driveways, as well as for the purchase and installation of appliances such as ranges, refrigerators, and clothes washers and dryers. Related facilities may include a maintenance workshop, recreation center, small infirmary, laundry room, day care center, and office and living quarters for a resident manager.

Section 514 loans are available at 1% interest for up to 33 years. Section 516 grants may not exceed the lesser of (1) 90% of the total development cost of the project, or (2) the difference between the development costs and the sum of (a) the amount the applicant can provide from its own resources, and (b) the maximum loan the applicant can repay given the maximum rent that is affordable to the target tenants.

RURAL RENTAL HOUSING (SECTION 515)

The Senior Citizens Housing Act of 1962 amended the Housing Act of 1949 by adding Section 515.[23] The law authorized USDA to make loans to provide rental housing for low- and moderate-income elderly families in rural areas. Amendments in 1966 removed the age restrictions and made low- and moderate-income families, in general, eligible for tenancy in Section 515 rental housing.[24] Amendments in 1977 authorized Section 515 loans to be used for congregate housing for the elderly and handicapped.[25]

Loans under Section 515 are made to individuals, corporations, associations, trusts, partnerships, and public agencies. The loans are made at a 1% interest rate and are repayable in 50 years. Except for public agencies, all borrowers must demonstrate that financial assistance from other sources will not enable the borrower to provide the housing at terms that are affordable to the target population.

The Housing and Community Development Act of 1987 amended the Housing Act of 1949 to state that occupancy of Section 515 housing, which has been allocated for low-income housing tax credits (LIHTC),[26] may be restricted to those families whose incomes are within the limits established for the tax credits.[27] If, however, USDA finds that some of the units have been vacant for at least six months and that their continued vacancy will threaten the financial viability of the project, then higher-income tenants will be authorized to occupy the units.

RENTAL ASSISTANCE AND INTEREST SUBSIDY (SECTION 521)

In 1968, Section 521 was added to the Housing Act of 1949.[28] Section 521 established an interest subsidy program under which eligible low- and moderate- income purchasers of single-family homes (under Section 502) and nonprofit developers of rental housing (under Section 515) may obtain loans with interest rates subsidized to as low as 1%.

Section 521 was amended in 1974 to authorize USDA to make rental assistance payments to owners of USDA-financed rental housing (Sections 515 or 514) to enable eligible tenants to pay no more than 25% of their income in rent.[29] Amendments in the 1983 Housing Act provide that rent payments by eligible families would equal the greater of (1) 30% of monthly adjusted family income, (2) 10% of monthly income, or (3) for welfare recipients, the portion of the family's welfare payment that is designated for housing costs.

The rental assistance payments, which are made directly to the borrowers, make up the difference between the tenants' payments and the USDA-approved rent for the units. Borrowers must agree to operate the property on a limited profit or nonprofit basis. The term of the rental assistance agreement is 20 years for new construction projects and five years for existing projects. Agreements may be renewed for up to five years. An eligible borrower who does not participate in the program may be petitioned to participate by 20% or more of the tenants eligible for rental assistance.

SELF-HELP HOUSING (SECTION 523)

The Housing and Urban Development Act of 1968 added Section 523 to the Housing Act of 1949.[30] Under Section 523, nonprofit organizations may obtain two- year loans to purchase and develop land that is to be subdivided into building sites for housing to be built by the mutual self-help method (groups of low-income families who are building their own homes). The interest rate is 3% for these loans. Applicants must demonstrate a need for the proposed building sites in the locality.

Sponsors may also obtain technical assistance (TA) grants to pay for all or part of the cost of developing, administering, and coordinating programs of technical and supervisory assistance to the families who are building their own homes. Each family is expected to contribute at least 700 hours of labor in building homes for each other. Participating families generally have low income and are unable to pay for homes built by the contract method.

Applicants must demonstrate that (1) there is a need for self-help housing in the area, (2) the applicant has or can hire qualified people to carry out its responsibilities under the program, and (3) funds for the proposed TA project are not available from other sources.

The program is generally limited to very low-and low-income families. Moderate-income families may be eligible to participate, provided they are unable to pay for a home built by the contract method.

TA funds may not be used to hire construction workers or to buy real estate or building materials. Private or public nonprofit corporations, however, may be eligible for two-year site loans under Section 523. The loans may be used to purchase and develop land in rural areas. The land is subdivided into building sites and sold on a nonprofit basis to low- and moderate-income families. Generally, a loan will not be made if it will not result in at least 10 sites. The sites need not be contiguous.

Sites financed through Section 523 may only be sold to families who are building homes by the mutual self-help method. The homes are usually financed through the Section 502 program.

DEVELOPING BUILDING SITES (SECTION 524)

In 1979, Section 524 was added to the Housing Act of 1949.[31] Under Section 524, nonprofit organizations and Indian tribes may obtain direct loans from USDA to purchase and develop land that is to be subdivided into building sites for housing low- and moderate-income families. The loans are made for a two-year period.

Sites financed through Section 524 have no restrictions on the methods by which the homes are financed or constructed. The interest rate on Section 524 site loans is the Treasury cost of funds.

HOUSING PRESERVATION GRANTS (SECTION 533)

The Rural Housing Amendments of 1983 amended the Housing Act of 1949 by adding Section 533.[32] This section authorizes USDA to make grants to organizations for (1) rehabilitating single-family housing in rural areas that is owned by low- and very low-income families, (2) rehabilitating rural rental properties, and (3) rehabilitating rural cooperative housing that is structured to enable the cooperatives to remain affordable to low- and very low-income occupants. The grants were made for the first time in FY1986.

Applicants must have a staff or governing body with either (1) the proven ability to perform responsibly in the field of low-income rural housing development, repair, and rehabilitation; or (2) the management or administrative experience that indicates the ability to operate a program providing financial assistance for housing repair and rehabilitation.

The homes must be located in rural areas and be in need of housing preservation assistance. Assisted families must meet the income restrictions (income of 80% or less of the median income for the area), and must have occupied the property for at least one year prior to receiving assistance. Occupants of leased homes may be eligible for assistance if (1) the unexpired portion of the lease extends for five years or more, and (2) the lease permits the occupant to make modifications to the structure and precludes the owner from increasing the rent because of the modifications.

USDA is authorized to provide grants to eligible public and private organizations. The grantees may in turn provide homeowners with direct loans, grants, or interest rate reductions on loans from private lenders to finance the repair or rehabilitation of their homes. A broad range of housing preservation activities are authorized: (1) the installation and/or repair of sanitary water and waste disposal systems to meet local health department requirements; (2) the installation of energy conservation materials such as insulation and storm windows and doors; (3) the repair or replacement of heating systems; (4) the repair of electrical wiring systems; (5) the repair of structural supports and foundations; (6) the repair or replacement of the roof; (7) the repair of deteriorated siding, porches, or stoops; (8) the alteration of a home's interior to provide greater accessibility for any handicapped member of the family, and (9) the additions to the property that are necessary to alleviate overcrowding or to remove health hazards to the occupants. Repairs to manufactured homes or mobile homes are authorized if (1) the recipient owns the home and site, and has occupied the home on that site for at least one year, and (2) the home is on a permanent foundation or will be put on a permanent foundation with the funds to be received through the program. Up to 25% of the funding to any particular dwelling may be used for improvements that do not contribute to the health, safety, or well-being of the occupants; or materially contribute to the long-term preservation of the unit. These improvements may include painting, paneling, carpeting, air conditioning, landscaping, and improving closets and kitchen cabinets.

USDA is also authorized to make Section 533 grants to organizations that will rehabilitate rental and cooperative housing. This part of the law, however, had never been implemented because USDA had not issued the regulations. Thus, the Congress, in 1987, passed legislation that directed USDA to issue the necessary regulations.[33] The final regulations were published in 1993.[34]

GUARANTEED LOANS FOR RENTAL HOUSING (SECTION 538)

The Section 538 program was added in 1996.[35] Under this program, borrowers may obtain loans from private lenders to finance multifamily housing, and USDA guarantees to pay for losses in case of borrower default. Section 538 guaranteed that loans may be used for the development costs of housing and related facilities that (1) consist of five or more adequate dwelling units, (2) are available for occupancy only by renters whose income at time of occupancy does not exceed 115% of the median income of the area, (3) would remain available to such persons for the period of the loan, and (4) are located in a rural area.

Eligible lenders include the following: (1) any lender approved by the Federal National Mortgage Association (Fannie Mae), the Federal Home Loan Mortgage Corporation (Freddie Mac), or the Federal Housing Administration (FHA), and currently active in their multifamily housing guaranteed lending programs; (2) state or local housing finance agencies; (3) members of the Federal Home Loan Bank System; and (4) other lenders that demonstrate to USDA that they have knowledge and experience with multifamily lending. In any case, the lenders must apply to USDA for permission to participate in the program. Eligibility must be verified every year.

Eligible borrowers include public agencies, Indian tribes, individuals, general partnerships (if formed for a term at least equal to the loan term), limited partnerships, for-profit corporations, nonprofit corporations, limited liability companies, and trusts. In addition, borrowers must meet the following requirements: (1) be a creditworthy single-asset entity[36] or have received prior written approval from USDA; (2) not be in default under any other agency housing program, or have performed well for six months in an approved workout plan; (3) be able to and intend to operate and maintain the project in accordance with program requirements; (4) be in legal and regulatory compliance with respect to any federal debt; (5) be a U.S. citizen or legal resident, a U.S.-owned corporation, or a limited liability corporation (LLC) or a partnership where the principals are U.S. citizens or permanent legal residents. Borrowers must contribute initial operating capital equal to at least 2% of the loan amount.

The eligible uses of loan proceeds include new construction; moderate or substantial rehabilitation and acquisition when related to the rehabilitation; acquisition of existing buildings for special needs; acquisition and improvement of land; development of essential on- and off-site improvements; development of related facilities; on-site management and maintenance offices; appliances; parking development and landscaping; limited commercial space costs; professional and application fees; technical assistance and packaging fees to and by nonprofit entities; board of director education fees for cooperatives; interest on construction loans; relocation assistance when applicable; developers fees; and refinancing applicant debt when authorized in advance to pay for eligible purposes prior to loan closing and approved by RHS. The program may not be used for transient or migrant housing, health care facilities, or student housing. Unless granted an exception by USDA, refinancing is not an authorized use of funds.

The interest rates on Section 538 loans must be fixed. The maximum allowable interest rate is as specified in each year's Notification of Funding Availability (NOFA). In order to help the Section 538 program serve low- and moderate-income tenants, however, at least 20% of Section 538 loans made each year must receive interest credit subsidy sufficient to reduce the effective interest rate to the Applicable Federal Rate (AFR) defined in Section 42(I)(2)(D) of the Internal Revenue Code.[37]

End Notes

[1] P.L. 81-171, October 25, 1949, 42 U.S.C. 1471, et. seq.

[2] P.L. 87-70, sec. 801, June 30, 1961, 42 U.S.C. 1472.

[3] P.L. 89-117, sec. 1001, August 10, 1965, 42 U.S.C. 1479.

[4] P.L. 90-448, sec. 1001, August 1, 1968, 42 U.S.C. 1490a.

[5] P.L. 9 1-609, sec. 802, December 31, 1970, 42 U.S.C. 1479.

[6] P.L. 95-128, sec. 502, October 12, 1977, 42 U.S.C. 1472, 42 U.S.C. 1487, 42 U.S.C. 1490a.

[7] P.L. 100-242, sec. 304, February 5, 1988, 42 U.S.C. 1472.

[8] P.L. 101-625, sec. 706, November 28, 1990, 42 U.S.C. 1472.

[9] Defined as those having incomes below 50% of the median income for the area.

[10] 42 U.S.C. 1474.

[11] P.L. 87-70, sec. 801, June 30, 1961, 42 U.S.C. 1474.

[12] P.L. 9 1-609, sec. 802, December 31, 1970, 42 U.S.C. 1474.

[13] P.L. 98-18 1, sec. 504, November 30, 1983, 42 U.S.C. 1474.

[14] P.L. 95-128, October 12, 1977, 42 U.S.C. 1479.

[15] P.L.101-625, sec. 709(b), November 28, 1990, 42 U.S.C. 1479.

[16] Colonia are defined as any identifiable community that (1) is in the state of Arizona, California, New Mexico, or Texas; (2) is within 150 miles of the border between the United States and Mexico (except for metropolitan areas with populations exceeding 1 million); (3) is designated as a colonia by the state or county in which it is located; (4) is determined to be a colonia on the basis of objective criteria such as a lack of a potable water supply, inadequate sewage systems, and a shortage of decent, safe and sanitary housing; and (5) was in existence and recognized as a colonia prior to November 28, 1990.

[17] P.L. 87-70, sec. 804, June 30, 1961, 42 U.S.C. 1484.

[18] P.L. 88-560, sec. 503, September 2, 1964, 42 U.S.C. 1486.

[19] P.L. 9 1-609, sec. 801(d)(4), December 31, 1970.

[20] P.L. 98-181, sec. 510, November 30, 1983.

[21] P.L. 98-181, sec. 513, November 30, 1983.

[22] P.L. 100-242, sec. 305, February 5, 1988.

[23] P.L. 87-723, sec. 4(b), September 28, 1962, 42 U.S.C. 1485.

[24] P.L. 89-754, sec. 804, November 3, 1966.

[25] P.L. 95-128, sec. 508, October 12, 1977.

[26] For background on the LIHTC, see CRS Report RS22389, *An Introduction to the Design of the Low-Income Housing Tax Credit*, by Pamela J. Jackson.

[27] P.L. 100-242, sec. 306, February 5, 1988. LIHTC provides a 10-year reduction in tax liability for owners of low-income rental housing based on the development costs of low- income apartments. In general, apartments financed using LIHTC cannot be rented to anyone whose income exceeds 60% of area median gross income.

[28] P.L. 90-448, sec. 1001, August 1, 1968.

[29] P.L. 93-383, sec. 514, August 22, 1974.

[30] P.L. 90-448, sec. 1005, August 1, 1968.

[31] P.L. 91-152, sec. 413(f)(1), December 24, 1969.

[32] P.L. 98-18 1, sec. 522, November 30, 1983.

[33] P.L. 100-242, sec. 310, February 5, 1988.

[34] 58 *Federal Register* 21894, April 26, 1993.

[35] P.L. 104-120, March 28, 1996.

[36] A single-asset entity is one that owns no assets other than the proposed project.

[37] The AFR is available at [http://ftp.fedworld.gov/pub/irs-utl /afrs.pdf], or in the *Wall Street Journal* on the third Wednesday of each month, labeled the "Long Term Monthly Rate."

CHAPTER SOURCES

Chapter 1 - This is an edited, reformatted and augmented version of a Congressional Research Service publication, RL34591, dated July 22, 2008.

Chapter 2 - This is an edited, reformatted and augmented version of a Congressional Research Service publication, RL33508, dated January 13, 2010.

Chapter 3 - This is an edited, reformatted and augmented version of a Congressional Research Service publication, R40118, dated April 9, 2009.

Chapter 4 - This is an edited, reformatted and augmented version of a Congressional Research Service publication, RL33764, dated July 8, 2009.

Chapter 5 - This is an edited, reformatted and augmented version of a Congressional Research Service publication, RL32284, dated January 29, 2008.

Chapter 6 - This is an edited, reformatted and augmented version of a Congressional Research Service publication, RL33929, dated January 26, 2010.

Chapter 7 - This is an edited, reformatted and augmented version of a Congressional Research Service publication, RL33421, dated July 27, 2007.

INDEX